THEORY AND INTERPRETATION OF NARRATIVE
James Phelan and Peter J. Rabinowitz, Series Editors

Towards the Ethics of Form in Fiction

Narratives of Cultural Remission

LEONA TOKER

THE OHIO STATE UNIVERSITY PRESS • COLUMBUS

Library of Congress Cataloging-in-Publication Data

Toker, Leona.
 Towards the ethics of form in fiction : narratives of cultural remission / Leona Toker.
  p. cm.—(Theory and interpretation of narrative)
 Includes bibliographical references and index.
 ISBN 978-0-8142-1122-9 (cloth : alk. paper)—ISBN 978-0-8142-9220-4 (cd-rom) 1. Literary
form. 2. Literature—Aesthetics. 3. Ethics in literature. 4. Hawthorne, Nathaniel, 1804–1864—
Criticism and interpretation. 5. Fielding, Henry, 1707–1754—Criticism and interpretation. 6.
Sterne, Laurence, 1713–1768—Criticism and interpretation. 7. Austen, Jane, 1775–1817—Criti-
cism and interpretation. 8. Dickens, Charles, 1812–1870—Criticism and interpretation. 9. Eliot,
George, 1819–1880—Criticism and interpretation. 10. Hardy, Thomas, 1840–1928—Criticism
and interpretation. 11. Conrad, Joseph, 1857–1924—Criticism and interpretation. 12. Joyce,
James, 1882–1941—Criticism and interpretation. 13. Kafka, Franz, 1883–1924—Criticism and
interpretation. 14. Shalamov, Varlam Tikhonovich—Criticism and interpretation. I. Title. II.
Series: Theory and interpretation of narrative series.
 PN45.5.T65 2010
 808.8—dc22
                          2009046695

This book is available in the following editions:
Cloth (ISBN 978-0-8142-1122-9)
CD-ROM (ISBN 978-0-8142-9220-4)

Cover design by Juliet Williams and Jennifer Shoffey Forsythe
Text design by Juliet Williams
Type set in Adobe Garamond
Printed by Thomson-Shore, Inc.

∞ The paper used in this publication meets the minimum requirements of the American National
Standard for Information Sciences—Permanence of Paper for Printed Library Materials. ANSI
Z39.48–1992.

9 8 7 6 5 4 3 2 1

To Iris Nadler, born July 19, 2009

CONTENTS

ACKNOWLEDGMENTS

The book is a product of reading, teaching, research, thinking, and changes of mind that I have gone through over more than a decade. The work alternated with studies of the narratives of Gulag and Holocaust survivors; in the end, those narratives gave my reading of classical English literature a new perspective. All this time I have been fortunate to benefit from consultations with my teacher and colleague Professor H. M. Daleski, sometimes engaging in minor controversies but always radically improving the results of my work with the help of his critical attention (for over thirty years).

Separate parts of this project have been amended as a result of constructive responses from June Sturrock (Simon Frazer University), Inge Leimberg (Münster University), Hans Ulrich Gumbrecht (Stanford University), Gennady Barabtarlo (State University of Missouri), Zephyra Porat and Meir Sternberg (Tel Aviv University), Amit Yahav (Haifa University), and my Hebrew University colleagues Shlomith Rimmon-Kenan, Emily Budick, Ruben Borg, and Yael Shapira. The work on this project also received intellectual stimulus from cooperation with Pekka Tammi (University of Tampere), Christine Raguet (Université Paris III), Matthias Bauer (Tübingen University), James Phelan and Peter Rabinowitz of The Ohio State University, as well as from the notes of the anonymous reviewer for The Ohio State University Press.

Special thanks go to my research assistants, Irina Lyan and Philip Podol-sky, without whose thoughtful help the project would have taken several more years. The necessary financial assistance was provided by a grant from the Faculty of Humanities of the Hebrew University of Jerusalem, the Rec-tor's Prize, and—in particular—by a generous grant (#903/01) from the Israel Science Foundation.

I take this opportunity to thank my husband, Gregory Toker, for his unflagging moral support—as well as massive help with computer technol-ogy. The younger generation of the family—Joni, Dana, and Moshe—have created a background of happiness that made many things possible.

I am particularly grateful to my mother, Nedda Strazhas, philologist by profession, who has read, critiqued, and proofread every part of this work repeatedly, and whose help attained particular value and profundity during our years of grief over the illness and death of my father, Aba Strazhas, whose own work on the period of World War I remained unfinished.

Earlier or partial versions of chapters 1, 4, 6, and 10 were published in, respectively, *Éclats de voix: Crises en représentation dans la littérature nord-américaine*, ed. Christine Raguet-Bouvart (La Rochelle: Rumeur des Ages, 1995); *Connotations*; *Victorian Literature and Culture*; and *Cold Fusion: Aspects of the German Cultural Presence in Russia*, ed. G. Barabtarlo (New York: Berghahn Books, 2000). I thank the editors and publishers of these journals and essay collections for permissions to reprint.

Exploration of a theoretical issue with the help of a variety of narratives ranging between the eighteenth and twentieth centuries leads to lagging behind the newest scholarship on one writer while catching up with the advances in the studies of another. This is my apology for possible oversights. *Ars longa vita brevis est;* but the length of art is not a burden—it is a source of the never-ending joy of discovery.

Remissions/Reprieves

It is in fact peculiar to Man to combine the highest and the lowest in his nature, and if his *dignity* depends upon a rigid distinction between the two, his *happiness* depends upon a skilful removal of the distinction.

—Schiller, *On the Aesthetic Education of Man,* Twenty Fourth Letter

CULTURE MUST SOMETIMES PAUSE. A non-genetically transmitted system of relationships that mediates between individuals and their world,[1] culture evolves more slowly than the conditions that it processes; as a result, cultural patterns tend to become inimical to individual human life. One of the correctives to the gelling of these patterns is aesthetic experience. By aesthetic experience I mean moments of self-forgetful aesthetic heightening; I do not use this term in the broad sense of aesthetic practice (see Levinson 2003: 4–7). The latter, whether as active attention to the aesthetic side of everyday life or as joining the audience of the arts, is a part of cultural constraints rather than a remission, though it contributes to the conditions under which a remission can take place.

When not reduced to complacent contemplation of personal possessions or skills or of collective cultural products, aesthetic experience is a "time-out" from the consolidation of sociocultural determinacies, a space of inner freedom. Rainer Maria Rilke's sonnet "Archaic Torso of Apollo" ends with the sense that "[y]ou must change your life": according to Rilke, in response to great works of visual art, offspring of individual creativity and cultural semiotics, one halts. One then reflects and backtracks before moving on.

1. See Lotman and Uspenskij 1984: x–xi, 3.

Great works of literature (which are not necessarily the same as canonical works) likewise constitute conditions for slowing down,[2] for moments of aesthetic self-liberation from the linear temporality of the perception-process. Such conditions are, I believe, a proper object for the study of the ethics of literary form,[3] though their actual fulfillment in individual reading is a matter of contingencies.

By the term "form" I mean not only style and those aspects of narrative structure that have been studied by descriptive poetics (Sternberg 1978, Genette 1980, Rimmon-Kenan 1983) but also what, following Hjelmslev, one might call "the form of content" in terms of the so-called Hjelmslev net:[4]

the substance of content	vs.	the form of content
	and	
the substance of expression	vs.	the form of expression.

The distinctions between these four coordinates cannot be watertight when applied to literary works, such as novels,[5] but they are, nevertheless, helpful as correctives to the traditional juxtaposition of subject matter and technique or even of the "fabula," as the sum total of information about the fictional world, and the "sjuzhet," as the sum total of all the devices that render this information (see Toker 1993a: 5–7). The *substance of content* can be roughly identified with the subject matter, the fields of reference (mainly, the External Field of Reference; see Harshaw 1984[6]), and the ideas that enter a narrative's "repertoire" (Iser 1978: 69). The *form of content* is to be sought in

2. Cf. Victor Shklovsky's (1965) rejection of the concept of the economy of (the reader's) effort and emphasis on the prolonged contemplation of details of a literary text.

3. Wayne Booth regarded preoccupation with ethical ideas in the repertoire of literary works as one of the reasons for the eclipse of ethical criticism in the seventies and the eighties (1988: 49–79); discussion of such ideas is not an *intrinsic* literary analysis so long as it is divorced from the study of the formal features that stage these ideas and pit them against one another. For a helpful recent survey of ethical criticism see Mendelson-Maoz 2007.

4. See Hjelmslev 1969; Deleuze and Guattari 1991: 43.

5. See also Algirdas Greimas's Aristotelian remark that "form and substance are merely operational concepts that depend on the chosen level of analysis: what will be termed substance on one level can be analyzed as form on a different level" (1974: 26; my translation).

6. Benjamin Harshaw's (Hrushovski's) 1984 article "Fictionality and Fields of Reference" has initiated the influential distinction between External Fields of Reference (history, geography, culture, philosophy, etc., which are accessible from sources external to a given text whose pertinent details claim referential truth value) and Internal Fields of Reference (a network of interrelated characters, themes, ideas, plot events) that the text constructs and refers to at the same time.

the relationships between the themes, patterns of imagery, the deployment of the motifs as parts of the Internal Field of Reference, and the corresponding shaping of the plot. The *substance of expression* is the verbal medium of literary communication; the *form of expression* is the style and such narrative techniques as the point of view, flashbacks, anticipations, heteroglossia, the monitoring of the flow of information, and the handling of blanks and gaps and of scene and summary. My 1993 book *Eloquent Reticence* was mainly concerned with the reader-response aspects of the form of expression. The current project will retain this concern but will shift its emphasis to the study of the form of content. Cora Diamond's influential statement that the moral philosophy of a narrative is bound up with the appropriateness of a particular form for a particular content (1991) actually points to the convergence of the aesthetic and the ethical in the congruence of the *form* (of both the content and the expression) with the *substance* of the individual work's content. It is suggestive that in his "Essays upon Epitaphs" William Wordsworth found in the congruence of the content and stance the explanation for the aesthetic effect of plain epitaphs written by the ordinary bereaved (1974: 63–93). The ethics of narrative form and the aesthetic experience of the reader are the solid base and the contingent epiphenomenon of the same conditions of perception.

The ethics of narrative form need not entail an expectation that a work should have a "moral in tow" (Nabokov 1970: 317). Nor is it solely defined by the novel's repertoire of ethical issues—these are, as noted above, part of the "substance of content." It is the congruence of a narrative's form (the form of both its content and its expression) with the substance of its content that creates conditions for aesthetic experience. Against many odds, I still believe that aesthetic experience has an intrinsic ethical effect, irrespective of the presence or absence of "message." Arthur Schopenhauer regarded aesthetic experience as morally positive because, for its (brief) duration, it silences the immanent Will (1969, I: 363). Subtracting the mystical touch of this theory, one can see the ethical value of genuine aesthetic experience in its momentary disinterestedness (cf. Kant 1946: 38–39ff.), its subject's reprieve from social interaction, from needs of survival and pressures of self-advancement, or from more extended personal interests.

Much criticism, mainly but not exclusively on ideological grounds,[7] was leveled at the notion of aesthetic experience in the past decades. This criticism was partly prompted by skeptical attitudes to disinterestedness, whether

---

7. See, in particular, Eagleton 1990. The opposite side of the debate is represented by, for instance, Isobel Armstrong 2000, George Levine 1994 and 2001, Tzachi Zamir 2006, and Thomas Docherty 2003—as well as by the present study.

personal, cultural, or sociopolitical. The only thing that I concede to such skepticism is that spans of liberating disinterest seldom last long. Indeed, audience response to a work of art is usually characterized by a to-and-fro movement, now transcending the self, now returning to the self and its physical or psychological needs and social and cultural commitments. This to-and-fro movement has no intersubjective structure except when monitored by the grooves provided by specific (mainly formal) aspects of the work. A work of literary art invites aesthetic self-forgetfulness, but there is no guarantee that an individual reader will respond to its felicities with the aesthetic heightening that they merit. In other words, there is no guarantee for the movement "to"—but the conditions that the text creates for the movement "fro" have a firmer intersubjective basis: the text can disrupt the aesthetic heightening that it induces. In *Eloquent Reticence* I have shown how narratives can maneuver that part of the reader's response which is not totally disinterested—the one that involves a power struggle with the text, the stakes being our sense of our own sagacity and our belief in the correctness of our own attitudes. Here I would like to emphasize that in addition to producing a variety of ethical effects, the text's *agôn* with the reader has the general effect of puncturing the reader's complacency—the virtual ivory-tower complacency that gives aesthetics a bad name.[8] Novels do not give us unalloyed aesthetic pleasure—they also strike at our belief in the correctness of our expectations or insights, our intellectual powers, our erudition, our Podsnappian habits of thought. Time and again they demand a counter-Narcissistic loss of disinterest and promote (without ensuring it) a self-critical self-reflexive twist—from reading the narrative to being read by it (cf. Toker 2008a).[9] The process of reading tends to oscillate between moments of self-forgetful appreciation and spans of self-involved agonistic engagement with the text.

Paradoxically, most kinds of aesthetic experience (like, for that matter, other kinds of cultural remission) are possible only on the basis of suf-

8. George Steiner has succinctly formulated what troubles several post–World War II generations: "We know now that a man can read Goethe or Rilke in the evening, that he can play Bach and Schubert, and go to his day's work at Auschwitz in the morning. To say that he has read them without understanding, or that his ear is gross, is cant" (1998: ix). The objection that such a person's enjoyment of his nation's high cultural achievements is not aesthetic experience but complacent enjoyment of his own understanding, his cultural proficiency (a version of the same self-aggrandizement through art that Browning has explored in "My Last Duchess") is irrefutable yet also insufficient. It must be complemented by the following claim: aesthetic experience merely creates the conditions for ethical growth—the actualization of this growth demands an appropriate prior ethical commitment (see Harrison 1994).

9. In practice, the conditions that promote a self-reflexive twist in some readers elicit the hostility of other readers, who choose, for instance, to accuse a writer such as Nabokov of cruelty and a writer such as Joyce of self-indulgence for the density of internal and external reference.

ficient cultural proficiency—which also threaten their purity by liability to self-congratulation. The ethics of narrative form is the other side of the to-and-fro undulation of aesthetic experience: as work-ethics it strives for the artistic feats that can *invite* cultural remissions; as ethics of interpersonal communication, it plants stumbling blocks that, on the contrary, *discontinue* such time-outs. The puncturing of aesthetic self-effacement may then lead back to aesthetic experience—in the shape of "meaning effects," that is, the shapely congruence of conceptual structures (the work's own, or ours in conceptual processing of the work) that is no less arresting than the "presence effects" (Gumbrecht 2004: 104–11) that, in a literary work,[10] are associated with style, varieties of emotional appeal, and dramatic illusion.

The above remarks about the aesthetical background of the ethics of form are a broad declaration of faith. I shall now turn to a statement of specific intention: this book examines narratives that simulate the effects of aesthetic experience by staging three kinds of culturally determined cultural remissions: the oppositional, the carnivalesque, and the ludic. These narratives explore and thematize detours from the logical course of sociocultural determinacy, ultimately leading to a conscious reendorsement of the dominant culture but with a degree-of-freedom openings for change. While creating the aesthetic conditions for such detours in the individual reading process—a work of art "suddenly tears" (or perhaps gently releases) "the person experiencing it out of the context of his life, and yet relates him back to the whole of his existence" (Gadamer 1989: 70)—these narratives provide models, each in its own medium and manner, of parallel cultural remissions.

My choice of materials is associated with a private microhistory of attempts to understand what the ethics of narrative form might consist in and how it might be sought. The work began subliminally when, on reading Jean-Paul Sartre's essay on Faulkner, I came across a sentence that would become the motto of several of my fiction courses at the Hebrew University of Jerusalem: "A writer's technique always relates back to his metaphysics" (1962: 84). This called forth the question whether such regularity would also be true of the writer's moral philosophy.

Trained as a structuralist, I have watched the *technique* of all the narratives that I read, seeking, among other things, an answer to that question but always finding that similar techniques can be associated with totally

---

10. Hans Ulrich Gumbrecht's (2004) strongest examples of the aesthetic effects of presence (rather than meaning) pertain to the visual arts and music.

different ethical theories. Things changed when my attention shifted from rhetoric to broader morphological properties of narrative—to the "form of content." Martha Nussbaum's *The Fragility of Goodness* provided a test for my incipient hypothesis by associating different *genres* of Ancient Greek literature, for example, tragedy, dialogue, essay, with specific philosophical perspectives on the possibility of restricting the role of chance in human affairs. Though Nussbaum's book (and her subsequent work) has been very stimulating for me, I found this kind of link between moral philosophy and literary genre tenuous—if only because it worked one way rather than both ways: it can be convincingly argued that Aristotle's position, in contrast to Plato's ethics, could best be presented in an essay rather than in a dialogue, but the genre of the essay is clearly amenable to representing sundry other ethical perspectives.

Yet Nussbaum also helpfully suggests that the relationship between the contents of an ethical theory and the kind of discourse suitable to it can emerge only given an appropriate classification of ethical theories—and that this classification should be based not on textbook distinctions between, for instance, rationalism and emotivism, or relativism and contractarianism, but on attitudes to specific issues. In *The Fragility of Goodness* such a touchstone is the topos of staving off the uncontrollable disruptions of the best-laid plans of men.

My touchstone in the following chapters is the *estimates of moral motivation.* The following regularity emerges, by way of induction, from the analysis of a series of literary works: a "high" view of human potentiality tends to be associated with the carnivalesque mode in narrative; and conversely, the carnivalesque mode can most often be read as a symptom of a high view of motivation.

I take the concept of the *high view* of human potentiality from Dorothea Krook's *Three Traditions of Moral Thought* (1959), a pioneering work that combines literary readings of philosophical texts from Plato to F. H. Bradley with philosophical readings of literary texts such as novels by D. H. Lawrence.[11] At stake is a belief in the efficacy of values that transcend self-interest and include "charity, or loving kindness (which is not the same as mere kindness); humility, which presupposes self-knowledge . . . , the desire to serve our fellow men before ourselves; the readiness to forgive those who have done us injuries; the power to renounce pleasure for the sake of good;

---

11. This book is seldom read these days; the changes in the tone of analysis and the effect of poststructuralism on philosophical vocabulary have relegated it to intellectual debris. Yet the brilliance of Krook's analysis and the pedagogical clarity of her discourse could set a standard for further ethical criticism.

and, above everything, the belief in the power of love to conquer and transform all the tragic disabilities which belong to man by the condition of his humanity" (Krook 4–5). These are the nondenominationally religious terms in which Krook defines humanism, which she distinguishes from the Platonic-Christian tradition of moral thought (Plato, St. Paul, St. Augustine) insofar as humanism dispenses with "the necessity of a supernatural sanction" (6) for its transcendent order of values and treats such values as accessibly human. It is in themselves that men and women can find the strength for selflessness; it is in themselves that they can find the freedom from the self-interested ambitions of the social world (the one that is too much with us). However, while giving human nature credit for the lofty flights of the spirit, the *high view* likewise envisages the depths of iniquity into which a human being can fall.

Krook regards this type of humanism (which she distinguishes from other types; 7–8) as religious because it amounts to a faith in the possibility of selflessness and because its cornerstone is love. One might add, however, that the high view of human motivation has no absolute need for the difficult idea of "love" beyond the domain of private life. As a motive-force in the public sphere and in the relationships with one's neighbors (in the scriptural as well as the municipal sense), *love* can be replaced by the more reliable secular idea of *respect.*

Such a replacement need not conflate the *high* and the *low* views of motivation, even though the "low" view of the human reach likewise replaces the unwieldy notion of love by approximations, such as friendship (Aristotle, Book VIII of *Nicomachean Ethics*) or social sympathy (Hume). The *low* view (Krook 3) is skeptical about the possibility of self-transcendence. "Low" here does not mean "sordid"; it means merely that motivation is traced to some form of self-interest, with self-sacrifice and idealistic supererogation reinterpreted in terms of extended personal interests, or contractarian calculation of reciprocity, or psychological egoism that redescribes the most selfless acts as those impelled by the subject's pursuit of a pleasurable self-congratulatory state of mind. Strictly speaking, this is a "middle" rather than a "low" view: its skepticism concerning idealistic motivation goes hand in hand with a readiness to ascribe evil, even the absolute evil that the twentieth century has celebrated with uncommon gusto, to the intensification of understandable and semiotically analyzable conflicts of interest. Indeed, novelists who write in the "biographical" rather than the "carnivalesque" mode (Bakhtin 1984: 101) tend to keep murderous hatred, sadistic violence, slaughter, genocide away from the painstakingly evolved civilities of their fiction.

The *high* view of human motivation is easier to maintain in thinking of fictional characters than of real people. It takes imagination to enter into the motives of fictional as well as of "real" people, but in the former case one may have narrative authority on one's side. In "real life," moreover, in these days of iconoclastic historiography and demystifying journalism, the public is trained to read human conduct in terms of a continuum between different scopes of self-interest and to withhold credit for disinterestedness: interests, we are taught to think, can be personal or variously extended—the welfare of the family, the group, or the nation is one's own delayed interest, whereas altruistic motivation is all too often reduced to psychological egoism—one of the closed conceptual systems within which everything can be adjusted to the foundational idea or else explained away.[12] Legends and novels, however, can still remind us that the agent's motivation may transcend the prison house of actual or psychological self-interest and be conceptualized as a commitment to the good of others, that actions can be evaluated deontologi-cally—as right or wrong in their own right rather than in terms of serving or impeding benevolent goals, that the self-congratulation at having done good can be perceived not as the purpose of doing good but as a byproduct (cf. Harrison 1994: 82–98). Since individual intention and the proportion of good and bad faith in its conceptualizations are seldom available to scholarly objectivity, literature, the work of imagination and memory, can supply no less workable material for the study of this subject than sociological fact-finding. And one of the numerous reasons why literature can overlap with moral philosophy (without providing an alternative for it) is that aesthetic impact involves a license for imaginative entering into human motivation and the kind of suspension of ethical skepticism that is akin to the suspension of disbelief in attending to the imaginary.[13]

Respect for others and commitment to the good of others are, of course, two-pronged notions. In the twentieth century, the utopian beliefs that priv-ileged a single notion of universal happiness led to massively murderous despotisms. Care for the well-being of others ("happiness" is a taller order) is "intrinsically" good—and yet not a few crimes have been committed in its service.

When in George Eliot's *Middlemarch* Dorothea Brooke must reconcile herself to being barred from benevolent social action (her resignation fol-lows several thwarted attempts at practical endeavor), she is aided by her

12. Bernard Harrison's work on the issue (1989, 1994) argues that the theory of psychological egoism cannot be refuted on its own ground, by counterexamples, but it can be abandoned in favor of viewing the pleasurable state of mind that results from a good deed not as the goal but as the bonus of that deed.

13. The 1983 special issue of *New Literary History* (15/1) was almost entirely devoted to these problems. They are taken up in Nussbaum's *Love's Knowledge* and her later work.

belief that "by desiring what is perfectly good, even when we don't quite know what it is and cannot do what we would, we are part of the divine power against evil—widening the skirts of light and making the struggle with darkness narrower" (1977: 270). A young intellectual praises this belief as "a beautiful mysticism" (271)—only to be asked not to give it categorizing names. With Kant, George Eliot is ready to grant moral credit to intention, even if the agent has no practical means of translating it into action. There may, indeed, be a touch of religiosity (some would say "superstition") in the formula "widening the skirts of light" for the idea of commitment to the good of others, yet this kind of religiosity does not conflict with a secular deontology; rather it constitutes an imaginative type of externalism—that is, in tune with Feuerbach's view of Christianity, it projects beyond the self what is the most noble, generous, and honorable in one's own inner life.

The high view of human motivation is deontologically oriented, but it need not reject the hedged-in validity of utilitarian principles. The utilitarian view of the good (as what serves the greatest happiness of the largest number) may be the necessary balance to deontology which, when carried to its logical extreme, is liable to lead to tragic consequences ("May the world perish but justice be done"[14]). If one believes, with Iris Murdoch (1956), that freedom of the will consists not in the choice of action but in the ideological choices *prior* to action, endorsement of cultural remission may lead one to opt for productive tensions between such clashing criteria for ethical value: an occasional rethinking of a rigid principle can ultimately reinforce this principle by replacing automatic consistency by conscious choice. By staging cultural remissions,[15] fictional narratives may loosen the hold of habitual maxims on individual conduct, subject the maxims to tests, and preempt their totalitarian control, whether over a society as a whole or over the moral economy of individual agents.

The structural pattern that applies to the principles of higher human motivation, namely the need to relax one's hold on what one wishes to consolidate, is parallel to and aesthetically congruent with the semiotics of the carnival—and with oppositional practices in general. Letting go in order to hold on is what festive carnival is about:[16] what it disrupts in order to

14. Cf. Kuhns 1983.

15. See Gumbrecht 2004: 85 on carnival as a self-suspension of the culture of presence.

16. But not only festive carnival; as H. M. Daleski has shown (1977), the theme of losing oneself in order to find oneself again recurs through the (predominantly non-carnivalesque) fiction of Joseph Conrad.

preserve is *individual discreteness* rather than social compartmentalization. The ruling classes of ancient Greece admitted the plebeian Dionysian festivities as a circumscribed safety valve: Euripides' *Bacchae* stages the dire consequences both of a king's rigid resistance to carnival culture and of the Bacchantes' failure to set a temporal limit to their vertiginous transports. In *The Birth of Tragedy* Nietzsche suggests that Greek tragedy celebrated a cooperative reconciliation of the Dionysian and the Apollonian impulses: the chorus in the orchestra part of the theatre extended the affects of the audience and enacted the ritual Dionysian intoxication whose outcome was the Apollonian dream of the gods and heroes on the stage. Nietzsche goes on to blame Euripides for destroying the classical tragedy by placing the audience on the stage, that is, by populating the stage not with the distilled artifacts of an Apollonian dream but with a mixed bag of human affects—an intellectual pabulum suitable for Euripides' target audience of one, who, according to Nietzsche, was Socrates. If Nietzsche's insight has truth value in addition to poetic appeal, it might further mean that when tragedy lost its function as an intellectually sublimating receptacle of Dionysian energies, this function may have been taken over, in a more diffuse way, by other literary genres. In modern culture, the circumscribed ritualistic carnival has likewise yielded to the less concentrated endemic carnivalesque that Mikhail Bakhtin, the leading interdisciplinary theorist of the carnival, traces back to Menippean satire and Socratic dialogue.[17]

This view of the carnivalesque should be distinguished from the conciliatory "safety-valve" theory of the festive, deservedly critiqued (see, for instance, Bristol 1985: 26–39) for the elision of other factors, such as the controlling influence of ancestral rituals in addition to that of the contemporary authorities. The main flaw of the "safety-valve" theory[18] lies in its suggestion that when the festivity is over, the valve closed, things return to normal. This is not a necessary consequence of seeing the carnivalesque as a cultural remission: the degree of self-liberation that is created during the remission cannot be totally canceled, nor can the things said be unsaid

17. Like numerous turn-of-the-century Russian intellectuals before him, Bakhtin was to a large extent influenced by Nietzsche (see Clowes 1988: 114–223; as well as Curtis (1986); Groys (1994); and Rosenthal 1986, 1994: 15–21). The Dionysian spirit described in Nietzsche's *The Birth of Tragedy* the syndrome of vertiginous transport, intoxication, blurring borderlines between personalities and their environment, of vitality that transcends itself in mystical moves, of excess in body language, reversal of hierarchies, and dissolution of the individual in the mass—obviously presides over Bakhtin's carnivalesque, especially in its Rabelaisian version, sharply contrasting with the Apollonian dream of discrete shape, individual grandeur, and hermetic finish.

18. See also Barbara Rosenwein's critique of what she calls "the hydraulic theories" of emotion (2002: 834–37; 2006: 13–15).

again. The temporary release of the sociocultural safety valve shares some of the structural features of the middle part of the rites of passage (Van Gennep 1960 [1908]), travel through liminal spaces that allows for an almost Saturnalian freedom and creates intervals "of pure potentiality when everything, as it were, trembles in the balance" (Turner 1982: 44) and the causal-temporal chain of necessity is loosened, pushed back, left in suspense.

The semiotics of the carnival presented in the chapter on genre in Bakhtin's *Problems of Dostoevsky's Poetics* and in his book *Rabelais and His World* may be seen as deployed along the horizontal and the vertical axes. On the horizontal axis, the carnival is defined as a pageant without footlights, a show during which the spectators merge with the participants. On the vertical axis, everyday hierarchical social order is turned, temporarily, upside down: kings are uncrowned and jesters elevated to thrones, comic mésalliances are formed and celebrated. The horizontal axis is characterized by the blurring of borderlines; the vertical by a volte-face, a radical role switch, often to the tune of profanation (Stallybrass and White 1986: 27–79). In fact, the distinction between the merging and the switching is more significant than the metaphors of the horizontal and the vertical: whereas social stratification is usually schematized in vertical terms, it can equally be seen as a matter of horizontal osmosis when people who usually stay in separate social compartments do not so much exchange places as enter into free and familiar contact with each other. The carnivalesque erasure of boundaries between classes and groups finds its extensions in the interpenetration of bodies and their physical environment, in the blending of individual minds into proximate intellectual niches, and in disruptions of self-containment, in temporary relinquishment of the discreteness of the self and its affects.[19]

The chronotope of the carnival (see Bakhtin 1981: 84–258) is that of circumscribed time and open communal spaces. In fiction, in contrast to actual carnival celebrations, the carnivalesque spaces are open not only in the *agora* fashion (marketplaces, public squares, streets) but also in a fashion suggestive of transition (liminal spaces, the threshold, the gate, the ha-ha) or of

19. This view presupposes the sense of self—not necessarily as a stable monolith but possibly, to adapt the language of George Eliot's *Middlemarch*, as a "centre of self"—whose ultimate circumference may be nowhere but whose fractal boundaries are sufficiently defined to know a breach when one occurs. For a useful discussion of the recent critiques of the notions of the self, identity, and individuality as well as of the philosophical approaches that rehabilitate them, see Rimmon-Kenan 1996: 12–18.

perilous communication (windows, judas holes, keyholes, permeable partitions, leaks in a boat). The diametrical opposite of the carnivalesque chronotope is that of the totalitarian prison, with its severely limited space and seemingly endless time: carnival is a time-space of free act and thought. As I show in the chapters that follow, the blurrings, reversals, and chronotopical features of the carnival overlap with the morphology of related phenomena, such as crisis situations, crowd experience, games of vertigo, empathy, and practices of Lent.

In the past decades Bakhtin's work has occasionally been criticized for factual imprecision or historically inaccurate conceptualizations (see, for instance, Berrong 1986, Averintsev 1992, Coronato 2003). Most of this criticism pertains to *Rabelais and His World,* which tends to put literary material at the service of anthropological analysis; in contrast, Bakhtin's application of the phenomenology of the carnival to the study of Dostoyevsky's art, demonstrating the value of anthropological notions in literary analysis, has been seldom challenged. But the present study is not devoted to Bakhtin: his notion of the carnival is here used instrumentally, for the sake of drawing a phenomenological link between narrative morphology and moral vision.

I see the carnivalesque as a literary mode rather than a genre. A "mode" can be broadly defined as the manner in which a literary text can be perceived as truth-telling. In *The Anatomy of Criticism* Northrop Frye shows how several genres may belong to the same mode while different works of the same genre may span more than one mode; he divides literary works into modes according to the relative status of the main heroes with respect to their environment and with respect to the reader. Other modal classifications can be made for specific purposes—thus, if one wishes to explore the limits of referentiality, one can classify narratives into those belonging to the factographic, realistic, experimental, and self-reflexive modes (Toker 1997b). Examination of the nature and intensity of the carnivalesque elements in narrative can likewise establish a modal scale, ranging from the carnivalesque via mixed or intermediate cases to the strictly non-carnivalesque (Bakhtin's "biographical"). As in Frye's model, the basis of distinction here is the form of content: in the carnivalesque works, the plots, character portrayal, and the deployment of motifs stage the two main carnival topoi, reversals and boundary-blurring. In contrast, the "biographical" pole of this modal scale tends to be dominated by the representation of solid hierarchies (albeit with a degree of vertical mobility) and, on the horizontal plane, social and psychic partitioning (with occasional switching of places). The distinction between the two is a matter of prevalence and emphasis; its modal character is bound up with the estimation that the works suggest concerning the stability or fluidity of ethical and sociocultural relations.

The intermediate cases are characterized by the absence of one of the two main carnival topoi.

Carnival and Lent are limited in time. On the expiration of the appointed period, the previous social and interpersonal relationships are restored, even though the psychological shifts produced by the interlude may remain irreversible. Unless carnival and (literal or figurative) fast are endemically contained and sporadically recurrent in a minor way amid everyday realities, the absence of the time limit for either feast or fast in individual narratives usually signifies *a corruption* of these phenomena: it is not so much what distinguishes the carnivalesque from the "biographical" as what signals the spuriousness or the deterioration of the carnivalesque, abuse of the values celebrated and enhanced by genuine festive expansion or by ritual self-purification. True carnival can be a vehicle of social protest, but a *fake* carnival may use the forms of a popular festivity for purposes of a radical attack on social structures (the case described in *Carnival in Romans* by Le Roy Ladurie, 1979). Carnival celebrates the liberty of the body and spirit even when there is an element of ad hoc secret power-play in the circumscribed license of specific carnival events. In contrast are the unhedged, corrupt, or fake carnivals that, instead of creating an interlude for such liberation, enact not cultural remissions but radical power struggles that seek to create their own legitimation.

Genuine carnival, like genuine Lent, is not revolutionary but "oppositional." The theory of oppositional practices evolved in Michel de Certeau's *The Practice of Everyday Life* (1984) has been fruitfully adapted to narratology by Ross Chambers.[20] Chambers's *Room for Manuever* (1991) discusses narratives that stage social oppositionality and have the potential of affecting the structure of the audience's desires.

Oppositional practices are "individual or group survival tactics that do not challenge the power in place, but make use of circumstances set up by that power for purposes the power may ignore or deny" (Chambers 1). They

20. See also Clabough 2003.

often consist in making subversive use of imposed structures or rules for unforeseen purposes:

> I am perhaps a waiter, at the beck and call of a demanding general public that forces me to smile (through gritted teeth sometimes) for the tips I demeaningly live on—but I can give myself the mild satisfaction of punishing my more obnoxious customers by selective application of the house rules, blandly denying them a second roll or their first choice of salad dressing. Or again I am a student, attempting to achieve an education in the face of academic rules and a computerized bureaucracy; but I can use nice old Dr. X in the clinic to get a certificate that will oblige Professor Y to give me the extension I need on my term paper so that I can study for Professor Z's final. (6)

Oppositional behavior eventually reinforces the prevailing systems "by making them livable" (7) and by helping preserve the individual dignity of the disadvantaged.[21] It is thus a radical alternative to "the worse the better" principle of the anarchist agenda.

Carnival celebrates oppositionality as a cultural remission, a respite from the straitjacket of everyday social contracts. However, as the institution of the Lord of Misrule suggests,[22] the disruptions that it wreaks usually proceed with reference to the prevailing power structures: *awareness* of the hierarchies that are turned upside down and of the borderlines that are transgressed is part of the *jouissance*. Oppositionality, however, is not always carnivalesque; when it is not carnivalesque, the ethical expectations behind it tend to be both more limited and, in a sense, less troubled. Carnival can be regarded as a special case of oppositionality.

21. Chambers goes on to say that oppositional practices "are in one sense what Michel Serres would call the 'noise' that seems to disturb the system but without which it would not work; they are in this sense needed by the system, and an integral part of it. Thus every rule produces its loophole, every authority can be countered by appeal to another authority, every front-stage social role one places has a backstage where we are freer to do, say, or think as we will. The *diffuseness of power*, in short, both makes 'opposition' possible and supports the structures of power that are in place. In this respect, however, it is worth noticing that there are societies whose power structure is relatively 'loose' and those where, to the contrary, it is relatively 'tight,' and in the latter the degree of tolerance towards oppositional behavior that characterizes 'loose' societies is replaced by an effort to stamp it out. In particular, in societies in which the dream of a concentrated power, centralized in a single person or office, presupposes absolute control of the population, the effort is to penetrate the 'backstage' areas of the personal, the private, the informal (the 'thought police'), to prevent the use of authority against authority (by making them all accountable to a central power), and to cut out loopholes (sometimes by abolishing rules themselves and substituting the reign of the arbitrary)" (7).

22. Tony Tanner (1977) discusses this institution as analogous to censorship.

Another form of cultural remission, compatible with the carnivalesque but constituting a new parameter, is the phenomenon of play—games, *paideia*, the ludic experience of make-believe. In *On the Aesthetic Education of Man* Friedrich Schiller discusses play as a corrective to culture, which he understands (with emphasis on the individual rather than social/cognitive dimension) as a search for balance between sense and emotion on the one hand and rationality on the other (1965: 68–69): play supplements distinction and equilibrium by a degree of osmosis between the "material impulse" and the "formal impulse" (72). Continuing, as it were, Schiller's suggestion that "Man shall *only play* with Beauty, and he shall play *only with Beauty*" (80), Hans-Georg Gadamer discusses aesthetic consciousness in terms of play, a to-and-fro movement as of light and shade within the game (1989: 101–10), noting that "in playing, all those purposive relations that determine active and caring existence have not simply disappeared, but are curiously suspended" (102). With aesthetic experience, as well as with the carnival and with oppositional loopholes, play shares the effect of "an intermezzo" (Huizinga 1955: 9) in our daily lives, a subversion of the grim logical determinacies of homeostatic need, invidious emulation, *ressentiment*, biographical mission-orientedness, or social regulation. Carnival, oppositionality, and games constitute circumscribed cultural remissions that ultimately both reinforce the dominant patterns and call them into question, sometimes opening mental avenues for reform.

In *Man, Play, and Games* (1961: 11–35 and 44) Roger Caillois develops Johan Huizinga's theory of play by classifying games into four types: (1) competition, or *agôn*, in which one relies only on oneself and one's efforts; (2) chance, or *alea*, in which one counts on everything except oneself, submitting to the powers not under one's control; (3) imitation, or *mimicry*, in which one imagines that one is someone else and invents an imaginary universe; and (4) vertigo, or *ilinx*, in which one "gratifies the desire to temporarily destroy one's bodily equilibrium, escape the tyranny of ordinary perception, and provoke the abdication of conscience" (44).[23] With the help

---

23. "Each of the basic categories of play has socialized aspects of this sort. . . . For *agôn*, the socialized form is essentially sports to which are added contests in which skill and chance are subtly blended as in games and on radio and as part of advertising. In *alea*, there are casinos, racetracks, state lotteries, and pari-mutuels. For *mimicry*, the arts involved are public spectacles, puppet shows, the Grand Guignol, and much more equivocally, carnivals and masked balls which are already oriented toward vertigo. Finally, *ilinx* is revealed in the traveling show and the annual or cyclical occasions for popular merry-making and jollity" (Caillois 1961: 41).

of Hans Ulrich Gumbrecht's *In Praise of Athletic Beauty* (2006) one can supplement such a scheme by the notion of *arête*, the striving for perfection, which may variously combine, in aesthetic experience, with each of the four types of games.

A pioneering application of Caillois's discussion of four types of games to literature was experimented with by Wolfgang Iser (1988: 94–106; 1989: 249–61; and 1993: 247–80). Iser distinguishes between the games *represented in* the text, the games *played by* the text, and the spirit of the game with which the reader approaches a particular text. The three need not coincide either in the same text or in the same reading experience. My discussion of *A Tale of Two Cities* will show, for instance, that though the motif of vertigo (*ilinx*) recurs throughout the narrative along with the recurrent representation of *mimesis*,[24] the narrative technique of the novel (the game played *by* the text) promotes *alea* and restrains *mimicry* in the audience response.

Though the game of *ilinx* is the closest to carnival morphology, in reader response it is *mimicry*, in the shape of sympathetic identification and vicarious experience (see Harding 1962), that actually constitutes the closest approximation to the carnivalesque boundary erosion and hierarchy reversal. "I was Raskolnikov," said a well-known American writer in a Faculty of Humanities elevator, recollecting his younger days. One frequently hears similar admission: "I was Holden Caulfield," or "I wanted to be Elizabeth Bennet, Prince Andrey, Scarlett O'Hara." In contrast, it would be rather uncommon to hear that someone "was" or "wanted to be" Lucy Manette, Isabel Archer, or Clarissa Dalloway. And what about Emilia Gould in Conrad's *Nostromo*? It is neither the traits of the character nor the morality of his or her conduct so much as the features of the narrative technique that allow or preclude vicarious experience—this is a major aspect of the ethics of literary form. For example, it is a shift in narrative technique that turns the reader who has identified with Dumas' Edmond Dantès into a detached curious observer of the same character as the Count of Monte Cristo.

The tendency of the carnivalesque on non-carnivalesque reading also depends on period tastes: the sentimentality of sundry Dickensian passages whether in *Little Dorrit* or *The Old Curiosity Shop* swept along the bulk of its nineteenth-century target audience; in the twenty-first century it rather "throws" the reader, disrupting the mimetic response. The types of game played by the reader are, moreover, affected by the background of media culture—the experience of what Marshall McLuhan called the hot media,

---

24. Caillois's use of the term *mimicry* is radically different from the use of the term *mimesis* in literary theory from Aristotle to Auerbach; in his system it is a type of game rather than a synonym of "representation."

such as films in movie theaters, tends to be significantly more aleatic and vertiginous (and largely carnivalesque) than the response to the cold media, such as novels have become in the age of what Wordsworth would have called "gross and violent stimulants" (1956: 155). At the candlelit desks of the past, novels had a greater power of casting a spell on the readers and carrying them away from their own predicaments and routines. These days "readerly" texts are more likely to match this effect, whereas the rhythm of reading the "writerly" text (Barthes 1974: 4)[25] is closer to a miniature model of sociocultural existence, with bittersweet daily discipline at times joyfully disrupted by interludes of fascination.

Works of fiction discussed in this book are instances of the carnivalesque, the intermediate, and the oppositional non-carnivalesque modes. Chapter 1 discusses the treatment of the carnivalesque in three of Nathaniel Hawthorne's stories in order to isolate the literary counterparts of the anthropological features of the carnivalesque—in particular, those features of the form of expression that tend to accompany the topoi of topsy-turvydom and horizontal osmosis (the carnivalesque traits of the form of content). The chapters that follow distinguish between the carnivalesque and the non-carnivalesque works on the basis of these formal features and examine the ethics of narrative form mainly in terms of the relationship between the form and the substance of content in each work (rather than in terms of reader response as in Toker 1993a). Starting with chapter 2 the materials are arranged chronologically: from the corpus of each writer I have chosen a work that marks a slot in the paradigm of cultural remissions. I discuss Fielding's *Tom Jones* as an oppositional narrative, but one that also displays numerous features of the carnivalesque. Sterne's *Tristram Shandy* (chapter 3) is my example of a somewhat diminished yet almost endemic *carpe diem* carnival, one that resurges as a compensation for the harshness of the human predicament. Jane Austen's novels *Sense and Sensibility* and, in particular, *Mansfield Park*

25. Barthes' distinction between readerly and writerly texts may be vividly illustrated by the Jewish parable I heard from my father. When a young man tells his father that he wants to be a writer, the father replies by asking, "What kind of writer do you want to be?" He then draws two images. One is of a young girl reading a novel on a Friday night: the candle will soon burn down (and it is forbidden to light a new one on a Sabbath); she wants to know how it will all end; feverishly, she starts reading and turning the pages faster and faster, until, the candle having almost melted, she peeps into the last page. The other image is of an old man wheeled out into the garden in his chair, reading a book, putting it away and thinking, dozing off, awakening and reading again, thinking and dozing off again. "So what kind of books do you want to write?"

are examples of the non-carnivalesque oppositional (chapter 4). Chapter 5 analyzes the ambivalent treatment of the "bitter carnival" (Bernstein 1992) in Dickens's *A Tale of Two Cities.*

Chapters 6 and 7 are devoted to narratives that prominently display one of the two central topoi of the carnivalesque: George Eliot's *Daniel Deronda* thematizes the horizontal blurring of boundaries between the self and the other (chapter 6); and Thomas Hardy's *The Mayor of Casterbridge* (chapter 7), set against the changes in the late-nineteenth-century agricultural trade, focuses on vertical reversals of hierarchies while also examining the submerged continuities of the past. *The Mayor of Casterbridge* can be regarded as a carnivalesque novel since the topos of horizontal osmosis is also present in it to some extent; *Daniel Deronda,* however, is an intermediate case.

Further down the modal scale, chapter 8 analyzes Conrad's "The Secret Sharer," which deals with a non-carnivalesque type of kinship between the self and the other—a kinship that excludes the pooling of affects. On the basis of this novella I also discuss the morphology of test situations, contrasting it with the morphology of carnivalesque crisis situations, and the narratological conditions for the games of *alea* and *agôn* played *in* and *by* the texts.

Chapter 9 moves from the carnivalesque to radical self-carnivalization. It analyzes an idea that Joyce's *Ulysses* shares with Bergson's *Creative Evolution*—and the way in which this novel carnivalizes not only the social mores it refers to but also the philosophical thought that is largely accountable for *its own* conceptual organization.

This chapter is followed by a remission, a caesura, an inter-section that points to a radical break in the history and the cultural history of the twentieth century. A short introduction precedes a reprinting of a story by Varlam Shalamov—to ease Anglophone readers' access to one of the stories that are discussed in the last chapter of the book. These stories, Kafka's "A Hunger Artist" and Shalamov's "The Artist of the Spade," shift the focus from carnival to Lent, or rather to forms of corrupted Lent. The former story foreshadows and the latter processes some of the atrocities that the logical cultural determinacies of the early twentieth century turned out to be powerless to anticipate or preempt.

Each of the ten chapters deals with ways in which the narratives explore cultural remissions and with the conditions they set for the reader's experience of aesthetic or intellectual self-liberation. Implicit (and at times explicit) in the analysis is the semiological model of semantics/syntactics/pragmatics (cf. Morris 1946: 217–20; Toker 2008b and 2010): the morphological features of the carnivalesque and the oppositional are discussed in relation to the semantics of the ethical vision, the syntactics of the aesthetic pattern, and, to a smaller extent, the pragmatics of the text–reader communication. Bakhtinian categories are, indeed, used instrumentally, but the narratives themselves are read not only as examples of phenomena that the book deals with but also for their own sake. The narratives discussed in the following chapters have been analyzed so often that an additional analytic iteration runs the risk of turning into what Umberto Eco has called Tetrapyloctomy, "the art of splitting a hair four ways" (1990: 64). To avoid that effect I focus on less discussed aspects of these works, and try to take advantage of their canonical status to show how a new theoretical framework can lead to new insights. Frankly, however, the relationship between a new theoretical basis and a new interpretive point is often etiologically circular.

Two more preliminary remarks:

(1) As is well known, the ethical system inferable from the text (and personified as "the implied author") need not be unambiguously ascribed to historical authors. As Sheldon Sacks noted in 1966, the "signals which influence our attitudes toward characters, acts, and thoughts represented in novels" are often "postulated upon rhetorical signals dictated by purely aesthetic considerations; the signals, then, would have no specifiable relationship to the ethical predilections of the novelist who employed them" (230). Yet narrative details capable of generating ethical inferences unacceptable to the historical author can be revised or neutralized: one can argue, for instance, that Jane Austen has Lady Catherine de Burgh pay an unreasonable visit to Elizabeth Bennet so that the happy ending of the novel should hinge on the results of this debacle rather than on the breaking of a promise (see Karen Newman 1983: 704). Specific rhetorical effects may or may not be introduced for purely aesthetic purposes, and may not have been adjusted to the ethical implications of the plot events. Here one treads the slippery ground of intentionality.[26] Indeed, formal considerations may have acted as search instruments for the author, as an aid to ethical reflection—just as in classical poetry meter and rhyme often served as means of philosophical outreach. However this may be, formal features can be viewed as guidelines, or, conversely, as "stumbling blocks" (Harrison 1993/1994), in the *reader's* construction of the ethical system for which the work has created a matrix.

26. For a new perspective on the issue of intentionality see Herman 2007: the idea of the concrete intentions of the individual author can be replaced by the operation of the craft "know-how" through which means are adjusted to goals, or rhetoric to poetics.

The *ethics of literary form* implies a *reciprocal* influence between the ethical ideas and the formal aspects of a literary work: not only does the idea-content call for a specific manner of articulation but the aesthetic subtleties of the shape of the discourse reflect back on, complicate, and adjust the ethical reality in whose creation the reader is invited to take part.

(2) The metaphor of "remission" for carnivalesque experience and oppositional practices implies that the logical determinacy of a cultural development is of the order of disease. Though emergent cultural self-organization can be beautiful in its own right, the ease of automatic cultural conformity (perceived as such when an individual's acculturation or social self-organization has reached an advanced stage) is, indeed, in the longer run, a dis-ease, whose revolutionary cures produce their own counterconformities, replacing one determinacy by another. It is in the loopholes that open up in cultural development—loopholes represented in carnivalesque and oppositional narratives and constituted by all genuine aesthetic and ludic experience—that the work of the sociocultural causes and effects is discontinued, giving play to the intuitive, the creative, baffling predictability and liberating new strands of individual and cultural potential.

CHAPTER ONE

Carnival and Crisis in Three Stories by Nathaniel Hawthorne

THE TOPOI OF VERTICAL REVERSALS and horizontal blurring of boundaries characterize the *form of content* in carnivalesque narratives even when the substance of the content is not carnival events. What are, then, the features of the substance of content that recur throughout the carnivalesque mode, and how do they connect with the form of both content and expression? I shall here suggest possible answers to this question on the basis of three of Nathaniel Hawthorne's stories set in New England's Puritan communities of the early and mid-seventeenth century. These stories do focus on carnivalesque events: the tar-and-feather procession in "My Kinsman, Major Molineux," the nocturnal foul-is-fair gathering in the forest in "Young Goodman Brown," and the maypole ceremony in "The Maypole of Merry Mount"; however, the carnival of the latter story is a corrupted relic and that of the former two is what Michael André Bernstein (1992) has described as the bitter carnival of resentment, the antipode of true festivity. In the three stories the anthropological characteristics of the carnival are associated with a number of themes (the substance of content) as well as formal narrative traits. In order to show that the connections between the carnival topoi and these particular themes and techniques represent regularities rather than specific cases, the analysis will be supplemented by examples from other narratives.

The features of the substance of content in carnivalesque narratives may be regarded as a translation of the features of the carnival as an anthropological phenomenon into the medium of verbal narrative.

Festive carnival takes place at an appointed, precisely circumscribed, and rather short period of time. Accordingly, the *time span* represented in carnivalesque narratives tends to be brief: its borderlines are approximately set by the beginning and the end of *crisis situations*.[1] This unity of time can stretch from a single afternoon as in "The Maypole of Merry Mount" to two days as in Solzhenitsyn's *The First Circle* or two weeks in Dostoevsky's *Crime and Punishment;* in any case, the story-time tends to be relatively short in comparison with the amount of the text devoted to it. Carnivalesque narratives are thus characterized by expansion, or deceleration (cf. Rimmon-Kenan 1983: 52–53). The relative slowness of the representational time—its *longueur,* what is perceived as an almost disproportionate amount of the text devoted to a certain episode—can become unbearably oppressive when the reader feels caught up in scenes of the carnival's bitter, violent corruptions—such as the interminable episode of the execution of the Blancos in Hemingway's *For Whom the Bell Tolls* or the episodes of mass murder and of delirium in Jonathan Littell's *The Kindly Ones*.[2]

Another feature of the carnival also largely reflected in carnivalesque fiction is its setting in *open or liminal spaces.* In non-carnivalesque narratives that *incorporate* crisis points (generally followed by a dénouement) but are not wholly devoted to them, the crisis points are usually also set in open spaces (e.g., Piazza St. Marco in Venice in Henry James's *The Wings of the Dove*) or in liminal spaces—on the balcony (James's *The Golden Bowl*), in the garden or shrubbery (Austen's *Pride and Prejudice*), at the threshold (E. M. Forster's *A Room with a View*). The phenomenology of the imagination associates even offstage crises in the life of secondary characters with liminal positions in space: in *Pride and Prejudice*, after Elizabeth Bennet has refused Mr. Collins, we find Charlotte Lucas *at the window,* listening to the uneasy conversation between Collins and Mrs. Bennet in the room behind her and getting ready for a turn in her own fortunes (91–92).

---

1. On "crisis time" as the subject of carnivalesque fiction, see Bakhtin 1984: 169.

2. This perception usually depends on the reader's emotional attitude to the type of events recounted: in most cases, certainly in the ones above, even if the text is read out loud the duration of the reading might still be shorter than the duration of the represented events. Not insignificantly, in Littell's novel the *longueur* of the wounded protagonist's delirium rather exceeds that of the representation of the slaughter of the Jews.

The chronotope of carnivalesque narrative (crisis times and open or liminal spaces) usually entails two more morphological features: (1) the theme of the growth of a tendency in the narrative opening, and (2) the theme of the subversion of individual discreteness in the main plot.

(1) The *opening* of carnivalesque narratives is characterized by the *refus de commencement.* Whereas non-carnivalesque biography-type fiction, especially by nineteenth-century writers, tends to start with an external event—an arrival or a departure that changes the deployment of the forces on the board, the action of crisis-type narratives usually begins with a version of an *in medias res* moment, when some tendency has come to a head, as if at "the appointed time."

Thus the action of *Crime and Punishment,* Bakhtin's major example of the carnivalesque mode, starts when the feverish workings of Raskolnikov's mind and the depletion of his body have reached a stage in which, to quote the dialectical principle, quantity turns into quality. Though his murder of the old woman is presented as stimulated by a few chance events and (in a bow, as it were, to the "biographical" tradition) by the arrival of his mother's letter after two months of silence, Dostoevsky makes it clear that if these events had not taken place, other incidents would have performed their function. Indeed, the murder of the old woman is not averted when Raskolnikov's plan to purloin an ax from the kitchen is thwarted—after a short while he is able to steal an ax from the caretaker's room: when a goal is obsessive, the means of pursuing it present themselves, one contingency being compensated by another.

Solzhenitsyn's *Cancer Ward,* a mildly carnivalesque narrative, is set in 1955, one of the transitional years in Soviet history, heralding the approach of the "Thaw." The action begins when the cancerous growths that have been developing in the bodies of the two main characters assume dimensions that can no longer be ignored. The actual arrival of the main characters at the hospital is the consequence of the swelling of the tumors rather than a self-contained trigger of further action.

Hawthorne's *The Scarlet Letter,* a novel that stages a tension between the carnivalesque and the anti-carnivalesque impulses in the individual soul, also starts soon after an event that has been, literally, in gestation: Esther Prynne has given birth to an illegitimate child. Her carnivalesque exposure to public shame coincides, however, with the arrival of Chillingworth, a kind of occurrence that usually initiates the action of non-carnivalesque narratives.

The pattern of *refus de commencement* is clearly discernible in Hawthorne's carnivalesque short stories: they start when a certain tendency, whether individual or cultural, with roots going back far into the fictional past, has risen to the pitch where it needs to be attended to or translated into action. In "The Maypole of Merry Mount" the relationship between Edith and Edgar has reached a stage when the midsummer night can double as the "appointed time" for their wedding. By confluence, the resentment of the Puritan community against the revelers of Merry Mount has likewise swollen to the point of bursting: indeed, the story makes no mention of any specific *casus belli* that may have provoked the Puritans to attack the Mount Wollaston settlement at this particular juncture. In "My Kinsman, Major Molineux" (in contrast to Dickens's *Nicholas Nickleby,* where it is after his father's death that the young protagonist goes to seek his fortunes in town), Robin travels to Boston not because something has happened in his family, nor because he has received any specific invitation in addition to the standing one from his uncle. Nor does his departure from home follow a specific age landmark that might call for a rite of passage: it is mentioned that Robin leaves home *before* he is eighteen, that is, while he is still immature,[3] yet the symbolism of a road to travel before he reaches maturity—or, rather, learns to toe the line—is complemented by the suggestion that his spirits have evidently reached a stage when he has to leave home, break away, seek his self elsewhere. In "Young Goodman Brown" there is likewise no specific trigger for the protagonist's expedition to the forest on that particular night "of all nights of the year" (1033)[4]—no reason apart from the stage reached by the psychosexual tensions of a young couple (only three months married) in combination with the unavowed animus against the patriarchal authority of the first Puritan settlers: the collective memory of their heroica is now threatening the third generation (see Crews 1966: 103–6). Goodman Brown's wife Faith also seems to be undergoing a crisis, both as a character of the story and as a personification of ideological attitudes that include imperfectly repressed religious doubts. Michael J. Colacurcio (1984: 289) reads the character of Young Goodman Brown as a product of the Half-Way Covenant, only recently granted a full, communing, church membership. However, the language of the text—in particular, the spectral Goody Cloyse's reference to the protagonist as "the silly fellow that now is" (1036)—suggests that such a passage may not yet have taken place: Goodman Brown therefore *needs* the self-test of turning to the wilderness for the certitude of his salvation. What he finds, however, is the ground for his suppressed resentment against the

3. Jane Austen anticipates such symbolism when making Emma Woodhouse and Elizabeth Bennet *almost* twenty-one, that is, just under age.

4. The night in question may, as Daniel Hoffman suggests (1961: 150), be imagined as that of October 31—All Saints' Eve.

pillars of his community.[5] The ambiguity of the spectral plot of the story (was it or was it not a dream?) parallels the doubts that the protagonist is left with in lieu of the desired *certitudo salutis.*

(2) The main body of a carnivalesque narrative is usually devoted to the cracking, breaking, bursting, of individual entities—the loss (usually temporary) of the discreteness of identity. The individual does not retain his hold on the sense of his or her separate self; the self opens up to the physical or mental environment and allows some layers to blend with the Other.

This critical erosion of the limits of the self may lead either to death or to a profounder understanding of reality—or to both. A suggestive account of this danger, and of the need to maintain a hold on one's identity lest it dissolve in the magma of the collective flow, is given in Vladimir Nabokov's humorously ambivalent remarks on the protagonist's heart attack in *Pnin:*

> I do not know if it has ever been noted before that one of the main characteristics of life is discreteness. Unless a film of flesh envelops us, we die. Man exists only insofar as he is separated from his surroundings. The cranium is the space-traveler's helmet. Stay inside or you perish. Death is divestment, death is communion. It may be wonderful to mix with the landscape, but to do so is the end of the tender ego. (1957: 20)

The passage deals, literally, with the inroads of physical disease, swooning, death (the pores and other apertures of the body open up to the environment, wounds bleed, consciousness fades); yet its symbolism also pertains to the possible loss of a person's intellectual discreteness within a collective discourse. The mixing of one's physical self with the "landscape" is an apt metaphor for the dissolution of one's identity in a crowd, in a collective emotional heightening, in a prevailing ideology, or in a mystical transport. It may be lethally irreversible: "the dead are good mixers" (Nabokov 1972: 93). Yet an entrenched rejection of invitations to loosen internal boundary control can lead to pettily self-interested emotional and intellectual sterility.

---

5. Colacurcio chooses to emphasize Goodman's presumptuously simplified version of Calvinism—for example, his theologically inadmissible belief in his own infallibility (1984: 290–95). He notes, moreover, that if the Devil claims to have helped the grandfather lash a Quaker woman through the village, in Goodman Brown's economy this means that the motif for the act (the woman would be half-naked) may have been "devilish" (1984: 293). Emily Miller Budick continues this line of thought, suggesting that Goodman Brown may be developing doubts not merely about the motivation for such an act but also about its general moral value; such a doubt would be radically subversive of Goodman's upbringing, according to which, if motivated by ideology rather than by psychological drives, "lashing a Quaker woman through the streets or setting fire to an Indian village would hardly have constituted the devil's work" (1986: 221).

Nabokov's texts enact the process of contact in which breaches in the armor of the individual self are at times, cautiously, allowed (see Toker 1999): like Hawthorne, Nabokov frequently stages dangerous tensions between the lure and the repulsiveness of the carnivalesque.

What any carnival sets the stage for is a mass merger of individuals into a whole, a respite from the sociocultural compartmentalization of everyday life. Associated with ancient fertility rites, it celebrates a natural life force—of the species or of the community rather than of separate individuals (Bakhtin 1968: 19, 88, 341). A pageant without footlights erases the divide between the participants and spectators (7), and, in a symbolic expression of belonging to a biological whole, the individual is swept along by the crowd—either physically, joining the movement of a street march or the transports of a demonstration in the square, or else psychologically, surrendering the discreteness and the intellectual autonomy of the self. The knowledge gained from this surrender is ambivalent—it may constitute a quasi-metaphysical insight but it may also amount to having one's reason overruled by popular drives or the party line. The loss of the sense of the separate self in yielding to the communal forces is a form of cultural remission—"the oceanic feeling" of Arthur Koestler's *Darkness at Noon* (1941: 256) or Freud's *Civilization and Its Discontents,*[6] "the discharge" in Elias Canetti's *Crowds and Power* (1978: 17–18; see also note 9 in chapter 5). In the framework of Schopenhauer's categories, it is an epistemological elevation (since it provides an insight into the illusory nature of individuality, which is nothing but an objectification of the will) and a moral debasement (since it aligns one with the workings of the amoral impersonal Will, red in tooth and claw). Post-Bakhtinian scholarship has, indeed, emphasized the close connection between the carnival spirit and the devastation wreaked by violent social or religious strife.[7] The carnivalesque is corrupted both when the misrule is not limited (e.g., in a gory rebellion represented as a dance in Bruno Jasieński's *The Lay of Jakub Szela*[8]) and when it is ritualized as an in-group's obligatory social routine (e.g., the "orgy-porgy" of Aldous Huxley's *Brave New World*).

---

6. Freud denied having firsthand experience of this religious feeling of the limitlessness of the whole to which one belonged as a grain to the sand; he attributed his awareness of it, as is now known, to Romain Rolland (see 1961: 8).

7. Cf. M. F. Bernstein: "The viciousness that can be released by the carnival's dissolution of the accumulated prudential understanding of a culture needs to figure in our thinking about the rhetorical strategies and ideological assertions within which utopian theorizing is articulated" (1992: 8).

8. See Krzychylkiewicz 2006: 165–83.

The three Hawthorne stories discussed here provide a paradigm of motifs pertaining to the discreteness of identity and to the factors that threaten this discreteness.

"My Kinsman" is to a large extent a story of initiation. A shrewd country youth, Robin Molineux, crosses a threshold (the river) and enters the town of Boston, where he plans to serve his political apprenticeship and make his fortune under the guidance of his high-placed uncle. After a number of puzzling trial-and-error encounters, he discovers that, as a representative of the British crown, his uncle has incurred resentment. Weird preparations for something are going on during the evening, and at nightfall the uncle, a uncrowned ruler, is driven through the town, in a tar-and-feather carnival pageant,[9] amid general derision. The procession stops in front of Robin and, as the eyes of the uncle and nephew meet in mutual recognition, Robin becomes the center of the crowd's attention: the roles of the participants and the spectator are now interchanged. Up to this point Robin has successfully resisted the multitude of sins personified by the various citizens of Boston (see Broes 1964). Now, however, he succumbs to the impulse of a self-protective dehumanization of the other. In order to suppress the pity and terror that seize him at the sight of his uncle's humiliation, Robin surrenders to the inarticulate psychological pressure of the crowd and joins the crowd's contagious brutal laughter at the dethroned ruler. The narrative parts ways with him at this juncture: the focus shifts to the perspective of the uncle, the scapegoat, a position from which Robin's laughter is registered as the loudest within this chorus.

The story is sometimes read as that of the young man's asserting his independence from a patriarchal authority figure, with Robin's experience possibly symbolizing the development of the young and self-assertive American nation. However, his laughter at a critical point is, conversely, a momentary but irreversible surrender of the separateness of his self, and an initiation into the guilt of the baiting crowd. His autonomy, moreover, turns out to be a mere change of allegiance: the last words of the story are an encouraging

---

9. Cf. John N. Miller's (1989a: 51–64) attack on the allegorical readings of the story and his conclusion that "pageantry in Hawthorne's historical fiction has lost its ritual innocence" (62) and, when "prostituted for questionable political ends in a particular colonial American setting," becomes "a nightmare" (63). The use of carnivalesque forms for popular social protest was, however, a well-known channel of violence in continental Europe up to the late nineteenth century—this is strikingly described in E. Le Roy Ladurie's *Carnival in Romans,* which deals with a history of tax-related mutinies in a fifteenth-century French town.

acceptance extended to him by an elderly person, another surrogate father figure, who has watched him before and during his near-tragic test. This patriarchal quasi-mentor, calm and apparently in the know, may well be seen as one of the conspirators who draw political profit from popular riots (Colacurcio 1984: 144–45). This interpretation of the story, reminiscent of Dickens's treatment of the forces behind the Gordon riots in *Barnaby Rudge,* rejects "the all-too-reassuring view that revolutionary politics recapitulates adolescent psychology: maturation is painful but it knows nothing of conspiracy" (152).[10] The would-be shrewd young provincial who bears the generic name of Robin (an eighteenth-century name for a stock character of a "country bumpkin") is initiated not into the out-of-the-limelight ruses of a cabal but into the exultation of the crowd, the discharge, the carnivalesque dissolution of the self, a letting-go that prefaces a redefinition of cultural personhood.

"The Maypole of Merry Mount" explores the opposite phenomenon— the reconsolidation of the individual self following the pressures of the carnivalesque dissolution of identity. The midsummer celebrations of the maypole in the Merry Mount community are supposed to represent a carnivalesque unity with fertile nature. Hence the grotesque animal masks worn by the celebrants; hence also the absent or minimal individualization of the characters. Yet here the generic stag, wolf, or goat masks do not so much express the wearers' genuine kinship with nature as hide and level out the features underneath; they thus facilitate the wearers' blending into the crowd yet also provide covers under which the individuals can remain secretly nonconformist. The masquerade is a part of the carnival, but a part that contains the seeds of the carnival's self-cancellation.

A *mandatory* permanent self-indulgence, such as that of the would-be Land-of-Cokaygne utopian community of Merry Mount,[11] is a *corrupted* carnival: true carnival is entered voluntarily and circumscribed in time. The celebrants' unity with nature is belied by the relative infertility of the community's cornfields: at harvest time their crop is "of the smallest" (885). The tone of the description of the celebrants is pensively alienated and melancholy rather than joyous.[12] Sadness amidst a carnival is a recurrent

10. Colacurcio refutes the parallel between Robin's rejection of his uncle and the Bostonians' rite of passage to maturity through active resistance to British colonial rule; Budick (1989: 117) adds that instead of exculpating Robin, the analogy inculpated the community.

11. On the difference between the Golden Age utopias and those of "moderation and restraint" see Kumar 1987: 7–9.

12. John N. Miller attributes this disparity between the subject matter and the tone to Hawthorne's residual Puritanical preferences (see 1989a: 111–23).

feature of Hawthorne's work (prominently thematized in *The Marble Faun*): Romantic individualism resists the festive Dionysian impulses of aggressive fusion, being all too keenly aware of their attraction.

No masks are worn by Hawthorne's May King and Queen, Edgar and Edith, whose marital union—not a carnival mésalliance yet vaguely reminiscent of the marriages of beggars in the cemeteries during plagues—is celebrated in the story. Nor does the young couple feel unalloyed happiness during the ceremony: "No sooner had their hearts glowed with real passion than they were sensible of something vague and unsubstantial in their former pleasures, and felt a dreary presentiment of inevitable change" (885). The narrative interprets their mood as the unavoidable concomitant of the acceptance of family responsibilities following frivolous adolescent joys, yet it also suggests that their sadness is consequent on the weaning of parts from the whole: true love (or "real" passion) is the love of separate individuals; it is anti-carnivalesque because nontransferable. The happiness of the communion in love both asserts and bridges the gap between the identities of the lovers (one has to be separate in order to unite), but it lays a moat between the private castle of the newly wed and the villages around it. The hostility of the traditional communities to those who live together "in sin" (powerfully evoked in Hardy's *Jude the Obscure*) is partly rooted in their resentment of the couples' self-excision from the whole. The communal ceremony of the wedding mitigates this self-excision by pretending to deny it, by appropriating the privacy of the young couple and turning it into a promise of its own self-perpetuation.[13] Hence even the most liberal community, such as that of Merry Mount, needs wedding ceremonies as ritual enactments of the sanction granted to the lovers to renege from the crowd.

Edgar and Edith try to hide their melancholy because it is "high treason to be sad at Merry Mount" (884); they reassert their separateness from the crowd of the celebrants by the very attempt to conceal their sadness. Nor do they blend with each other: their love is presented as a caring companionship of two discrete individualities. However, unknown to themselves, their mood may be a projection of the concealed spirit of the whole Merry Mount community on which the frivolous, carnivalesque, and "masterless" state has, to some extent, been imposed from without.

Thus, upon the emergence of their individual selves as *separate*, Edgar and Edith remain *representative* of their community. Or rather, they remain what Joseph Conrad might have called its "secret sharers" (see chapter 8),

---

13. Cf. Tanner on marriage as offering "the perfect and total mediation between the patterns within which men and women live" (1979: 16).

as they discover, firsthand, an aspect of that universalizable "truth of the human heart" (243) which transcends individual differences: the heart needs both the moods of "L'Allegro" and those of "Il Penseroso" (see Birk 1991). The people of Merry Mount who know that carnival has lost its meaning by becoming perpetual have to keep their awareness concealed. Their utopia has turned into a repressive ideology,[14] a cultural remission into a social disease.

Paradoxically, the turning of utopia into an ideology also characterizes the Puritans who come to arrest the merrymakers. The Puritans have to suppress their "Anglo-Pagan" neighbors not only in order to demonstrate their independence of the King (whose relatively recent edict permitted May-games) but also because in this forest "Comus crew" they recognize a rejected aspect of their own psyche. Despite their valorization of the individual self, Endicott's Puritan saints and warriors remain parts of the human whole—in terms of psychological kinship, or "secret sharing" rather than in terms of ecological symbiosis or cultural uniformity. Denying themselves a cultural remission, they remain in the grip of a social disease that is the photonegative of the Merry Mount indulgence.

Yet at the moment of crisis the Massachusetts Puritans do not retain the discreteness of their selves; they too melt—not within the congregated body of biological humanity but in the body politic of the posse. Significantly, they are shown making their entrance into the arena of the story's action as shadows that detach from the shadows of the forest around the maypole clearing ("some of these black shadows" rush forth in human shape, 887). Only two of the shadows are then granted individual identities and names: Governor John Endicott and Peter Palfrey, the latter variously defined as "the Ancient of the band," "the lieutenant," and "the officer" (888). Yet even this crystallization of personalities is not final, especially since Endicott seems to recognize in Edgar and Edith a part of himself, a part that he does not wish to suppress. By an ingenious authorial footnote, text masking as paratext, Hawthorne alerts us to the fact that the man whom Endicott addresses as Blackstone (and whom he arrests) could not have been the historical Rev. Blackstone (who never lived in Mt. Wollaston, alias Merry Mount): he thus sends us to background sources—and they tell us that the person arrested at Mount Wollaston was one Thomas Morton, the gun-peddling founder of the Saturnalian community after Captain Wollaston's departure.[15] The

---

14. Cf. Mannheim 1955.

15. William Bradford recounts that Thomas Morton "got some strong drink and other junkets and made them a feast; and after they were merry, he began to tell them he would give them good counsel. 'You see,' saith he, 'that many of your fellows are carried to Virginia, and if you stay till this

person who arrested him was not Endicott but Miles Standish; Endicott came along later to hack down the symbolic maypole (see Colacurcio 1984: 260–77). Thus, as the borders between the text, the paratext, and the External Field of Reference (Harshaw 247–49) dissolve, the Endicott of the story dissolves too, fading away in the diffuse historical oblivion that self-assertive personalities have always tried to retard.

"Young Goodman Brown" likewise explores the consolidation of personality, but here the focus is on the kind of consolidation that rejects even the "secret sharing," the non-carnivalesque consciousness of kinship with one's neighbor. The story also examines the consequences of the suppression of "L'Allegro" in the Puritan community. Denied institutionalized expressions, misrule breaks out in somber shapes, such as the tar-and-feather violence in "My Kinsman, Major Molineux" or the skimmington ride in Hardy's *The Mayor of Casterbridge*. Here it takes the shape of an internalized fantasy of the witches' Sabbath, a prelude to the Salem witch trials.

This story is an example of what Tzvetan Todorov has called the genuine fantastic (1980: 25–42): it makes the reader hesitate between accepting the supernatural (Goodman Brown meets the devil and attends a spectral carnivalesque parody of a church ritual in the forest[16]) and reading the bulk of the story as an account of a dream. Whatever the case, the unusual experience gives Goodman Brown what he regards as a true insight into the sinful nature of his neighbors and friends. The insight may be a projection of his own secretly seething subversiveness; it may be crassly exaggerated; yet it may also be, to some extent, true. Throughout the story Goodman Brown struggles to dissociate himself from the evil that, as the devil tells him, is the nature of mankind. He is willing to concede that the elders of the community are lost souls but insists on his own salvation. Yet when he begins to doubt his wife, the Faith to whom he is wedded, his erstwhile cherished certainties are reversed: "My Faith is gone! . . . There is no good on earth; and sin is but a name. Come, devil; for to thee is this world given" (1038). In a mixture of despair and pride, chief of the deadly sins, he continues to assert his identity, now turned upside down: "Let us hear which will laugh loudest. Think not to frighten me with your devilry. Come witch, come wizard, come Indian powwow, come devil himself, and here comes Goodman

---

Rasdall return, you will also be carried away and sold for slaves with the rest. Therefore I would advise you to thrust out this Lieutenant Fitcher, and I, having a part in the Plantation, will receive you as my partners and consociates; so may you be free from service, and we will converse, plant, trade, and live together as equals and support and protect one another,' or to like effect. . . . And Morton became Lord of Misrule" (1967: 204–10).

16. Cf. also David Levine (1962) and Harvey Pearce (1954).

Brown. You may as well fear him as he fear you" (1039). Without realizing it, however, he comes to share the "if-you-can't-beat-it-join-it" impulse of many of his fellow congregationists (e.g., Martha Carrier, rumored—in the story's Internal Field of Reference—to have "received the devil's promise to be queen of hell," 1040). The story can be read as suggesting that it is Goodman Brown's suppressed doubt about his own identity as one of the elect that has sent him on his own "errand into the wilderness" (see Christophersen 1986). His predicament may represent that of his fellow congregationists, who, owing to a vague sense of guilt, are unable to come to terms with the indeterminacy and so choose a potentially carnivalesque "foul-is-fair" reversal to stabilize their identities, even if negatively defined.[17] The description of Goodman's rush through the forest to the witches' meeting presents his demoniacal self-assertion as delusive—even one person alone can enact a dark bacchanalian pageant in which the borderlines between himself and the evil that he celebrates dissolve: "On he flew among the black pines, brandishing his staff with frenzied gestures, now giving best to an inspiration of horrid blasphemy, and now shouting like demons around him. The fiend in his own shape is less hideous than when he rages in the breast of man" (1039).

Goodman's attitude to his fellow sinners remains one of alienated resentment. For him "the communion with [his] race" means only the power of insight into the evil in others: the devil, indeed, ascribes a ledgerful of iniquities to the Salem congregation and concludes with a promise: "By the sympathy of your human hearts for sin ye shall scent out all the places . . . where crime has been committed. . . . It shall be yours to penetrate, in every bosom, the deep mystery of sin" (1041).

At what is presented as the penultimate moment before the quasi-baptismal clinching of the "communion," Goodman Brown rallies, calls on his Faith to "resist the wicked one" (1041),[18] and awakes in the solitude of the forest path. Instead of baptismal drops on his forehead, cold dew falls from a branch upon his cheek.

This cooling liquid comes from the outside world—as a surrogate for the warm tears that a painful insight into sinfulness and suffering ought to call forth from the depths of the self (see Easterly 1991). Young Goodman's

17. Cf. Colacurcio: "Especially in the latter days of Puritanism, when so many people lived out whole lives of spiritual tension in a half-way status, the temptations must have been both strong and various: simply to get the whole business settled; or authentically to accept the highly probable import of one's unremitting sinfulness (and perhaps to enjoy some sense of true significance in the world); or even to join the Devil's party out of sheer rebellion against such singularly infelicitous figures of covenant authority as Cotton Mather" (1984: 300–301).

18. See Paulits 1970 on Goodman Brown's motivation for this act of resistance.

bodily self retains its discreteness. It is not bruised; symbolically, it does not connect with the environment, not even to the extent of fusing tears with dew: Goodman Brown continues to insist on his separateness from his neighbors, a separateness that takes the shape of suspiciousness and gloom. Even if the spectral evidence of his neighbors' sinfulness is understood as a projection of his own suppressed drives, its result is his complete dissociation of himself from the others (cf. Tritt 1991): as it often happens in the cases of psychological projection, he steels himself against all suggestions of his own guilt. If we believe Schopenhauer (1969, I: 372), the wicked person is one who totally dissociates himself from the life of others, denying the community of human experience. The rejection of the carnivalesque impulse of familiar contact and imaginative indulgence of forbidden carnivalesque drives are thus presented as conducive to the witch-hunt mentality—Goodman Brown's snatching a little girl away from the pious instruction of Goody Cloyse may be the first motion towards the Salem trials. Like Arthur Miller a century later,[19] Hawthorne represents the psychology of the witch hunt as a morbid convulsion of repressed carnivalesque impulses.

In the three Hawthorne stories discussed (as in, for example, Solzhenitsyn's *Cancer Ward*), the crises in the lives of the protagonists overlap with the crises in the lives of their respective communities: it is as if, in order to participate in the formation of the national or communal identity, the individual temporarily surrenders his identity. The confluence of the personal and the political imposes limitations on the high view of human possibility that underlies Hawthorne's carnivalesque narrative mode. "The Maypole of Merry Mount" and "My Kinsman, Major Molineux" refer to communal landmark events which, despite the attendant ethical problems, might be seen as sociocultural remissions that foreshadow the cataclysm of the War of Independence. By contrast, "Young Goodman Brown" emphasizes an entrenched self-assertion combined with a resistance to the call for relaxation of cultural/ideological control, a resistance aligned with the mysterious determinacy of developments leading up to witch trials.

Whereas "My Kinsman, Major Molineux" conjures up the sense of the variegated city life and stages a bitter carnival of urban abjections and resentments, "The Maypole" and "Young Goodman Brown" are part of Hawthorne's

19. Miller's *The Crucible* offers a different interpretation of the psychological roots of the Salem witch hunt, yet there too the corrupt carnival is traced back to a lack of legitimated oppositional loopholes for the suppressed resentments of the underprivileged.

attack on utopianism, which, judging by his two years at Brook Farm, may, at times, have held an attraction for him. Both the soft Garden-of-Eden/ Land-of-Cokaygne utopia of Merry Mount and the stern City-on-the-Hill utopia of the Puritans demand visible outward conformity from their members. As Isaiah Berlin has pointed out (1990: 1–48), the decline of Utopian thought in the twentieth century is linked with a new consciousness of the incommensurability yet possible coexistence of different culturally and psychologically determined needs or views of happiness. One should perhaps not go as far as claiming that Hawthorne may have anticipated this modern development in the history of ideas, but he evidently sensed the threat of utopianism to the discreteness of the self. Hawthorne's Romantic deontology recurrently betrayed a doubt that supererogation risks violating—in the language of *The Scarlet Letter*—the sanctity of the human heart. It also betrayed a doubt, more intimately understandable in the twentieth century than in the nineteenth, that spectacular supererogation can often be shot through with egoism or sociopolitical interest.

Thus, to extrapolate from the three stories, the main, mandatory but insufficient feature of the substance of content in the carnivalesque mode is not the representation of a carnival event but the theme of the individual identity's loss of discreteness, usually a temporary loss, a remission before a reconsolidation. The carnivalesque elements in the works of Dostoevsky, Hardy, Solzhenitsyn, and even Dickens, are likewise associated with a variety of moral problems pertaining to the disruptions of individual discreteness, wholeness, inner independence, self-possession; these disruptions take the shape of scandal scenes, confessions, melodramatic dialogues, emotional lacerations, emotion-fraught ideological arguments, all often leading to radical character transformations. The associated formal features (meter suited to matter) are focus on crisis situations, limitations of the temporal frame of the narrative (a version of the classical unity of time), and the prevalence of open and liminal spaces in the topographical setting. The *refus de commencement* and the motif of the swelling of a tendency in the narrative *incipit*—features of the form of expression in which the substance of the content and the form of the content intersect—are early signals of the carnivalesque mode.

CHAPTER TWO

Oppositionality in Fielding's *Tom Jones*

Dost thou think, because thou art virtuous there shall be no more
cakes and ale?
—Shakespeare, *Twelfth Night* 2.3.115–16

IF THE MAJOR FEATURE of the substance of content in the carnivalesque mode is the theme of the loss or relinquishing of the individual
identity's discreteness, then Fielding's second great "comic Epic-Poem in
Prose" (1987: 4), the hilarious *Tom Jones,* is not, by and large, carnivalesque,
even though it admits such inroads of the carnival as picaresque adventure,
scandal scenes, slapstick, sexual license, mock-epic battles, convivial gatherings, and liminal scenes complete with keyhole, arras, and closet. Whatever
changes of status the novel's protagonist undergoes, his essential self is presented as always remaining intact. Nor need Tom really *change* in the course
of the novel; what he needs is to learn prudence and mend his boisterous
ways. The closest he comes to losing himself is when his instinctive generosity conflicts with his other values; the resulting surface wounds heal quickly,
as does, it seems, the *"Hiatus in manuscriptis"* (Book VIII, chapter 4: 268)
that the barber finds on Tom's skull after his fight with Northerton.

Yet, even more intensely than the more earnest eponymous hero of Fielding's *Joseph Andrews,* Tom Jones displays the type of nobility of spirit that
necessarily clashes with the social mores of the iron age: like many a well-
meaning *jeune premier* in later fiction, he is impetuous, by nature good-
hearted, and motivated by "the glorious Lust of doing Good."[1] So long as he

1. Fielding, "Of Good Nature" 1972: 31.

finds it difficult to learn the prudent appearance of virtue, his most altruistic acts, such as protecting Black George, are all too readily misinterpreted as self-interest; his joyful intoxication at the news of his benefactor's recovery from illness is misrepresented as inconsiderate brawling; the ideas of chivalry that keep him from rejecting the advances of a lady endanger his reunion with his true love. Though of illegitimate birth, misguidedly banished, and (apparently) disinherited by Squire Allworthy, Tom never regards himself as disadvantaged or downtrodden: whatever happens, he is always a gentleman who has fallen on bad times rather than a picaro or a rebel. "Fielding,"[2] the Lord of Misrule in the novel's carnival enclaves, takes the liberty of rewarding Tom's generous spirit by ultimately allowing him the happy marriage to the gentlewoman he loves as well as a position of social prominence, yet this breach of class conventions is circumscribed: the happy ending of the love story is allowed to happen only after it is revealed that Tom's origins are genteel. The "stain" of his illegitimate birth, to use Jane Austen's ironic vocabulary,[3] is "bleached" by class.

In the first of the novel's prefatory chapters, the narrator assumes the metaphorical role of the owner of an "ordinary"—that is, a *restaurateur*, a modestly lower-rung counterpart of the Master of the Revels (cf. Wright 1965: 31). His "bill of fare" is "human nature," but the paying guest's cannibalism is no more than an extended metaphor associated with the extended eighteenth-century meaning of "appetites": the reader is given a "taste"[4] of class-cultural manners, innate moral tendencies, acquired commitments, and varieties of (im)prudence, sufficiently varied to prevent satiety. This combinatorial deployment of character traits is to a large extent the product of the sheer gusto of a witty, mystifying, surprise-rich story, one whose festive energies can open up loopholes in any "awful, impersonal Morality" and place Fielding, like most great artists, considerably ahead of his own epoch and class.

Loopholes, however, are not carnivalesque but oppositional phenomena, and it is on the latter that this chapter will focus. The oppositional stance

2. In this chapter (but not in the one on Jane Austen) I use the novelist's name as the personification of the system of values that informs the novel—in the sense in which Wayne Booth has used the term "the implied author" (1961: 71–76, 215–18).

3. Cf. Austen's *Emma* on Harriet's birth: "The stain of illegitimacy, *unbleached* by nobility or wealth, would have been a stain indeed" (*E* 317; my italics).

4. The conceit of the novel as a restaurant meal (I: 1) is further extended in the use of the metaphor of educational degustation—of, for instance, Mrs. Wilkins's resentful complaints: "Much more of the like Kind she muttered to herself; but this Taste shall suffice to the Reader" (V: 8, 161).

may be largely accountable for the uneven fortunes of this novel. For more than a century after its composition, the cakes and ale of *Tom Jones* seemed to call its ethical value system into question; as late as 1956 John Middleton Murry (9–52) still considered it necessary to play advocate to the book in an imaginary court of morality. By contrast, Henry James described this novel as "a vast episode in a sermon preached by a grandly humorous divine; and however we may be entertained by the way, we must not forget that our ultimate duty is to be instructed. With the minister's week-day life we have no concern: for the present he is awful, impersonal Morality" (1987: 21), softening this dictum by a compliment to "Fielding's fine old moralism, fine old humour and fine old style, which somehow really enlarge, make every one and every thing important" (41). Elsewhere, with the help of Cora Diamond's distinction between morality and moralism (1997) and Bernard Harrison's 1975 analysis of Fielding's ethical system and its place in the history of British moral philosophy, I have argued that Fielding's "fine old moralism" is, in fact, "fine old ethics" which could be roughly constructed as a three-dimensional paradigm with the axes made up of "the good heart," the deliberate commitment to the good of others (Harrison), and the checks and balances of prudence[5] (Toker 1996a). Here I shall show that the novel's moral stance, worked out through the deployment of character, event, and theme, is supplemented by the oppositional play that results from the dynamics of mystification when the potential side effects of mystification are turned to advantage in creating thematic patterns of the oppositional kind: like some of his characters Fielding gets away with breaking the rules.

At issue is not the obvious oppositionality inscribed in the protagonist's neglect of conventional moral poise. Nor is the kind of oppositional maneuver that I shall discuss to be conflated with the circumscribed licentiousness of the masquerade (cf. Terry Castle 1984) evoked in Book XIII. Like the carnival, the masquerade is an institutionalized safety valve for pressures that accumulate underneath the pieties of everyday life; its participants wear masques while often playing out those aspects of their character that, while wearing their own faces, they tend to conceal. Yet in *Tom Jones*, the masquerade is not a cultural remission; here masquerade roles are oneiric stylizations

---

5. On Fielding's treatment of genuine prudence, one of the cardinal virtues, as opposed to the false self-seeking prudence, and on the relationship of prudence and wisdom, see Battestin 1974: 145–92; a shorter version appears in Fielding 1995: 733–49.

of the participants' actual roles in the plot. It is only from the hypocrisy of everyday life, not from its structural irregularities, that they provide ludic relief: the characters can now mimic themselves while in real life they mimic idealized images.[6]

In the middle between the masked self-revelation and the barefaced hypocrisy one may find different shades of role-consciousness: thus Thwackum truly identifies with his role as a guardian of Christian virtue but suppresses the realization that his fervor is fueled by a penchant for cruelty; Partridge seeks his own advantage while genuinely believing that he is promoting the welfare of another; Mrs. Deborah Wilkins combines bad faith with downright hypocrisy; and Dowling and Black George succumb to temptations knowingly, without self-delusion. The paradigm of possible combinations of self-delusion and hypocrisy has received considerable attention in fiction, literary scholarship, philosophy,[7] and "real life"; what is more difficult to account for is the motivation of characters who deliberately play the moral reprobates that they are not[8]—or rather the artistic "know-how" (Herman 2007: 255–57) that creates such motivation. In *Tom Jones* such a character is Jenny Jones, a disadvantaged exponent of protofeminist oppositionality.

Jenny is one of the novel's women characters who take recourse to oppositional practices, including mystification, in the struggle for their rights to happiness and dignity. Sheridan Baker (1967) has demonstrated that keeping the secret of Tom's birth necessitates a certain kind of seemingly uncharacteristic behavior on the part of Miss Bridget Allworthy and that Fielding endows her with exactly the sort of disposition that renders her conduct consistent on a deeper psychological plane. But the underhand behavior of Jenny Jones is as vital to the mystification as is Miss Bridget's, and as consistent with Fielding's principle of the "conservation of character" (VIII, 1: 261): the pragmatic deployment of temporary informational gaps that underlies the novel's games of mystification may be viewed as a ran-

---

6. Lady Bellaston's masque of the Queen of Fairies, for instance, combines her roles of Tom's fairy godmother with that of Queen Omphala to his Hercules (see Ek 1979: 152–54). By contrast, the masques worn by the languid merrymakers in Hawthorne's "The Maypole of Merry Mount" (see p. 28 above) express features of the imposed and no longer fully endorsed personhood.

7. Cf. Marcus 2005 on the treatment of self-delusion in fiction and philosophy.

8. But see a melancholy philosophical treatment of such a theme in Borges's "Three Versions of Judas" (1964: 95–100).

domizing search instrument that provides access to unexpected ethical and psychological complexities.

———

Can the character of Jenny Jones be granted a convincingly coherent psychological makeup that would explain her consent to take upon herself the role of a "fallen woman"? Is her character consistent with her later identification with that role in the guise of the merry Mrs. Waters, whose entrances and exits are timed with theatrical skill, delaying and then precipitating the novel's comic anagnorisis? As a Borges character notes, reality may avoid the obligation to be interesting but "hypotheses may not."[9] Though Miss Bridget purchases Jenny's services for money, the hypothesis that money is the only motivation for Jenny's taking the fall for Miss Bridget's romance is not aesthetically satisfying. The novel, however, creates conditions for more engaging meaning-effects. Indeed, the episodes in which Jenny Jones appears in the novel suggest that considerable artistic care has been invested in their patterns of recurrent motifs, analogies, antitheses, and displacements.

Jenny emerges as a comic counterpart of Miss Bridget: neither is good-looking, and both are gifted scholars who cannot put their learning to constructive use. Yet if for Miss Bridget book-learning is largely a matter of sublimation of a passionate nature, in Jenny's case sexual promiscuity seems to be a gallows-humor displacement of an unsatisfied intellectual appetite. Jenny's sexual conduct is oppositional—more radically oppositional than Sophia's plight. The novel contains sufficient evidence for reading it as one of the ways in which Jenny struggles to restore her sense of dignity after it has been trampled by the community around Allworthy's Paradise Hall.[10]

Jenny starts her working life as a servant in the house of the schoolmaster Partridge. She is endowed with "a very uncommon Share of Understanding" and a "great Quickness of Parts," displays intellectual curiosity, "an extraordinary Desire of learning (for every leisure Hour she was always found reading in the Books of the Scholars)." Partridge has "the Good-nature, or Folly (just as the Reader pleases to call it)" to undertake her instruction (I, 6: 35–36). When her achievements exceed those of her master, Mrs. Partridge misreads the resulting tension between scholarly vanities as a symptom of a love affair. Here begins the pattern of *displacements* in Jenny's story. Curiosity

9. Borges, "Death and the Compass" (1964: 77).

10. "Oppositional practices help us to maintain *some* sense of dignity and personhood" (Chambers 1991: 7).

and vanity become her leitmotifs, but they are soon displaced from the sphere of scholarly achievement to that of sexual adventure.

Like Miss Bridget, Jenny finds herself at an impasse: the social structure denies the two women regular avenues of self-actualization through learning,[11] whether the learning is a result of intellectual "curiosity" (Jenny) or a sublimation of other appetites (Miss Bridget). One is free to imagine that it may be out of genuine sympathy rather than long-term calculation that Miss Bridget makes Jenny a status-determined yet also otherwise symbolic gift of her own silk outfit.

In these clothes vanity brings Jenny to church—and arouses the resentment of her neighbors (Molly Seagrim will, a generation later, appear in Sophia Western's dress, in a reprise of this effect). Like Mrs. Partridge, the parishioners misinterpret Jenny's flaunting her difference from them; they displace its cause from superior education to love-start privilege. As a result, Jenny becomes a likely scapegoat when the foundling baby appears in Paradise Hall.

Jenny's response to the hostility provoked by the secondhand finery is a keynote for her further biography: she bears malicious "Affronts to her Chastity" patiently, and is angered only when a woman remarks that the man "must have a good Stomach, who would give Silk Gowns for such Sort of Trumpery" (I, 6: 36). One can read Jenny's anger at this remark as showing that her vanity is stronger than her concern for reputation. Yet it can also suggest her resentment of the contemporary prejudice against learned women—against the belief that they were physically flawed, disfigured, unsexed (see Hill 2001: 81–95). It is as if to prove this prejudice false—as well as to satisfy her displaced curiosity—that Jenny needs sexual victories in later life. Her private predicament thus reflects a contemporary cultural blueprint, and the implied author of *Tom Jones* seems to find himself in sympathy with her maneuvers against it.

It is one thing to lose one's reputation and quite another to have nothing to show for it, which is what happens when the shame of illegitimate motherhood is displaced from Miss Bridget to Jenny. But the reverse side of this situation is that, for Jenny, banishment to a distant parish—a geographical displacement in consequence of displaced public opprobrium—means liberation rather than punishment: in her own parish, though maddeningly above her peers in intellectual capacity, she seems destined to remain at the bottom of the social hierarchy. If one adopts the interpretive principle

---

11. Cf. Barnard 2009. This is not to deny exceptional cases among Fielding's contemporaries— such as that of Marquise du Châtelet (1706–49) on the other side of the English Channel.

according to which the incurred punishment may have been not a failed deterrent but, conversely, a hidden motivation for the "crime," the prospect of such a move may be regarded as one of the motives for Jenny's conspiracy with Miss Bridget.[12] The banishment, indeed, offers new vistas for her displaced curiosity—she soon lives up to her reputation by going off "in company with a recruiting Officer" (II, 6: 67). When she reappears in the novel as Mrs. Waters, she seems to have learned to adapt to the prejudice against women's classical education by not making a show of her own learning.

The leitmotifs of "curiosity" and "vanity" duly recur in the episodes involving Mrs. Waters. Here another kind of displacement takes place: we do not immediately identify Mrs. Waters as Jenny Jones because these leitmotifs do not seem to directly pertain to her. Instead, they are displaced to "human nature" in general: chapter 7 of Book IX opens with the observation that "[t]hough Nature hath by no Means mixed up an equal Share either of Curiosity or Vanity in every human Composition, there is perhaps no Individual to whom she hath not allotted such a Proportion of both, as requires much Arts and Pains too, to subdue and keep under" (334). Together with the ensuing reference to Tom's good manners in subduing his curiosity about Mrs. Waters, this serves as a preamble for a flashback on Mrs. Waters's recent past. The flashback allays the curiosity of the reader, and also diverts the reader's attention from the comment on vanity in the opening sentence ("curiosity or vanity in every human composition"); only on a rereading does this sweeping generalization get anchored in Jenny's lack of prudent moderation, in particular, her failure to "subdue and keep under" her vanity and curiosity.

On meeting Tom, Mrs. Waters takes full advantage of the disarray in her clothes and of the expressiveness of her "lovely blue Eyes" (IX, 5: 330), still seeking to get even with the world for having been considered plain. It is as if in response to the early insult ("the man must have a good stomach, etc.") that her seduction of Tom takes place, literally, at the dinner table, at a high point of Fielding's carnivalesque play on "appetites."[13]

In the final Book of the novel, Jenny's vanity receives a blow when, on a visit to Tom in prison, she cannot dissuade him from his new pledge of fidelity to Sophia. However, the discovery that Tom is the baby whose

12. In the eighteenth century, for young women migration was one way of "escape from the confining restrictions and intrusive surveillance of village life" (Hill 2001: 27), yet they needed contacts and some financial help to smooth their first steps.

13. The link between conviviality and "conversation" in the two senses of the latter word starts as early as in the first chapter, where the narrator, the Lord of Misrule playing an innkeeper, reinterprets the "dress" in Pope's "True wit is nature to advantage dres't" as a culinary reference.

mother she once pretended to be causes her even more distress: the tone of her letter to him is consistent with such an emotional upheaval. To delay the solution of the novel's central enigma, Fielding keeps Jenny temporarily ignorant of the fact that Partridge has recognized her and has already put Tom into the thorny sandals of Oedipus—"you must suspend your Curiosity till our next Meeting" [XVIII, 2: 597]), she writes to Tom. On the first reading, the wording of her contrite letter actually seems to confirm the fact of incest—Jenny suspends her power to disabuse Tom (and the reader) of the belief that he has committed incest because she is not aware of Partridge's panic that necessitates such reassurance.

Here too the principle of the conservation of character is maintained: in her relations with soldiers Mrs. Waters has been conflating the roles of lover and mother figure. As a sergeant tells the company assembled in the kitchen of the inn at Upton, she has been unfaithful to Captain Waters but "to give the Devil his Due, is a very good Sort of Lady, and loves the Cloth, and is always desirous to do strict Justice to it; for she hath begged off many a poor Soldier, and, by her good-will, would never have any of them punished" (IX, 6: 331)—she has treated "the Cloth" in both amorous and maternally protective ways. As the novel moves towards its dénouement, Jenny must limit the misrule by playing roles that would be more easily compatible with each other. One may note that in reference to her future clergyman husband the meaning of "cloth" is restricted to that of the table covering.

Foreshadowing the less daring but likewise witty endings of Jane Austen's novels, acceptance of moderation eventually allows Jenny to be conveniently married off to Parson Supple—one may wonder whether he is not the same clergyman whom Allworthy had meant for her many years ago. The metaphor of the man's "good stomach"[14] is here literalized again: Parson Supple has excellent digestion and greatly appreciates Squire Western's dinner table. He is described as

> a good-natured worthy man; but chiefly remarkable for his taciturnity at the table, tho' his mouth was never shut at it. In short, he had one of the best appetites in the world. However, the cloth was no sooner taken away, than he always made sufficient amends for his silence: for he was a very hearty fellow; and his conversation was often entertaining, never offensive. (IV, 10: 122)

14. This interplay of motifs convinces me that my reading of Jenny Jones cannot be explained away by the doubtlessly great "power of the interpretive habit to preserve the mimetic" (Phelan 2005: 28). The aesthetic pleasure that such a reading yields is an apt illustration of the kinds of "effects of meaning" (Gumbrecht 2004: 104–11; see p. 5 above) that are produced by intellectual constructs of the reader's own creation in response to textual stimuli.

At Upton, it should be recalled, Mrs. Waters has to wait for Jones to eat his fill before a different "conversation" can begin between them. The title of the chapter that contains this sequel to the Battle of Upton is almost a giveaway: "An Apology for all Heroes who have good Stomachs, with a description of a Battle of the amorous Kind" (IX, 5: 327): Fielding's conservation of character extends to the unfailing recurrence of leitmotifs.

The final scene in which Mrs. Waters makes her appearance contains another case of displacement. In chapter 8 of Book XVIII, she has her chance to be readmitted into Allworthy's good graces. Her concern for Tom's welfare is evident to all, but to complete the reconciliation she has to explain away her sexual promiscuity. A woman of quick intellect, she does so by an extension of the oppositional technique that she used in Upton where, caught *in flagrante,* she cried out "Murder! Robbery! and more frequently Rape!" (X, 2: 340). Now she again plays the victim, saying that she was first misled into a cohabitation with the recruiting officer by "the most solemn Promises of Marriage"; she goes on to the casuistic argument that "after much reading on the Subject" (the motif of the displacement of curiosity) she became convinced "that particular Ceremonies are only requisite to give a legal Sanction to Marriage, and have only a worldly Use in giving a Woman the Privileges of a Wife."[15] After a little difference with Allworthy concerning such fruits of her education, she adds that upon her companion's death her way back to virtue was cut off, there being little left for "a Woman stript of her Reputation, and left destitute." "Necessity," she says, "drove me into the arms of Capt. *Waters,* with whom, though still unmarried, I lived as a Wife for many Years, and went by his Name" (XVIII, 8: 616). This presentation of the story, followed by due expressions of gratitude to Tom for saving her from Northerton's assault, gives Allworthy an official justification for admitting the stray sheep into the fold—especially because it fully confirms his somber warnings to Jenny Jones in the first interview between them in Book I, chapter 7. Jenny thus makes skillful use of the oppositional technique of turning the oppressiveness of social mores to her advantage.

In the same chapter, Allworthy's interview with Mrs. Waters is immediately followed by his talk with Dowling, in which the latter gives his version of how Tom's true parentage was suppressed, casting himself in the role of another victim of Blifil's deceit. The narrator comments:

> We have remarked somewhere already, that it is possible for a Man to convey a Lie in the Words of Truth; this was the Case at present, for *Blifil* had, in Fact, told *Dowling* what he now related; but had not imposed on

15. Possibly an allusion to a contemporary topical issue; see Starr 1971: 118–20.

him, nor indeed had imagined he was able to do so. In Reality, the Promises which *Blifil* had made to *Dowling,* were the Motives which had induced him to Secrecy; and as he now very plainly saw *Blifil* would not be able to keep them, he thought proper now to make his Confession, which the Promises of Forgiveness, joined to the Threats, the Voice, the Looks of *Allworthy,* and the Discoveries he had made before, extorted from him, who was besides taken unawares, and had no Time to consider of Evasions. (XVIII, 8: 619)

Being pressed for time is, of course, Dowling's steady leitmotif, which at one point in the novel (XII, 10: 428) is displaced onto Tom (see Toker 1993a: 115–17). In this episode, the narrator's exposure of Dowling's subtle mendacity is a displacement of the exposure that he spares Mrs. Waters, whose brief autobiography in the first half of the chapter likewise elides inconvenient facts. As Jane Austen would have put it, the account "contained nothing but truth, though there might be some truths not told" (*Emma* 106). One of such "truths"—about the cakes and ale of the Waters couple—has already been sketched by the sergeant at Upton: the captain, he said, "may go to heaven when the sun shines upon a rainy day. But if he does, that is neither here nor there; for he won't want company." As to the lady, "to be sure, ensign Northerton and she were very well acquainted together. . . . But the captain knows nothing about it; and as long as there is enough for him too, what does it signify? He loves her not a bit worse" (IX, 9: 331).

In her autobiographical exercise for the benefit of Allworthy, Mrs. Waters dwells on her disastrous affair with Northerton because it is convenient for presenting herself as a victim once again, but she hushes up her adventure with Fitzpatrick, in which no stretch of imagination could cast her in that role. Thus, in the atmosphere of broad amnesty, Mrs. Waters's promiscuity is swept under the carpet, so that the rewarding of her good will should be less offensive to the moralistic reader, the novel's "hurdle audience."[16]

The convention of the happy ending further distracts the reader from the oppositional sleight of hand by which the merry female rogue is allowed to win her pardon. Looking backward from the similar pragmatic practices of Jane Austen, it may, indeed, appear that both a literary convention and a conventional moral tone are elements of a "cover story" (cf. Gilbert and Gubar 1979: 146–83), while the real story is to a large extent subversive of both. Jenny Jones has learned to pose as a victim—but this surface role is actually another case of displacement: she is, indeed, a victim—not of

---

16. On "hurdle audience" see the end of chapter 4 as well as Toker 2005.

the sexual mores of her society but of its cultural schemata or, in Fielding's terms, "the received Notions concerning Truth and Nature" (XII, 8: 422), and the resulting lack of possibilities for an intellectually avid young woman, especially of the lower classes, to gain education and take good practical advantage of it. This is not what Allworthy means by "I am sorry, Madam, . . . you made so ill an Use of your Learning" (XVIII, 8: 616), but the words have been said and cannot be unsaid. Allworthy chooses not to deconstruct Jenny's story because at the moment he is not dispensing strict justice but living the life of the heart.[17] Almost as in a masquerade, the role of the victim that Jenny assumes as a preface and price of her readmission into the normative mainstream is a stylized literalization of her actual disadvantage.

If the characters sometimes interpret Tom's generosity as corrupt self-interest, the novel supplies ample sanction for reinterpreting Jenny's promiscuity as, among other things, generous repayment to those who help to buttress her self-esteem. Her disadvantage is not only social: she seems to lack an *innate* moral fiber (the "good heart" that in Fielding is all too often emblematized by good looks). Yet she compensates for this by an *acquired* commitment to the good of those around her, a commitment no less genuine for being acquired than it would have been if innate. The limits that the novel imposes on her (and its own) carnivalesque misrule may be associated with the prescriptive touch in the value system of Fielding's comic epic—the recommendation that the "good heart" and the benevolent principle, and, in particular, the combination of the two, stop short of *imitatio Christi;* a deontological basic principle is to be constrained by rule-utilitarian circumspection (prudence). This recommendation is not the central principle of Fielding's system; rather, it represents a rational limit on, and thus a subsidiary to, the principle of the emotionally fueled active benevolence. This hybrid economy is loosely identifiable with "the great, useful, and uncommon Doctrine" (XII, 8: 422) that *Tom Jones* ironically promises the reader. Articulated through the narrative rather than formulated as its tutelary proposition, it represents a somewhat regretful opting for the middle way. In contrast to the golden mean valorized in Austen's novels (see chapter 4), this ethical stance privileges not moderation in the intensity of character traits but the checks and balances in which the practice of one's favorite moral/ideological principles is to be held: the less enthusiastically

17. See Bernard Harrison's discussion of Fielding's rejecting the dichotomy of Appetite and Principle and constructing "an array of cases in which Appetite wields the sceptre of Principle, passion turns out to lie at the heart of goodness, morality turns out to demand worldliness (in a certain sense) of us, and unworldliness (in a certain sense) stands under moral condemnation" (1993/1994: 162).

endorsed maxims may claim equal respect and enter into what may be seen as a dialogue with an individual's commitment to the dominant definition of his or her integrity.

Yet the presence of the carnivalesque touches in Fielding's novels in general may also suggest that the ethical vision behind them is not identical to the latitudinarian views within the Church of England. The latter tended to be rather too "flattering to human nature" (Battestin 2000: 234) in postulating "an active charity as a condition to salvation" (237), a "practical morality by which a sincere man or woman might earn salvation by the exercise of those compassionate and benevolent feelings that were natural to them—though, regrettably, too often suppressed by bad education and bad custom" (234). These beliefs were clearly much closer to Fielding than the nonconformist postulate of faith rather than good works as a way to salvation. Yet Fielding's narratives also allow for the possibility of innate and largely incurable *ill nature*.[18] The partly supererogatory and partly appetitive "lust for doing good" is ineluctably shadowed by unnamable desires of the opposite kind, in people such as Blifil, Thwackum,[19] or the Noble Lord of *Amelia*. However, the oppositional practices associated with Fielding's carnival are directed less against vicious usurpers of power than against the cultural customs and prejudices that obstruct the justice of the laws of the land, of human nature, and of the Low Church—cultural conventions that the wicked can take advantage of for their own goals.

By itself, the Jenny Jones plot line would be an insufficient basis for arguing about the oppositional tendency of the novel. However, the case for oppositionality may be amply supported by the novel's portrayal of its central woman character, Sophia Western.[20] A runaway daughter whose self-protective conduct is oppositional rather than rebellious, Sophia uses some sociocultural regularities to counteract others. She does not propose to marry against the wishes of her father but insists on her right of refusal: her resistance to marriage without love is a semantic pointer to the slow cultural shift

---

18. This view is not a side effect of including comedy villains among the cast of characters; it is expressed directly by, for instance, the protagonist of *Joseph Andrews:* "if a Boy be of a mischievous wicked Inclination, no School, tho' ever so private, will ever make him good" (III, 5: 180).

19. Cf. Alter 1968: 61–97 on the stylized darker complexities of Fielding's character portrayal.

20. Fielding's presentation of Tom's generous good heart as balancing his moral lapses is likewise part of the novel's oppositional agenda. It has been done full justice in critical literature and is therefore not part of the present discussion.

from dynastic to companionate marriages among the gentry. Sophia's flight from home to the house of a female relative of higher social standing lends support to the law that prohibits forcing a woman into a marriage against her will; it is oppositional in the sense of using the available loopholes in arbitrary patriarchal power. Her transgression against filial pieties is largely justified by the fact that she opposes not the order but the disorder in her social enclave, not the law of the land or of the church but the anachronistic feudal ambitions of an individual who slips into the stock role of a tyrannical father, despite his own better feelings. Indeed, the theme of rebellion, unavoidable in the semantic repertoire of the novel, is safely channeled off to the Jacobite invasion at the background of the plot: references to Jenny Cameron drain the theme of rebellion away from Sophia and even from her adulterous runaway cousin Harriet. By ironic analogy, Squire Western is himself presented as a loud-mouthed opponent of the Hannoverian dynasty yet not one who might go over to the Jacobite side.

Sophia is also the character with the strongest claims to identification on the part of the reader. The game in which Fielding's treatment of her progress through the novel invites the reader to engage is what Caillois classifies as *mimicry*—vicarious experience, with the reader's affects and valuations following those of a character. This is the most carnivalesque of the ludic reading-responses: we enter the character's situation approvingly, empathetically, and with a large, though unstable, degree of self-forgetfulness.[21] The reason for this effect lies in the wholesomeness of Sophia's impulses and her freedom from shameful emotions—except for the not unjustifiable jealousy (which brings her even closer to the average mortal reader), and occasional haughtiness with her servant. The *mimicry* is not disrupted by surprises, as it often is in the case of Tom. The narrator frequently delays information about Tom's commitments and predicaments, distancing him from the reader, but Sophia remains almost totally transparent for us. The fact that the medium of vicarious experience and one of the novel's main exponents of energetic oppositionality is the woman who loves only where she can respect is an important feature of Fielding's narrative ethics.

In an earlier essay (Toker 1993a: 108–26), I have traced the novel's *agonistic* play with the reader, a (rigged) competition in sagacity. The imagined narrator-reader dialogue, with its sense of mutual cordiality yielding to tugs of war, *aleatic* surprises, possible resentments, and reconciliations, is a matter of direct, nonvicarious reading-and-rereading experience. The techniques

21. Cf. Bakhtin's notion of *vzhivanie,* projecting oneself into the character (1979: 78). The relationship between this notion and that of empathy is usefully discussed by Russell Valentino (2005).

that create the conditions for such a dialogue are a major aspect of the ethics of narrative form. Likewise ethically significant is the oscillation between the two kinds of reader-response—the direct and the vicarious. These oscillations are partly contingent and partly structured: contingent insofar as cultural conditions promote sympathetic identification with some characters rather than others; structured insofar as narrative techniques produce an intersubjective platform for the *subversion* of vicarious experience—narrative itself can puncture sympathetic identification, distancing us from the character either by way of disapproval or by way of cognitive gaps such as dramatic irony and signaled mystification. A character may also be denied sufficient prominence to invite vicarious experience in the first place, though we may still remain concerned for her welfare. The reader's attitude to Jenny Jones/Mrs. Waters tends to remain distant because attention to her image is insufficiently sustained, because her role in slapstick scenes is comic, because in the later chapters she may have one or two love affairs too many (not a universal deterrent for sympathetic identification), but also because of cognitive gaps between her and the reader, who always knows that she has secrets not divulged. Nevertheless, the narrative consistently influences the reader in her favor, inviting a degree of admiration for her picaresque talents and preempting harsh judgment (in striking contrast, for instance, to Elizabeth Gaskell's treatment of the unfortunate Aunt Esther in *Mary Barton*). Our positive attitude to Jenny Jones, starlet of the supporting cast in the novel's drama of oppositional energies, may be partly an effect of the aesthetic enjoyment of the meaningful comic reprises that cluster around her image (the pattern of displacements; the motifs of vanity, curiosity, and of a good stomach), even if this aspect of the novel's syntactics is not consciously registered in the process of reading.

As noted above (p. 14), the carnivalesque is always also oppositional but not every instance of the oppositional is carnivalesque. The carnivalesque remissions staged *in* the novel (the brawls, the passions, the intrigues) are distinct from those staged *by* the novel (intermittent sympathetic identification, surprises, stylistic felicities); both, however, add gusto to the oppositionality of the characters and playfulness to the narrative's own pragmatic orientation. Yet if the main lines of oppositionality practiced by the characters are accepted and, to a degree, intellectually replicated by Fielding's target audiences and the modern reader, the troubled history of Fielding's reception has shown that the pragmatic camouflage of these cultural remissions was not sufficient to disarm the hurdle audience of *Tom Jones*.

CHAPTER THREE

Carnival Diminished

The Secret Springs of *Tristram Shandy*

The question that he frames in all but words
Is what to make of a diminished thing.

—Robert Frost, "The Oven Bird"

THE LETTER OF ADVICE THAT WALTER Shandy writes to his brother Toby contains a warning not to let Widow Wadman, whom Toby is courting, read "Rabelais, or Scarron, or Don Quixote": "They are all books which excite laughter; and thou knowest, dear Toby, that there is no passion so serious, as lust" (VIII.xxxiv: 537). Yet the literary presences that are monitory for Walter are tutelary for Tristram—or rather for Laurence Sterne behind him. *Tristram Shandy,* with its witty *mésalliance* of eschatology and scatology, its *reductio ad absurdum* of contemporary topical issues, its "deconstructive resistance to the philosophical dogma" of its age (Harrison 1991: 76), the oppositional subversiveness of its treatment of authority, and its comic peripeteia, is a carnivalesque work, though less festive than *Gargantua and Pantagruel* and even *Don Quixote.* Sterne's is a *diminished* carnival: its social base is narrow, and its "appetites," mainly sexual (references to food are sparse in this novel, especially in comparison with *Tom Jones*), are more likely to be defused, short-circuited, or thwarted than fulfilled. The pattern starts with the novel's opening episode, a version of *coitus interruptus.*

The carnivalesque interface of the body and the environment is massively explored in the novel—not as a joyful overflow[1] but rather as painful

---

1. There are, of course, exceptions: for example, when, in a discussion of legendary *Wunder-*

incursions—by way of asthma that Tristram is said to have got skating (oppositionally?) against the wind, the wounds Toby and Trim get in the war and Tristram from the obstetrician's forceps and a window sash, a nocturnal musket shot that kills Le Fever's wife in his arms in the tent,[2] the illness of which Le Fever himself dies in an inn, the intrigues that break the endurance of Parson Yorick, and so forth. On the sunnier side, the environment affects the self by way of somatic expressions of contagious emotion.

Nor is the laughter that rings in Sterne's novel entirely festive. It is, *par excellence,* the kind that can help turn "nauseous thoughts about the horror and absurdity of existence into notions with which one can live" and which may be seen as constituting "the artistic discharge of the nausea of absurdity" (Nietzsche 1966: 60).[3] If we believe the narrator (who in this instance is mimicking Corporal Trim), the "book is wrote, an' please your worships, against the spleen" (IV.xxii: 270). Like most oppositional writing, it clears a well-lighted livable space in "this scurvy and disasterous world of ours" (I.v: 10): physical circumstances and cultural patterns are diseases, yet not without remissions. Here I shall discuss two kinds of such remission in Sterne's novel: the comic (anti-aphrodisiac?) treatment of lust and the peculiar type of leaping wit with which it overlaps.

Tristram's father's hobby-horsical theory of laughter as an impediment to desire contrasts with Tristram's own description of sexuality as intrinsically comic. Indeed, upon enumerating the features of Love in alphabetical order,

A gitating
B ewitching
C onfounded
D evilish affairs of life—the most
E xtravagant
. . .

---

kinder Yorick refers to "the great *Lipsius*" who "composed a work the day he was born," Uncle Toby's remark is "They should have wiped it up" (VI.ii: 371).

2. The image of the tortured victim of the Inquisition (in whom Trim sees his brother Tom) in Yorick's sermon and Trim and Toby's memories of unmercifully flogged soldiers likewise belong to this strand of motifs, associated less with the enclave of the Shandys' Yorkshire neighborhood than with Sterne's contemporary Voltaire's "best of all possible worlds."

3. The sublime, which Nietzsche names in the same breath (as "the artistic taming of the horrible"), is in Sterne's world reduced to the sentimental.

P ragmatical

S tridulous

R idiculous (VII.xiii: 500–501)

Tristram adds that "the R should have gone first" (501). What it may please Walter to call "lust" and Tristram to call Love is, *mutatis mutandis,* first and foremost, Ridiculous.

Yet in his own witty way Sterne subscribes to the tradition of viewing love as a step to higher things. He has his Tristram object to the macrometaphor of "falling in love" (which, incidentally, signals a peculiarly English catachresis[4]). The phrase, says Tristram,

> is not at all to my liking: for to say a man is *fallen* in love,—or that he is *deeply* in love,—or up to the ears in love,—and sometimes even *over head and ears in it,*—carries an idiomatic kind of implication, that love is a thing *below* a man:—this is recurring again to *Plato*'s opinion, which, with all his divinityship,—I hold to be damnable and heretical;—and so much for that. (VI.xxxvii: 422)

The passage is part of Sterne's game of carnivalizing language by reviving and literalizing dead metaphors such as "would not hurt a fly" or "at the drop of the hat."[5] Yet Tristram's reflection on the metaphor of "falling" in love also rejects the Platonic notion of spiritual self-transcendence through love of the higher order: regular earthly love, says Tristram, is *not* a lower-order phenomenon. It is only via our general *fallen* state (since Adam) that "falling" in love can connect with all the other "falls" in the novel—those of Dr. Slop, the midwife, the stone that wounds Toby, the sash window that circumcises Tristram, the sermon that slips out of a book, and the hot chestnut that gets inside the pompous Phutatorius's breeches (cf. Burkhardt 1961: 70–75 on gravity). Though the carnivalesque explicitness of the link between sexual attraction and the lower regions of the body is, for Tristram, an inexhaustible source of jest, throughout the novel the literally somatic and the figurative motion associated with sexual desire take the direction opposite to "falling": things *rise*—like the Phoenix from its ashes. A veritable paradigm of micromotifs of upward motion—open or hidden, actual or

---

4. In most other languages the notion tends to be expressed by a single verb, usually reflexive, for example, *vliubit'sia* (Russian), *sich verlieben* (German), *įsimylėti* (Lithuanian), *lehitahev* (Hebrew).

5. In the novel's most famous pleonastic paragraph Toby apostrophizes a fly and releases it through the window (II.xii: 100); later his servant Trim regulates the other servants' feeling on the sudden demise of Bobby Shandy by dropping his hat on the floor by way of visual aid (V.vii: 325).

virtual, literal or metaphoric—is presented in the story of Trim's recuperation from the near-lethal wound in his knee with the help of a beautiful
nun's ministrations:

> The fair Beguine . . . continued rubbing with her whole hand under my
> knee—till I feared her zeal would weary her—"I would do a thousand times
> more," said she, "for the love of Christ"—In saying which she pass'd her
> hand across the flannel, to the part above my knee, which I had equally
> complained of, and rubb'd it also.
>
> I perceived, then, I was beginning to be in love—
>
> As she continued rub-rub-rubbing—I felt it spread from under her
> hand, an' please your honour, to every part of my frame—
>
> The more she rubb'd, and the longer strokes she took—the more the
> fire kindled in my veins—till at length, by two or three strokes longer than
> the rest—my passion rose to the highest pitch—I seiz'd her hand—
>
> —And then, thou clapped'st it to thy lips, Trim, said my uncle Toby—
> and madest a speech. (VIII.xxii: 521–22)

In *Tristram Shandy,* the erection ("Call it by it's [*sic*] right name, my
dear," as Walter Shandy might say to his wife in the context of keyholes,
VIII.xxxv: 539) is an emblem of *resilience*—suffice it (or almost) to recollect
that in the eighteenth century the verb "to die" still retained memories of
its earlier sense of "spending." This function of the theme of male sexuality
is practically "laid bare"[6] in Volume VII of *Tristram Shandy,* in which the
protagonist is literally running away from death to the south of the European continent, pursued by death, this "*son of a whore*" that, like a bailiff
sent to collect the debt of nature, "has found out [his] lodgings" (VII.i:
432). Weak and ill, in a hurry to reach warmer climes, Tristram cares little
for the standardized tourist traps of the towns on his way but always notes,
and courts the notice of, attractive women—they are the landmarks on his
way to recuperation. He enjoys the very fleetingness of these encounters,
as the women walk away or as the coach carries him on. When, during a
country dance, Nannette, the "nut brown maid" with a slit in her petticoat,
makes advances to him, he dances off, and then dances away further south
(VII.xliii: 485). One need not read this as a sign of Tristram's impotence

---

6. This term for autometadescriptive touches in a work of fiction, a calque of the Russian
obnazhenie priema, was practically launched by Victor Shklovsky's 1921 article on Tristram Shandy
(see Shklovsky 1968). Sterne's own account of the principle is as follows: "never do I hit upon any
invention or device which tendeth to the furtherance of good writing, but I instantly make it public;
willing that all mankind should write as well as myself" (IX.xii: 560).

or his trailing a morality in tow: his agenda on this journey is only instru-mentally erotic—it is the resurgence of desire rather than its consummation that gives him the sense of being alive. And it is this resurgence, and this "picaresque resilience" (Bloom and Bloom 1984: 59), this rebounding, that Walter Shandy, elsewhere in the novel and with something else in mind, refers to as the "secret spring" that lifts one up from prostration (IV.viii: 251).[7]

True, impotence may well be read into the passage where Tristram is reflecting "upon what has *not* pass'd"—and Jenny reassures him that she is, nevertheless, "satisfied." What exactly has not passed, however, is suppressed; and Jenny's utterance is hidden by a line of undecipherable asterisks (VII. xxix: 466): these particulars do not matter, Sterne may be saying to the reader along with Jenny.[8] What does matter is the symbolic *garters* that Tristram is holding in this episode: "*Honit soit qui mal y pense.*"

Anticipating Henry Bergson's belief that the source of the comic effect lies in the combination of the living and the mechanical,[9] the somatic "jack-in-the-box" (1956: 105–10) resurgence of desire is also, for Sterne, an ample source of comedy. This resurgence is, of course, but *one of the many* cases of literal and figurative springing up of hobby-horses out of the black box of human consciousness, the thing-in-itself which (to save us, as it were, the window tax) is not equipped with "*Momus's* glass" (I.xxiii: 65)—"by their playthings ye shall know them" (Reed 1981: 152–53). The homographic "spring" refers to the revival of nature after winter, to the "jumping" of bod-ies and wits, to "a source" (of vitality, of inspiration, and of water—which Eugenius is recommended to drink), as well as a mechanical implement that signifies elasticity and impels both the grandfather clock and the jack-in-the-box "Ruling Passion." A comic hobby-horse/jack-in-the-box duet is performed in the episode in which, following Trim's suggestion that Toby

7. My interpretation of the "secret spring" as resilience, whatever mixture of psychic forces or intellectual interests it may be based on, has the merit of establishing the common denominator between the application of this clockwork metaphor both to Tristram and to his father. It thus differs from Martin Battestin's view that for Walter, "the 'secret spring' that smoothes the rough passages of life is his irrepressible Hobby-horse," whereas for Tristram it is "another sort of mechanism by which the happiness of others is made our own and colours our perception of the world, dissolving the boundaries that separate us and harmonizing the self with Nature" (1974: 257).

8. In his discussion of Sterne's bawdy puns as the fuel for the heightening of imagination and a method of activizing the reader, Robert Alter (1984: 101–2) interprets occasional impotence (an instance of the minor vexations with which fortune pelts the protagonist) as expressive of the common human condition.

9. Bergson's comments on the tension between sympathy and humor and on the corrective ef-fect of comedy are remarkably similar to some of the views of humor in the eighteenth century (for a useful survey of the latter, see Iser 1988: 106–20).

should go to his brother's Yorkshire estate, where models of fortifications can be built on the bowling green, Toby wishes to waste no time and prepare for departure, whilst Trim first wishes to harangue about it. The comedy involves a *double entendre:* variations on Toby's "say no more" are attempts to press Jack, or rather Trim, back into the box, at the same time also expressing Toby's turgescent concurrence in Trim's enthusiasm. "My uncle Toby," says Tristram,

> was fired with Corporal *Trim's* project and description.—*Trim!* said my uncle *Toby,* thou hast said enough.—We might begin the campaign, continued *Trim,* on the very day that his Majesty and the Allies take the field, and demolish 'em town by town as fast as—*Trim,* quoth my uncle *Toby,* say no more.—Your Honour, continued *Trim,* might sit in your arm-chair (pointing to it) this fine weather, giving me your orders, and I would—Say no more, *Trim,* quoth my uncle *Toby.*—Besides, your Honour would get not only pleasure and good pastime,—but good air, and good exercise, and good health,—and your Honour's wound would be well in a month. Thou hast said enough, *Trim,*—quoth my uncle *Toby* (putting his hand into his breeches-pocket)—I like thy project mightily;—and if your Honour pleases, I'll, this moment, go and buy a pioneer's spade to take down with us, and I'll bespeak a shovel and a pick-ax, and a couple of—Say no more, *Trim,* quoth my uncle *Toby,* leaping upon one leg, quite overcome with rapture,—and thrusting a guinea into *Trim's* hand.—*Trim,* said my uncle *Toby,* say no more;—but go down, this moment, my lad, and bring up my supper this instant. (II.v: 86–87)

The springing of the hobby-horses that the characters ride through the novel is, figuratively speaking, largely mechanical and deterministic. In a novel by Virginia Woolf it would be replaced by the more abstract and earnest notion of "compensation"—something that helps a person get through, and by, the multiple vexations of life. In *Tristram Shandy,* however, the hobby-horse-in-the-box palliates misery by causing an upsurge of adrenaline, but in other novels it also often leads to further misery and mischief. If Virginia Woolf's Mrs. Dalloway has learned to submerge conceptual abstractions in the flow of reality, the problem of Walter Shandy is the para-Lockean tendency of "isolating meaning from situation. . . . In his refusal to recognize difference [between meaning and situation] he becomes comic, especially since he is constantly confronted with it through his proliferating and contradictory theories. The comedy . . . consists in the continual bombardment of theory by the realities that theory excludes, for nearly every theory brings about a misfortune which then needs to be neutralized by another theory" (Iser 1988: 39).

The common denominator of Walter's theories and Tristram's fascination with desire (about which Walter tends to "pish, and huff, and bounce, and kick," VIII.xxvi: 525) is not a hobby-horse itself but its propelling mechanism, the "secret spring." As Mark Loveridge (1992) has demonstrated on the example of the "cock-and-bull" ending of the novel, far from being merely a competitive in-joke for Sterne, Hall-Stevenson, and their circle,[10] or merely an attack against tartuffery, Tristram's covered-way license is over-determined. Each case has a local function in its context and serves a specific local felicity. Cumulatively, however, sexual references represent, and humbly carnivalize, human powers of resilience. Though Tristram complains that, instead of giving him great griefs, fortune has been "pelting" him, "like an ungracious duchess" with "so many small evils" (VII.xxix: 466), it is not to be forgotten that the prospect of early death of consumption, of being "cut short in the midst of my days" (VII.xiv: 446), is a rather grievous circumstance (both Tristram's and Sterne's own). Though we are all "driven, like turkeys to a market" V.vii: 327), it is with an unobstructed prospect of early death that he spins his yarn.[11] Death is a major presence in the novel, and not only in the episode where it knocks at Tristram's door and is requested to "come again" (VII.i: 431). The long story of Tristram's birth, complete with references to the disasters that can overtake the mother and the child, ties the motifs of birth and death into faster knots than those of Obadiah's over Dr. Slop's green baize bag.[12]

Indeed, Mrs. Shandy's refusal to have Dr. Slop attend to her and her preference for the old midwife (whose license does not include the use of instruments such as a crochet and forceps) can be read as representing Mrs. Shandy's hobby-horsical pose of "Injured Virtue"[13] in response to her

10. Sterne's relationship with Hall-Stevenson, partly reflected in Tristram's friendship with Eugenius, uncannily anticipates that of the Joyce–Gogarty and Stephen Dedalus–Buck Mulligan pairs, with their strange mixture of care, affection, rivalry, and suspicions of betrayal.

11. Edward A. and Lillian D. Bloom discuss Tristram's "picaresque resilience" with an emphasis of the minor rather than the major disasters of his life (1984: 59–61). I read Tristram's foregrounding of the former as a diversionary maneuver; another such maneuver is his mock-heroic cataloguing of his complaints in such a way that "grief" should get diluted among the homogeneous parts of the list: "What a jovial and a merry world would this be, may it please your worships, but for the inextricable labyrinth of debts, cares, woes, want, grief, discontent, melancholy, large jointures, impositions and lies" (VI.xiii: 390).

12. For the information in the following paragraph I am indebted to Arthur H. Cash's (1968) and Bonnie Blackwell's (2001) explanations of eighteenth-century topical issues concerning obstetrics and their bearing on the narrative of Tristram's birth.

13. See Harrison 1994: 94; this interpretation of Mrs. Shandy's choice pits Mr. and Mrs. Shandy's

husband's refusal (sanctioned by a clause in the marriage settlement) to take her to London where she could be attended by first-rate doctors. But it also gives rise to an exercise of bawdy wit following Toby's unwittingly obscene reference to her modesty: "My sister . . . does not care to let a man come so near her * * * *" (II.vi. 89)—a comic reference to the contemporary theory that a woman experiences an erotic heightening during childbirth and can direct it towards a male attendant. More seriously speaking—and positing a grain of truth underneath most jokes, including the bawdy ones—it may also be Slop's religion, or perhaps popular conceptions of Catholic values among Protestants, that makes Mrs. Shandy shun him: in the contemporary Catholic environment, the choice between the life of the mother and that of the infant during a catastrophic birth was believed to be routinely decided in favor of the infant, since the mother is already baptized while the infant still needs to be thus saved. Despite her blandly consistent jack-in-the-box resistance to her husband's learned discourses, Mrs. Shandy seems to be aware of such eventualities: she grows ash pale at her husband's reference to Caesarian section (which was, at the time, still fatal to the mother).[14]

And yet, as in the case of Walter's auxiliary theories that try to bridge the gaps between his previous concepts and new contingencies, the comic discourse on baptism *in utero* actually comes to salvage Slop's professional standing. It is, after all, by parents rather than babies that Slop is retained—and the mother, surprisingly enough, may have a say in the matter. Dr. Slop *can* be trusted to choose in favor of the mother since his green baize bag (the one that undergoes a displaced Caesarian section when Dr. Slop impatiently cuts the knots with which Obadiah had secured it—see Blackwell 2001: 111) is said to contain implements of "salvation and deliverance"—that is, not only forceps (deliverance) but also a *"squirt"* (II.xi: 97), a *"petite Canulle"*—for baptism *in utero* (salvation). The question whether one needs to be born, separated from the womb, in order to be baptized is Tristram's seriocomic scatology-cum-eschatology touchstone for distinguishing between Roman Catholic ("popish") and Anglican attitudes.

(and Dr. Slop's) "deliberative individualism" (72–82) against Toby Shandy's commitment to the good of others.

14. Characteristically, Walter Shandy immediately "dismounts" from this hobby-horse on seeing his wife's response: genuine feeling is consistently shown to break through fossilized attitudes in the world of the novel. It is likewise characteristic, however, that, in contrast to Swift, who, through Gulliver's account of Laputa, mocked contemporary science for its irrelevance to moral life, Sterne, through Walter Shandy's sundry scholarly and parascientific theories, mocks the opposite phenomenon—the all-too-ready *application* of hobby-horse hypotheses to flesh-and-blood individual lives.

Dr. Slop's squirt is also associated with the novel's thematic strand of *trust:* the question whether a woman in labor can trust a Catholic obstetrician is complicated by the question whether the Almighty cannot be trusted with a stillborn infant's salvation even without baptism. It is distrust that causes the complications of the Shandy marriage settlement—a monumental caricature on legal and personal prudence in dealings with the Other. A popular version of theological distrust leads to the hasty baptism of the protagonist (frustrating his father's plans for his name) when, on the night after being born, he has a fit and seems to be on the verge of death.

The seriousness of the theme of trust in *Tristram Shandy* is emphasized by Yorick's skeptical sermon on "trusting" rather than "knowing" that one has a good conscience, yet, like every serious issue, it does not escape carnivalization—along with the concept of *defining* to which it is juxtaposed:

> —Here are two senses, cried *Eugenius,* as we walk'd along, pointing with the fore finger of his right hand to the word *Crevice,* in the fifty-second page of the second volume[15] of this book of books,—here are two senses,—quoth he.—And here are two roads, replied I, turning short upon him,—a dirty and a clean one,—which shall we take?—The clean,—by all means, replied *Eugenius. Eugenius,* said I, stepping before him, and laying my hand upon his breast,—to define—is to distrust.—Thus I triumph'd over *Eugenius;* but I triumph'd over him as I always do, like a fool.—'Tis my comfort however, I am not an obstinate one. (III.xxxi: 196–97)

Tristram's triumph is foolish because, among other things, it absolutizes the virtue of "trusting." The downfall of the other holy fool of the novel—Sterne's alter ego, Parson Yorick—is caused precisely by his undue trust in being taken at his own valuation. The sermon that argues that one can only trust but never know that one has a good conscience deliberately subverts itself by showing that even (or perhaps particularly) self-trust is, as often as not, misplaced. The main drive of Tristram's "triumphant" sally is, however, against Locke's agenda of defining the terms of discourse before doing philosophy.[16] As the metaphor of the roads suggests, defining means cutting off one of the options, reducing one's freedom (or license), limiting one's possibilities—all through distrusting the road that looks dirty at a distance. Taking the dirty-looking road, like trusting the innocuousness

---

15. The reference is to "a small crevice, form'd by a bad joint in the chimney-piece" at which Toby looks when pondering the meaning of Walter's phrase about knowing "the right end of a woman from the wrong" (II.vii: 90–91).

16. On Sterne's subversive responses to Locke in *Tristram Shandy* see Mullan 1988: 164–70.

of the bawdy implications of "crevices," might be a minor leap of faith, if only faith in noncontagion. It might also mean trusting the language to lead one to thoughts and felicities that no preconceived intention and no a priori intuition could generate unaided and which conventional decorousness would obstruct.

Tristram's triumph is also "foolish" in the cap-and-bells sense (see II.ii. 77): a court jester's wit may smuggle in wisdom by a back window as it carnivalizes the portly gravity of "proper" discourse (in French, one might note, *propre* conflates the meanings of "decent" and "clean").

As Lakoff and Johnson have shown, a metaphor hides something as it highlights something else (1980: 10–13). While the metaphor of the two roads emphasizes the motifs of choice, option, and the walking of the straight and narrow, it downplays the fact that in semantic practice one may walk both the roads at the same time. *Tristram Shandy* actually gives us a whole paradigm of semantic relationships in which two or more meanings can be activated simultaneously. This paradigm includes

- Polysemy: one may or may not choose to ignore one of the meanings of "ejaculation" (IX.ix: 556) or "shift" (VI.iii: 372); one may associate the word "bridge" with one's hobby-horse (as in the case of the broken drawbridge on Toby's bowling green) or, more pertinently, with the broken bridge of Tristram's nose (III.Xxvi: 192–93); one may wonder who hears what "in the beds of justice" when Mrs. Shandy says that she "cannot conceive" (VI.xix: 395);
- *Double entendre:* are we to think of the sex act taking place "in the beds of justice"? In other words, is it only figuratively, as part of the argument, that Walter Shandy "presses the point home to" his wife (VI. xix: 396)?[17]
- Common associations clustering around words with a single dictionary meaning—or around images signified by these words: when, in a case of straight-faced *prétérition* (Fontanier 1977: 143–45), the narrator stipulates that when he uses the word "nose" he means "a Nose and nothing more, or less" (III.xxxi: 197), he can trust his readers to come up with other ideas—in Slawkenbergius's tale Strasburg falls because its inhabitants distrust the genuineness of Diego's nose;

17. See New 1994: 101. Cf. Jacques Berthoud (1984: 25): "Blameless locutions like 'rise up trumps' or 'get it out of him' or 'to make ends meet' turn into ideas we can scarcely permit ourselves to entertain." Berthoud distinguishes between paronomasia and *double entendre* in terms of the fully admitted ambiguity of the former and, in the latter, the suspension of the "sexual sense" between the text and the reader who can choose to disown one of the meanings or opt for a collusion with the text (29).

- Uncommon associations that can debauch intrinsically innocent mono-semic words, such as "whiskers"; the resulting mistrust is dramatized in Lady Baussiere's rigid obtuseness to the sundry applications for charity (V.i: 312–13) as she rides off from a linguistic *coup d'état* that turns "whiskers" into a phallic symbol at the court of Navarre;
- Homonymy: in the episode of the nuns of Andoüillets, the *meaning,* or rather the intention, of the phonetic combinations *bouger* and *fouter* is to get the mules to move; out of the fear of an iconic relationship between the mule-prodding sounds and the sexual acts that they can signify, each of the nuns pronounces only half of each word, thus actually reinforc-ing this relationship (hence, though the mules do not hear them, "the Devil does," VII.xxv: 459). One may add that "noses" is a homophone of "gnosis" (Iser 1988: 89), and "nosology" is a science of diseases and their classification.

In each particular instance (the examples given above are a representative cross-section), the narrator chooses to *trust* the reader as to which semantic path to take—or whether to take two or more at the same time.

It is not that Tristram can expect the reader to follow the play of his verbal wit at all times: his *agônistic* "triumph" is undiminished if his jokes remain underread—it is only special wits that "jump" (III.ix: 150) every which way. Tristram's wit, like that of his father, is largely enthymematic:[18] it skips or subverts one of the terms in would-be syllogisms. This technique is demon-strated in Walter's "triumph" over Obadiah. The household expects thunder and lightning to shower on the head of the unfortunate groom through whose negligence Walter Shandy's favorite thoroughbred mare has given birth not to an appropriately eugenic colt but to a mule (the hybrid of a horse and a donkey). Aristotle says that if "Nurse not immortal wrath" is a maxim, "Oh mortal man, nurse not immortal wrath" is an enthymeme (1954, 1394b: 21–23). It is however, through another enthymeme that Wal-ter manages to follow the Attic maxim:

My mother and my uncle *Toby* expected my father would be the death of *Obadiah*—and that there never would be an end of the disaster.—See here!

18. The *enthymeme* is an argument in which, in contrast to a syllogism, one of the premises is either implicit, absent, or nonvalid, and the conclusion is, therefore, a matter of probability rather than certainty. See Toker 2006 for a more detailed discussion of rhetorical and narrative enthymeme in Sterne and Joyce.

You rascal, cried my father, pointing to the mule, what you have done!—It was not me, said *Obadiah*.—How do I know that? replied my father.

Triumph swam in my father's eyes, at the repartee—the *Attic* salt brought water into them—and so *Obadiah* heard no more about it. (V.iii: 318)

The enthymeme works as follows:

The mule is the offspring of the mare and a donkey.
[Missing but implied term: Obadiah is an ass.]
How do I know Obadiah is not the father?

Walter is so pleased with the jumping of his wit that the butt of the joke is let off easy. And yet his triumph is also "foolish." In the story of Bobby's death, Obadiah and the other retainers get their revenge. Their minds take predictable little leaps as well—Susannah's first undisciplined thought, leaping over intermediary stages, is about Mrs. Shandy's almost new green nightgown (which she will get when her mistress goes into mourning). Obadiah's mind leaps to the other practical implication of Bobby's death: (Aunt Dinah's legacy will not be needed for Bobby's Grand Tour; therefore, the funds can be used for the improvement of the estate; hence) "we shall have a terrible piece of work of it in stubbing the ox-moor," says Obadiah (V.vii: 325). Several chapters later, however, Obadiah is spared even that punishment, since Walter's love of the *mot juste* boomerangs: upon Trim's reciting the Ten Commandments,

> I will enter into obligation this moment, said my father, to lay out all my aunt *Dinah*'s legacy, in charitable uses (of which, by the bye, my father had no high opinion) if the corporal has any one determinate idea annexed to any one word he has repeated.—Prythee, *Trim,* quoth my father, turning round to him,—What do'st thou mean, by "*honouring thy father and mother?*"
>
> Allowing them, an' please your honour, three halfpence a day out of my pay, when they grew old.—And didst thou do that, *Trim?* said *Yorick*.—He did indeed, replied my uncle *Toby*. (V.xxxiii: 354)

A man of his word, Walter can now be fully expected to lay out the thousand pounds in philanthropic donations, expanding, as it were, Trim's *caritas* in honoring his father and his mother instead of improving his real estate (possibly to the detriment of the peasants).

Whatever doubts arise in the reader's mind concerning Tristram's legitimacy or DNA (see New 1994: 99–100), he clearly proves to be his father's son in his ability to use leaps of wit to compensate himself for practical losses. If a pecuniary loss is sustained, one can at least "say some smart thing upon the occasion, worth the money" (VII.xxxv: 475).[19] Wit is Tristram's only resource when he needs to regain his self-esteem after the French tax collector ("commissary") first causes a rip in his breeches and then demands that he pay for the stage horses that he would have used had he not changed his mind about the mode of traveling:

—By all which it appears, quoth I . . . that if a man sets out in a post-chaise from Paris—he must go on traveling in one, all the days of his life—or pay for it.—Excuse me, said the commissary, the spirit of the ordinance is this—That if you set out with an intention of running post from Paris to Avignion, &c. you shall not change that intention or mode of traveling, without first satisfying the fermiers for two posts further than the place you repent at—and 'tis founded, continued he, upon this, that the REVENUES are not to fall short through your *fickleness*—

—O by heavens! cried I—if fickleness is taxable in France—we have nothing to do but to make the best peace with you we can—

AND SO THE PEACE WAS MADE (VII.xxxv: 475–76)

In this joke on the 1763 Peace of Paris that ended the Seven Years' War Tristram surpasses his father in the elegance and complexity of the enthymeme:

In France tax is levied on fickleness.
[The French are famously fickle].
[Hence the French treasury must have collected a great deal of money.]
[Hence France must be a very rich and strong state.]
We had better make the best peace with them we can.

A large part of Tristram's enthymematic wit, however, involves different semantic varieties of bawdiness, which he comes to regret on one occasion, when he cannot help joking at the expense of the deranged Maria near Moulins (IX.xxiii–xxiv: 574), an episode reminiscent of Walter's remorse on his jocular imputation of something beyond curiosity to his wife's wish to watch

---

19. Cf. Alter on wit in Sterne: "if nothing very hopeful can be done in or about the human condition, we at least afford ourselves through our human posturings an endless spectacle for delighted contemplation" (1984: 103).

Toby's courtship through a keyhole (VIII.xxxv: 539). After the episode with Maria, Tristram vows future adherence to Wisdom rather than to Wit: "I swore I would set up for Wisdom and utter grave sentences the rest of my days—and never—never attempt again to commit mirth with man, woman, or child, the longest day I had to live" (IX.xxiv: 574). Indeed, in most of the remaining portion of the novel, it is the other characters, and mainly in direct speech, who provide the comedy—of Toby's frustrated courtship or the "cock-and-bull" ending: Tristram himself "commits mirth" only as the narrator, not as a character. It is difficult to imagine that Tristram's sentimental compunction will keep him uttering only "grave sentences," but the turning-point episode is prefaced by a suggestion that jack-in-the-box wit and desire are not the only secrets of Tristram's emotional resilience: on the way to Moulins, he says, "every thing I saw, or had to do with, touch'd upon some *secret spring* either of sentiment or of rapture" (IX.xxiii–xxiv: 573; emphasis added).

Both Toby's loss of interest in Mrs. Wadman and the moratorium on Tristram's wit signify the approaching end: both the emblems of resilient vitality begin to dissolve in the milk of human kindness, quite like Aunt Dinah's legacy. The bull in the "cock-and-bull" finale alludes to Christopher Smart's verse fable about the old bull condemned to slaughter after being baited with dogs to make his flesh tender, as was the custom (see Loveridge 1992: 39–43). The "son-of-a-whore" grim reaper who had found out Tristram's (and Sterne's own) lodging is preparing to re-visit.

The license of *Tristram Shandy* is, indeed, limited and somewhat melancholy beneath its cheerful notes—it is the best one can do with that "diminished thing," the life still at one's disposal.

Yet Tristram will not be caught dead moaning about the approach of the unwelcome caller. The resilient sexuality rhythmically evoked in the novel, and the equally resilient comedy, bawdy or otherwise, stand for a kind of humble stoicism in accepting one's curtailed lot. Despite the contrary pulls of human nature, most characters of the novel sooner or later live up to decent humane sentiments. With most of them, these sentiments are not hypocritical but form a continuum with their real feelings: in any case, as Uncle Toby maintains, "God only knows who is a hypocrite, and who is not" (VI.vii: 380): in recognition of the better potential of the human heart, we are invited to *trust* the sentiments of the others (and their carnivalesque somatic expressions—the body does not lie[20]) until given hard evidence that the trust is misplaced. And not even then, perhaps, seeing how the hard fact of the hot chestnut and Yorick's stooping to get it are misread by Phutatorius, sealing Yorick's fate.

The diminished nature of Sterne's carnival is also evident in that the butt of his attacks is the tartuffery of Phutatorius and similar rulers of the church and the state, the grave and massive pillars of society. The shabby though landed country gentleman puts on a cap and bells to defuse the pomp of his "betters." By contrast, the novel never calls into question the essentially feudal class structure on which the residue of this gentleman's standing is based. Despite all the carnivalesque free and familiar contact between the masters and the servants, there is a clear distinction between the parlor and the kitchen. Some of the servants, such as Trim, may be smarter than their masters; yet they are all grateful to be serving the Shandys, whom they consider the best masters in the world, and, for all their occasional leaks and lapses, are uniformly faithful to them. In fact, it may be precisely the confidence in the stability and, as it were, legitimacy of the class strati-fication that allows for that free and familiar but nonegalitarian contact, with the coins (usually crowns—in a defusion, as it were, of the theme of uncrowning) passing from the masters to the servants for special efforts or feats—seigniorial gifts[21] rather than middle-class "perks." And when Trim is suffered to make his long speeches or tell his stories to the distinguished company, he dutifully interpolates verbal bows such as "an' please your honour(s)" or "With humble submission to his honour's better judgment" (V.xxxviii: 360).

Nevertheless, even the diminished carnival destabilizes the upper-class privilege of the Shandys, if not through the events of the fictional world then through the narrative patterns. A great deal of the novel's irony lies in that Toby Shandy, the gentlest of souls alive and totally committed to the good of others (see Harrison 1994: 96–98), is equally strongly committed to the

20. "The anchorage of morality in the body would seem to undermine the reason-orientated principles of eighteenth-century ethics, but in fact it radicalizes their mainspring, which was to 'natu-ralise' morality by grounding it in man himself. What is more natural than the body, which alone can express the naturalness of morality? The manifestation of morality by bodily signs indicates a cor-respondence between the two—relieving morality of any need for substantiation as to its naturalness. Consequently, instead of abstract references like commandment, reason, rationality and definition, Sterne takes morality to be action" (Iser 1988: 46–47).

21. As Carolyn Steedman notes, domestic "service was a component of the eighteenth century's modern labor relations, in which contract individualism only slowly replaced older forms" (2002: 134). In the Shandy household that process may have been even slower than usual.

art of warfare, which, not ignoring the death and suffering that wars bring about, he regards as "the getting together of quiet and harmless people, with their swords in their hands, to keep the ambitious and the turbulent within bounds" (VI.xxxii: 416). On another occasion, Uncle Toby adds that the art of war is needed in order to "intrench the lives and fortunes of the *few,* from the plunderings of the *many*" (IX.viii: 555), that is, to protect upper-class privilege.[22] Both the ideas are reduced *ad absurdum* when Toby's and Trim's delight in reenacting contemporary sieges on the bowling green is accounted for by "the consciousness" that "in carrying them on," says Toby, "we were answering the great ends of our creation" (VI.xxxii: 416) and when the expense incurred is waived as insignificant "so long as we know 'tis for the good of the nation" (III.xxii: 185).[23]

The latter two astounding statements, however, invoke an irrational but all-too-human belief in sympathetic magic, which, incidentally, it might have behooved Walter to recollect during Tristram's birth: in terms of symbolic gestures, it is not right of Walter to make Slop read Ernulphus's systematic curse while Mrs. Shandy is in labor upstairs—it is, in fact, particularly wrong in view of the numerous suggestions that for Walter, in contrast to Toby, the ultimate end of our creation is to "be fruitful and multiply" and thus consolidate a country squire's standing. For a variety of reasons, both the brothers serve their respective principles somewhat indifferently. Walter's new hobby-horse theory in the novel's last chapter holds that the trouble with social conventions is that the implements of the destruction of life are cultivated, gilded, carved, inlaid, enriched, and paraded, whereas the sundry implements of the production (or generation) of human life are

22. Cf. John Traugott's view of Toby's attitude to the war beyond the maneuvers on his bowling green (1968: 4) with the response of Melvyn New (1994: 68). Jonathan Lamb places Toby's idealization of war into the context of Swift's pamphlets "The Conduct of the Allies" and "The Character of Richard Steel" and notes that to "the ambitious and the turbulent, who Toby's war was aimed at restraining," war actually "offered unparalleled opportunities for pelf and political manipulation" (33). Lamb goes on to suggest that "Sterne's hatred of deceit and hypocrisy did not lead (as it did with many civic humanists) to the enshrinement of the ideal of absolute personal integrity that somehow survives corruption to sustain what is left of the *patria*" (34).

23. In the eighteenth-century context this statement is not as absurd as it may sound now. When military theory calls for matter to be made mental—it may mean not merely devising a vocabulary for redescribing physical violence beyond recognition (cf. Scarry 1985: 60–108) but also, and perhaps mainly, the art of using artillery and fortification not to increase but to reduce casualties: "Chivalry stood for an attempt to endow instinct with a kind of correct deportment. Warfare in the classical age of Western Europe was conducted with great formality because there was a wish to reserve and renew this correct deportment, notwithstanding the advent of inhuman factors. Following the desolation left by the Thirty Years' War, there was a desire to keep expenditure within bounds—men cost dear!—and to avoid alarming the population so thoroughly as to render recruitment impossible" (de Rougemont 1956: 254–55). The agenda of modern total warfare tends to dismiss such principles as obsolete.

jealously hidden from view (IX.xxxiii: 587). His oral dissertation on this subject is duly interrupted by the sudden appearance of Obadiah[24] with complaints about the Shandy bull (if not about the "Irish bull" of the novel). If Toby's belief in the divine right of privilege is reduced *ad absurdum* earlier in the novel, Walter's witty *double entendre* about the hairiness of Obadiah's baby[25]—meant to save the old bull from ignominy and slaughter (cf. the fate of the old horse in Orwell's *Animal Farm*)—ultimately points to the intellectual sophistication that, for all its hobby-horse tangents and capers, may be the last bastion of the social class that claims trusteeship of the cultural heritage of their country.

The example of *Tristram Shandy* shows, among other things, that the reading of a carnivalesque narrative need not be a carnivalesque experience. The characters of the novel, including the narrator-protagonist, may attract sympathy but are too systematically distanced by their own eccentricities and the proto-Borgesian learned narrative complications to sustain sympathetic identification. The irritations of the first reading—spell disrupted by shock, manner competing with matter, a profusion of explicit and submerged allusion that constantly humbles the never sufficiently informed reader, the sense of being in the room where people are laughing and we may be missing the joke, and repeated calls for backtracking and catching up—create a predominantly *agônistic* experience (cf. also Iser 1988: 94–120), even for Sterne's immediate target audience, a narrow enclave of the well educated with a free choice of reading matter. The modern reader's wrestling with the text for control of meaning is made still harder by the need to reconstruct the cultural codes of the period and its literary and philosophical contexts in order to understand the narrative's semantics—its references to humors, homunculi, squirts, sieges, enclosures, commissaries, window taxes, its staging of the association of ideas, and its dialectics of book learning and "authenticity" (Lamb 1989: 40–51ff). On a repeated reading, with initial difficulties overcome, there still remain numerous puzzling passages and

---

24. This interruption is one of the reasons why I disagree with Melvyn New's ascription of Walter's belief "that a society more ashamed of its sexuality than of its violence, a society always ready to make war but ashamed of making love, is in moral and social peril" to Sterne himself (1994: 81).

25. Obadiah has expected his own baby to be born at the same time as his calf, and this does not happen. The fact that the baby is hairy is interpreted to mean that it is premature—or, continuing the joke of Obadiah and the mule, that it has been sired by the bull: in both cases, the bull is cleared, on the basis of reasonable doubt, of the accusation of sterility.

hence a large residue of interpretive struggle, yet the element of *alea* is enhanced—not by the shock of flouted convention as on the first reading but through moments of discovery: meanings fall into place (e.g., the polysemy of "the secret spring," or the recurrence of the micromotif of "falling"), mental dice hitting expectant narrative grooves. In a sense, the experience of the first reading parallels the characters' doomed attempts to stave off the chance and accident that constantly disrupt their best-laid plans; the second reading is, by contrast, one of gratitude for the unexpected moments at which we realize that what flows in the seemingly random stream of narrative detail and opinion is actually knotted into a vertiginous complexity by a multiplicity of consistent semantic, thematic, philosophical, and intertextual strands.

Such moments of triumph, in which, paradoxically, the enjoyment of *alea* and *ilinx* amount to a concession of the reader's defeat in an agonistic wrestling with the text, create the aesthetically heightened meaning effects, which complement the presence effects produced by the novel's imagery and style. In *The Birth of Tragedy* Nietzsche talks about the cheerfulness of the Greeks as one that can only be based on the knowledge of horror. The cheerfulness of *Tristram Shandy* is of this kind as well. It is offered us against the background of intrigues and enclosures at home, the Inquisition, icy winds, and absurd entrapments abroad, the grim logic of war, fever, consumption, and inequality everywhere. The remissions that such aesthetically distancing cheerfulness offers are almost religiously oppositional: their grateful pleasure flows unevenly from a "secret spring" through loopholes in the ill-starred ("disasterous") overlap of the flawed human condition and inept social contract.

CHAPTER FOUR

Non-Carnivalesque Oppositionality
Jane Austen and the Golden Mean

The poetry of aesthetic reconciliation must seek its own self-conscious-
ness against the prose of alienated reality.

—H.-G. Gadamer, *Truth and Method*, 83

FOR A SCHOLAR'S TREASURE TROVE of the non-carnivalesque
oppositional mode one can turn to the fiction of Jane Austen. Though
faintly carnivalesque features are present at the crisis points of her novels
and sometimes in the dénouement (where declarations of feeling and attitude are set in liminal spaces, observers and participants exchange roles,
rigid superordination is modified, and individual minds come ajar to admit
considerations that have been resisted), such episodes usually unfold within
the constraints of etiquette, with but minor oppositional loopholes. Moreover, it is not to every reader that Austen's novels give a sense of cultural
remission; more generally, they create a reassuring impression of a way of
life that continues from generation to generation—in particular, since their
one major rite of passage culminates in a judicious channeling of desire to
a suitable marriage. This, in addition to Austen's unforgettable character
types, is one reason for the special place of her novels in the culture of her
country.[1]

Austen's novels combine features of the comedy of manners with those of
the traditional *Bildungsroman*. The conventions of the former genre underlie

1. As Rudyard Kipling's short story "The Janeites" shows, amidst the bitter mangling carnival
of World War I, to the British officers Jane Austen's novels represent what they are fighting for (cf.
Claudia Johnson 1993: 99–100) and provide a basis for solidarity across class boundaries.

their romantic plots; with the latter, a markedly non-carnivalesque genre, they share stories of the characters' progress towards maturity, which, when achieved, is rewarded—or confirmed, as if by a matriculation certificate—by a happy marriage. The *Bildungsroman* pattern observable in most of the novels consists in isolating the potentially dangerous tendencies in the heroines' dispositions, creating circumstances in which these tendencies grow and lead to the threshold of personal disasters, and then watching the heroines' reflective anagnorisis and attempts to modify their "disposition" while courageously facing the bleak consequences of their errors. The personal integrity displayed at the latter stage brings the heroine the approbation of the general reader[2] and vindication in the eyes of her hurdle audience—the authorities who stood between her and her target readership. The same pattern[3] can, however, be viewed as oppositional insofar as it suggests that the disabling blow received by a heroine, usually as a consequence of her ethical experimentation, reduces her energies sufficiently for her to give up some of her spiritual independence and, in the words of Congreve's Millamant (*The Way of the World,* Act IV), "dwindle into a wife."

Such an *oppositional* reading is most appropriate to Austen's "problem novel," *Mansfield Park,* whose heroine, Fanny Price, receives a deenergizing blow early in her life, through no fault of her own: at the age of nine she is transplanted from an impoverished but relatively happy home to the elegant and affluent estate of the Bertrams, where she has to assume the liminal role of a dependent relative. Her docility and retiring disposition seem largely to be a consequence of this blow; her moral integrity is interpretable as a success of an Evangelical upbringing, according to which a young lady's mandatory compliance and self-effacement in company should, instead of weakening her ethical principles, enhance them by an unobtrusive cultivation of her intellectual and religious inner life.[4]

2. Robert Polhemus has described Austen's novels as dreams "of individual integrity in which self-interest and morality coincide" (1982: 39).

3. An alternative description of Austen's recurrent plot formula is given in Phelan 2003: 67–70. See also Hinnant (2006) for a survey of the ways in which Jane Austen novels rework seven traditional types of "courtship plots" that conventionally involve the characters' having to undergo "a traumatic experience, a violent shift from innocence to self-knowledge before their union can be consummated" (294).

4. *Mansfield Park* was written in the period when Jane Austen partly relented towards Evangelicalism, which was, in itself, an oppositional movement within as well as outside the established church. For a relatively recent discussion of the refraction of Evangelical principles in this novel see Waldron 1999: 85–87; for an opposite argument (less convincing) see Monaghan 1978. John Wiltshire notes that the literary innovation of *Mansfield Park* is the creation of a heroine "whose quiet and acquiescent exterior is matched by an inner life of complex and agitating feeling, a dutiful heroine conceived with an ego, with strong convictions and emotional demands" (2005: lxxviii). Acquaintance with Evangelical literature may have been part of the etiology of this artistic feat.

The end of the traditional *Bildungsroman* usually confirms the end of the adolescent misrule and leaves the protagonist and her (or, most often, his) natural milieu safely adjusted to each other. Though Austen's protagonists are women, her version of the *Bildungsroman* differs from that of the female model of *Bildungsroman* (such as, in much later versions, Kate Chopin's *The Awakening* or Alice Walker's *Color Purple*) which stages not the protagonist's reconciliation with the logic behind absurd social restrictions but, on the contrary, her awakening from social conformity (see Abel, Hirsch, and Langland 1983: 3–14).[5] However, the "male"/"female" dichotomy may be void of gender content—Joyce's *A Portrait of the Artist as a Young Man* arguably belongs to the latter variety.

As a novel of character development, the *Bildungsroman* is a "biographical" genre that tends to emphasize the movement towards (or away from) the mainstream social standard and that has little space for carnivalesque remissions. This empirical regularity (not invulnerable to counterexamples, especially when the *Bildungsroman* is also a *Künstlerroman*) is usually associated with the ethical system of the author. The cautiously non-carnivalesque character of Austen's novels corresponds to the rationally limited moderate view of human possibility that they construct, adjust, and refine. For Austen ethical value is, ideally, a version of the Golden Mean, with a tinge of rule-utilitarianism: the stable functioning of the social structure is seen as dependent on civility, the middle-way self-limitation of social groups, and the personal integrity of their members. Yet Austen's mildly anti-Jacobin or rather "centrist" (Knox-Shaw 2004: 5) agenda of perpetuating the social order involved oppositional liberalization of social routines in the spirit of an idealized cultural tradition that could justify the privileged status of the gentry.[6] I shall here discuss some of the ethical and social implications of Austen's valorization of the middle way and then, focusing on *Mansfield Park,* turn to different facets of her non-carnivalesque oppositionality.

In Aristotle's *Nicomachean Ethics* (II.vi–vii), positive ethical value is presented as the average between the extremes of the same quality: courage, for

5. For a different account of the specificity of the British female *Bildungsroman*, one that emphasizes its responses to courtesy books, see Fraiman 1993: 1–31.

6. The plot pattern in which a "moment of self-discovery and self-abasement" is followed by "the resolve in future to follow reason" constitutes the climax of the majority of anti-Jacobin novels (Marilyn Butler 1990 [1975]: 166). This plot formula is, however, complicated by the sense that the genteel marriage that rewards the practice is somewhat Procrustean.

instance, is a positive value, the mean of the quality that, if insufficient, is known as cowardice and, if excessive, as rashness.[7] This principle of ethical evaluation was eventually developed into the notion of the Golden Mean sung by Horace.[8]

As noted, in Austen's novel ethical value is a matter of measure (see Tave 1973: 29–30): a little finesse is a mandatory social accomplishment; too much finesse is self-serving manipulativeness (Toker 1993a: 84–104); lack of neighborly attention is shameful neglect, too much of it is officiousness; too much self-confidence is obstinacy, too little is spinelessness; the right amount of attention to class distinctions is sophistication; its excess is prejudice.[9]

Numerous examples of valorized moderation can be found in *Mansfield Park*—for example, Fanny's pious and near-morbid introspection is a mean—though not entirely a Golden one[10]—between Rushworth's comic lack of self-awareness (or Edmund's self-delusions) and Mary Crawford's cynicism.[11] Austen's most sustained exploration of the golden mean is conducted in *Sense and Sensibility,* where the two title qualities are unequally distributed between the two heroines as well as among the supporting cast. The heroines do not represent extremes of sense or of sensibility. Indeed, Elinor has just the right amount of sense: it is her half-brother John Dashwood whose hypertrophy of "sense" turns into a syndrome of opportunism, stinginess, and covetousness. Occasionally, a slight overstatement of sense on Elinor's part results in a rigid self-control that not only hides but also distances her feelings (cf. also Copeland 2006: li).[12] And yet it is not Elinor but Mrs. Palmer who is presented as radically out of touch with her real

---

7. Austen's implicit ethical theory does not, however, share the ideals of the Aristotelian *heroica;* accordingly, the presentation of the development of her protagonists departs from Aristotle's view that character deteriorates rather than improves with experience—a view that, however, is often applicable to her presentation of the older generation, for example, Mr. Woodhouse in *Emma.*

8. *Odes* II.x. I am sometimes tempted to replace the metaphor of the Golden Mean with that of the so-called golden ratio (1.62:1), the mysterious number yielded by the Fibonacci series, which also underlies the aesthetic appeal of, for example, standard rectangular frame proportions.

9. Cf. Judith Shklar's definition of snobbery as "making inequality hurt" (1984: 87).

10. "Between the extremes of selfhood by extinction of feeling and selfhood entirely created by feeling, Fanny stands as a slightly tarnished golden mean" (Fleishman 1967: 50).

11. Austen's preference for the middle way is to a large extent culturally determined; cf. Kate Fox on the "distinctively English" rule of moderation, according to which "too much of anything" is to be deplored (2004: 32). It may be that her novels not only *reflected* this social value but actually helped *to form and disseminate* its practice.

12. Elinor's reserve should be read against the background of the *ideological* doctrine of the women's "passionlessness," which, as Nancy F. Cott (1978) has persuasively argued, served women's interests in the late eighteenth century and the first half of the nineteenth, even if its relationship to reality was tenuous.

feelings, who laughs when she has reason to feel miserable or offended—not out of magnanimousness but because of intellectual deficiency (cf. Humphrey 1991). Nor is Elinor's antipode sister Marianne a case of maximum emotional self-indulgence: she has, at least, more sense and self-control than the younger Eliza, who is seduced by Willoughby.[13] Indeed, in all of Austen's novels secondary characters display some of the protagonists' features in different degrees of intensity. The characters are deployed thematically: each facet of the protagonist is a motif also trailed by several other members of the troupe (see Phelan 1987: 287–92).

Yet the sense and the sensibility are not only character traits in Austen's novel; they are also *ethical commitments*. Elinor's "sense" is a socially oriented version of the cardinal virtue of prudence, combined, as in Fielding, with a commitment to the happiness, or at least the comfort, of those around her. Marianne's "sensibility" is a Romantic valorization of intensity, sincerity, and spontaneity, as well as a determined Romantic rejection of the encroachments of society on her inner life. This consciously endorsed disposition is not alien to Elinor either; what Elinor objects to in her sister is not the principle itself but exaggerations in its practice: Marianne's sincerity often means rudeness and inconsiderateness (for which Elinor has to atone); spontaneity gets translated into comic tactlessness (of which Elinor is the victim); intensity slips into morbidness (against which Elinor's good sense is helpless). The radical change that Marianne undergoes after her illness is all the more credible insofar as it is not only a remolding of the self but also, predominantly, a conscious shift in her practical ideology—from the romantic cultivation of the intense experience to constructive civility.

In *Sense and Sensibility*, moreover, the preference for moderation has sociopolitical implications. It pertains to the limited social ambitions of the Dashwood sisters (and, by extension, of Edward Ferrars): what both Elinor and Marianne want is not wealth or lofty status but genteel "competence," though the two define it in different ways. Marianne states that

"money can only give happiness where there is nothing else to give it. Beyond a competence, it can afford no real satisfaction, as far as mere self is concerned."

"Perhaps," said Elinor smiling, "we may come to the same point. *Your* competence and *my* wealth are very much alike, I dare say. . . . Come, what is your competence?"

13. See also Rachel Brownstein's discussion of the contrasts between the Dashwood sisters and two other pairs of sisters in the novel—as well as of the associated motif of interchangeability (1997: 45–49).

"About eighteen hundred or two thousand a year; not more than *that*."

Elinor laughed. "*Two* thousand a year! *One* is my wealth. I guessed how it would end." (88)

Though Marianne's definition of competence is on the "noble" side, she is right about what it would take for Willoughby, the gentleman of leisure she is in love with, to remain content with domestic life. Elinor's estimation of what would suffice for her material well-being is geared up to the character of Edward Ferrars—a thousand a year would ensure the reasonable standard of consumption that would keep her and her family within the lower gentry and allow them to maintain the cultural, social, and religious activities that endow this class affiliation with idealized meaning. This moderation of financial status also implies a utopian dream of defying the first law of economics: there just might be enough for everyone. However, the patriarchal disposition of property discussed in the first chapter of the novel (along with the entail that motivates Mrs. Bennet's agenda in *Pride and Prejudice*) sacrifices the interests and cultural commitments of gentlewomen such as the Dashwood sisters to the principle of consolidation of patriarchical landed estates and transmission of political power.

Elinor and Marianne combine leisure-class cultivation with the peaceable ethics of activity and contentment. The goals of the sisters are contrasted with those of their half-brother John and his wife and mother-in-law—pursuit of the expansion of property and elevation of social status. John Dashwood is an exponent of the atavistic mentality that Norbert Elias describes by what was once "said of the American pioneer: 'He didn't want all the land; he just wanted the land next to his'" (1982: 160). This too is an ideological commitment—John conceptualizes the enhancement of the estate in terms of "duty"—which excuses him, as it were, from the small expenses that might add to the comfort of his sisters and totally absolves him from concern about the peasants who might be hurt by the enclosures:

"The inclosure of Norland Common, now carrying on, is a most serious drain. And then I have made a little purchase within this half-year—East Kingham Farm, you must remember the place, where old Gibson used to live. The land was so very desirable for me in every respect, so immediately adjoining my own property, that I felt it my duty to buy it. I could not have answered it to my conscience to let it fall into any other hands." (219)

John Dashwood's greed is thus presented not as a personal vice but as a status-determined commitment. His expenses during the stay in London are a matter of *noblesse oblige:* "we must live at a great expense while we are here" (219). His wife likewise considers a certain standard of living not as a comfort but as a duty, so that she can even pretend to envy Mrs. Dashwood and her daughters' exemption from the burden of status symbols: "They will live so cheap! Their housekeeping will be nothing at all. They will have no carriages, no horses, and hardly any servants; they will keep no company, and can have no expenses of any kind! Only conceive how comfortable they will be!" (10).

Mr. and Mrs. Dashwood's talk of their own obligation to buy adjacent property, maintain large households and equipages, and enclose the commons is not entirely describable in terms of a hypocritical double standard. Theirs is a clear expression of the *invidious emulation* that in Thorstein Veblen's *The Theory of the Leisure Class* (1899) is analyzed as a distinctive feature of the *predatory* leisure class—the tendency to compare people "with a view to rating and grading them in respect to relative worth or value— in an aesthetic or moral sense—and so awarding and defining the relative degrees of complacency with which they may legitimately be contemplated by themselves and others" (34).[14] Versions of invidious emulation are one of the dominant issues in the English novels of the nineteenth century (Thackeray's *Vanity Fair,* Dickens's *Martin Chuzzlewit* and *Our Mutual Friend,* George Eliot's *Middlemarch,* among others), where they reflect not the attitudes of the nobility (to which Veblen traces them) but, mainly, the social ambitions and insecurities of the middle and upper middle classes.

Austen's cumulative portrayal of her own class and of the cultural legacy of the Augustan age involves a privileging of the domestic ideal (Romantically tinged yet desentimentalized, with disinterested public service restricted to setting the ethical standards in one's own parish), over a truculent ambitious quest for vaster power and "consequence."[15] She opts for what almost a century later Veblen would call the peaceable culture as opposed to the

14. Veblen here neglects the Kantian distinction between a person's "worth" and a person's "value" to others (see Kant 1946: 63–64).

15. "Consequence" is one of the insistently recurrent key words in *Mansfield Park* (see McKenzie 1985), along (to a smaller extent) with the words "evil" and "connections" (see Fleishman 1967: 51–54) and the word "struggle" associated with the Malthusian "struggle for existence" (Knox-Shaw 2004: 176), the way the derivatives of "exert" are in *Sense and Sensibility* (see Tave 1973: 113), the derivatives of "exhibit" in *Pride and Prejudice,* and those of "perfect" in *Emma.*

predatory one. Veblen, indeed, reduces the social hierarchy to two classes: the leisure class (scions or imitators of the once-predatory social prominents) and the toilers, people who maintain themselves by their industry instead of enjoying the spoils of belligerence.[16] Though Austen's characters belong to the former class, and the few working professionals among them (clergymen, a barrister such as John Knightley, army and navy officers, governesses) are still closely linked to families in which primogeniture usually meant exemption from the need to make a living, most of her protagonists cultivate the values of the peaceable culture, and hence find themselves in opposition to authority figures in their environment. The ethical and personal goals of Austen's protagonists are, indeed, pitted against the invidious emulation that, according to Veblen, commonly takes the shape of "conspicuous consumption" and "conspicuous leisure." In discussing Jane Austen's corpus, this scheme must be supplemented by conspicuous sexual charisma, or what may be called *invidious sexuality.*

The less demonstrative version of "conspicuous consumption" is behind the regularity with which a gentleman, who can pride himself on overcoming multiple hardships abroad, will tend to perceive minor hardships in his own home as indignities. The more demonstrative version is often resorted to by the so-called new money as well as by frauds and charlatans, such as Montague Tigg with his Anglo-Bengallee Life-Assurance company in Dickens's *Martin Chuzzlewit* (see Toker 1998) or Becky and Rawdon Crawley, who know "how to live well on nothing a year" in *Vanity Fair.* With the exception of Mrs. Elton in *Emma* (a *parvenue* who takes vicarious pride in her brother-in-law's estate and barouche-landau and sneers at the small quantity of white satin and lace at Emma's wedding), Austen tends to delineate the less showy version of conspicuous consumption, still almost always critically. In *Persuasion,* for instance, despite his debts, Sir Walter Elliot cannot stoop to giving up his carriage and some of his servants while staying in his family mansion but will not feel the discomfort of living in a

---

16. Veblen's description of social stratification offers an alternative both to the English traditional view of social hierarchy (upper, middle, and lower classes—with the subtleties of the distinction forming the daily substance of etiquette in Jane Austen's milieu and surviving to this day) and to the Marxist nomenclature of class as related to the means and forces of production. In modern societies Veblen's distinction between the leisure class (whatever the sources of its income) and the citizens who have to work in order to make a living is no longer (if it ever was) watertight, but Veblen's theory is still illuminating in application to consumer culture, in addition to being useful for the analysis of the representation of society in realistic nineteenth-century fiction, whose authors responded to empirical data similar to those observed by Veblen himself. Peregrine Worsthorne's 2004 *In Defense of Aristocracy* is an interesting counterstatement to Veblen's view of the aristocracy (as well as to the Marxist view).

much smaller house in Bath because there the relatively cramped quarters are not a retrenchment but a general rule. Conspicuous wealth is Sir Walter's "spiritual" need;[17] by contrast, his daughter Anne, the protagonist of the novel, is disinclined to invidious emulation of any kind. The "competence" desired by Elinor Dashwood in *Sense and Sensibility* amounts to the minimal level of consumption that would still be classifiable as genteel.

In *Mansfield Park* the motif of conspicuous consumption includes Sir Thomas's sending Fanny to the dinner at the Grants in his carriage—not because it may rain or because the order of the day is kindness but because it does not suit his status to have a niece of his *walk* half a mile to a formal dinner engagement. Maria and Julia Bertram hold Fanny "cheap" on finding that she is not interested in music (musical training belongs to the semiotics of "conspicuous leisure") and has only two sashes (12). In the Mansfield circle it is unthinkable to make do without a necklace at a ball. If Henry Crawford makes his horses, carriage, hunting dogs, and jewelry available to his friends, he is, among other things, enjoying a benevolent version of conspicuous consumption: his friends' consumption is an extension of his own.

Veblen's theory does not apply to all national leisure-class cultures in a uniform way. Among the English gentry, partly owing to Protestant suspiciousness of lavish display, consumption tended to be less conspicuous than the cultural signs of leisure.[18] In literature, showy wastefulness was an unfailing butt of satire—as in Smollett's *Humphry Clinker.* The semiotics of leisure, on the other hand, entered into a dialectical tension with the negative view of "idleness." The resulting confusion is comically caricatured in Rushworth's disparagement of the theatricals: "I am not as fond of acting as I was at first. I think we are a good deal better employed, sitting comfortably here among ourselves, and doing nothing" (128). A suave *reductio ad absurdum* of the paradox of diligent leisure (also explored in the portrayal of Rosamond Vincy in George Eliot's *Middlemarch*) is Henry Crawford's elegantly cynical remark that because he does not like "to eat the bread of idleness" (157) he will set himself the challenge of seducing the affections of Fanny Price.

17. "Very much squalor and discomfort will be endured before the last trinket or the last pretence of pecuniary decency is put away. There is no class and no country that has yielded so abjectly before the pressure of physical want as to deny themselves all gratification of this higher or spiritual need" (Veblen 1899: 85; see also 167–68, 190).

18. To this day the so-called U-culture in Britain dispenses with a great deal of material appurtenances considered necessary for the display of successful middle-class status. This regularity is recurrently noted in Fox 2004.

A lady, in particular, needs always to be occupied, although, in contrast to the occupation of the "spinsters" of olden times, not in a way that would increase the family's income or force her to change into work clothes.[19] The "great deal of carpetwork" and "many yards of fringe" that Lady Bertram produces, Penelope-like, during her husband's absence from Mansfield Park are useful mainly for demonstrating how "her own time had been irreproachably spent" (124); even so, it is Fanny, essentially in her role of an errand-running dependent, who must smooth My Lady's "work" by untangling knotted threads. Insofar as the conduct of a gentleman's wife is expected to be analogous to that of his upper servant,[20] Fanny is, in fact though not in intention, trained accordingly while at the service of her aunts. Veblen's remark that the servants' ("vicarious") leisure is not their own but an extension of the leisure of their masters (1899: 59–60) is foreshadowed in Henry Crawford's commendation of the "unpretending gentleness" with which Fanny takes it "as a matter of course that she [is] not to have a moment at her own command" (202).

In a young lady's home education in eighteenth- and early-nineteenth-century England, the emphasis on "accomplishments" (spelling, writing in a small hand, decorative needlework, drawing, music, dancing, French, and—as befits the age of imperial expansion—geography) rather than on academic or professional training was geared to the conspicuousness of leisure. Excellence in drawing and musical performance could be real amenities in the pretechnological times, and writing in a small hand saved postage, but in the absence of real talent or love of the art, most other accomplishments were social props and facilitators, or decoys for minor vanity (see Poovey 1984: 29), or just sanctioned ways of passing the time:[21] the elegant constraint of Mrs. Grant's tambour frame (47) supplements and attenuates the grimmer

19. Cf. Nancy Armstrong on "labor that is not labor" (1987: 75–81).
20. "The servant or wife should not only perform certain offices and show a servile disposition, but it is quite as imperative that they should show an acquired facility in the tactics of subservience—a trained conformity to the canons of effectual and conspicuous subservience. Even to-day it is this aptitude and acquired skill in the formal manifestation of the servile relation that constitutes the chief element of utility in our highly paid servants, as well as one of the chief ornaments of the well-bred housewife . . . trained service has utility, not only as gratifying the master's instinctive liking for good and skilful workmanship and his propensity for conspicuous dominance over those whose lives are subservient to his own, but it has utility also as putting in evidence a much larger consumption of human service than would be shown by the mere present conspicuous leisure performed by an untrained person" (1899: 60–61).
21. Jane Austen's metaphor for her fiction as the "little bit (two Inches wide) of Ivory" (*Letters*, 16 December 1816, p. 469), a version of the traditional "modesty topos" (cf. Curtius 1953: 83–85; Wolosky 2004: 155–99), also constitutes a claim to inoffensiveness by aligning her writing with the ladies' recognized pastimes (see Gilbert and Gubar 1979: 107–9).

symbolism of the iron gate in front of which Fanny is seated in Sotherton. In Austen's *Emma,* the recoil of the intelligent Jane Fairfax from the position of a governess may have as much to do with this curriculum as with the indignities and vexations of that ambiguous status.[22]

Fanny Price, whose happiest hours are spent in the unheated East Room (formerly a schoolroom) with her plants and her books, seems to endow a selected part of her own "accomplishments" with a genuine spiritual significance. The by-product of her being treated as "the child of the attic whose wicked stepmother (Aunt Norris) allows her no fire to keep her warm" (Meyersohn 1983: 226) is the absence of privacy—on cold days Fanny has to go down to the warm main drawing room, and stay there in attendance on her aunts. Thus if Fanny's early education provides her with intellectual resources to compensate for social disadvantage, her position in the Bertram household tends to prevent her from falling back on those resources—until Henry Crawford's courtship heightens her "consequence," calls Sir Thomas's attention to her, and induces him to overrule Mrs. Norris's ban on a fire in the East Room.[23]

Jane Austen can be described as a "connected critic" (Walzer 1987: 38–40ff.) of the gentry at the margins of which she lived most of her life (see Collins 1994: ix–x), a critic whose relative well-being largely depends on this society.[24] If, according to Veblen, the leisure class is an outgrowth of the primeval bellicose *predatory* aristocracy of greedy merit that, by force or fraud, had made its fortune and won positions of dominance over the peaceable population who eat their bread in the sweat of their brow (1899: 1–21),[25] Austen's

22. On the in-between position of the nineteenth-century governess see Poovey 1988: 126–63 and Hill 2001: 54–66.

23. Mrs. Norris's name may be an allusion to a notorious slave dealer about whom Austen must have read in Thomas Clarkson's *History of the Abolition of the African Slave Trade* (see Gibbon 1982: 303). The name undergoes an intertextual carnivalization when given to a cat in J. K. Rowling's *Harry Potter.*

24. A milder fictional portrayal of such a critic is the protagonist-narrator of Elizabeth Gaskell's *Cranford,* affectionately critical of the elderly ladies who offer her her confidence and seedcake.

25. This poetic anthropology is in tune with the history of the medieval heroica and the distribution of landed estates among the kings' faithful. Fanny nostalgically romanticizes this past when disappointed by Sotherton's modern chapel (61). Her ideals of chivalrous generosity are associated with Walter Scott's characters and with romantic figures by the name of "Edmund," which her beloved cousin happens to share with the anti-Jacobin author of *Reflections on the Revolution in France* (see Kelly 1982: 34): "'It is a name of heroism and renown—of kings, princes and knights; and seems to breathe the spirit of chivalry and warm affections'" (145). The predatory ways of the distinguished ancestors of the older upper-class families actually occupy her mind as little as the Shakespearian use

favorite social setting is the unranked gentry, with a marginal sprinkling of knights and baronets. Her favorite characters are indifferent to the peerage (cf. Greene 1953);[26] only the unredeemed Sir Walter Elliot and the social climber Mrs. Ferrars are presented as actively seeking "connections" with the aristocracy. Ideally, people belonging to the stratum ranging from the Bertrams of *Mansfield Park* to the Bennets of *Pride and Prejudice* were in a better position to effect a convergence of the genteel sense of responsibility with the values of the peaceable culture, especially since resident landownership imposed practical duties and counteracted the restlessness of unlimited leisure.[27] The idealized conception of the commitments of the rural gentry involved the cultivation of family pieties, paternalist respect for the tenants of the estate, and the life of the spirit in which love would hold pride of place. Austen's circumscribed oppositionality consists in her sympathy with those members of the leisure class who opt for peaceable moderation and thus, as the money talk in *Sense and Sensibility* shows, for the agenda of expanding the ranks of the cultivated upper class instead of reducing them by concentration of property.

The morphology of Austen's novel-of-manners "courtship" plots can be described in the framework of this oppositionality and in a way different from that of the *Bildungsroman* plots in the same novels. The heroines find themselves in conflict with the authority figures, usually of the older generation, who restrain their freedom, but this conflict is outwardly displaced by one with the predatory rival in the same age group. There is little supererogation in Austen's novels and even less absolute evil. The "wicked" figures such as John Thorpe in *Northanger Abbey,* Willoughby in *Sense and*

---

of the name "Edmund" in *King Lear* (though her own story develops as a cross between Cordelia's disposition to love and be silent and the patient Griselda's vindication).

26. Marilyn Butler believes that Austen "shows no love for the great aristocracy (as represented in Darcy's family) or for the very rich (the Rushworths); and pride of rank, whether in an earl's daughter or a baronet, is evidently anathema to her. Jane Austen's attitude to social distinctions in the upper reaches of society has been called that of a 'Tory radical': which is accurate provided we recognize that over all in the novels her Toryism carries more weight than her radicalism" (1990: 165). However, the Darcy branch of Lady Catherine's family clearly commands Austen's respect: as their unostentatiously noble "grounds" and rich library suggest, they see themselves as guardians of a cultural tradition.

27. This milieu was congenial to families of genteel professionals such as Austen's father and brothers, yet part of Austen's social duties was attention to the higher-ranking influential relatives to whom such professionals had been or would be indebted. "Whenever it is time for the family to go into mourning for even the most distant relation of consequence, Jane Austen weighs in with black lace, ribbons and every accoutrement needed to maintain the family connection. When a niece or nephew needs prompting to produce a gift or a letter for one of the living worthies, Austen is ready with the reminder. When she must attend on the demands of her unpleasant but very rich aunt she grumbles, but makes her plans accordingly" (Copeland 2006: xlvii–xlviii).

Sensibility (a role-confusing namesake of the Sir Clement Willoughby in Fanny Burney's *Evelina)*, Wickham in *Pride and Prejudice,* Henry Crawford in *Mansfield Park,* Mr. Elliot in *Persuasion,* and to some extent even Frank Churchill in *Emma* are mild comedy-of-manners versions of traditional villains or rakes; they act not as adversaries but as catalysts, indirect facilitators of the heroines' victories over the rival camps. As befits "cover stories," such victories are usually crowned by the favor of the novels' representatives of patriarchal authority. The positive male agents, the eligible *jeunes premiers* of *Northanger Abbey* and *Sense and Sensibility* (Henry Tilney and Edward Ferrars, respectively), function as prizes of the struggle; in *Pride and Prejudice, Emma,* and *Persuasion,* they (Darcy, Knightley, Wentworth) eventually replace the paternal authority figures; in *Mansfield Park,* Edmund Bertram combines these two functions.

The main issue of contention between Austen's heroines and their rivals (Isabella Thorpe, Lucy Steel and the John Dashwoods, Caroline Bingley, Mrs. Elton) and rulers (General Tilney, Sir Thomas Bertram, Sir Walter Elliot and Lady Russell) is motives for marriage. Austen's protagonists want to marry for love, or not at all; their antagonists are committed to the pursuit of "advantageous" marriages that raise one's "consequence." The most unabashed spokesperson for this principle in marital choice is Mary Crawford, Fanny's rival in *Mansfield Park,* whose better feelings eventually conflict with her own maxims. Quite wealthy herself, Mary desires a marriage that will enhance her social position ("every body should marry as soon as they can do it to advantage" [32]), and considers a clergyman ineligible because, in her economy, "a clergyman is nothing" (66). Her conscious agenda is thus in tune with the upper-class politics of power expansion through a network of connections and alliances. Her best friends are women who have contracted loveless marriages and whom Edmund's letter defines in terms of invidious emulation:

> I do not like Mrs. Fraser. She is a cold-hearted, vain woman, who has married entirely from convenience, and though evidently unhappy in her marriage, places her disappointment, not to faults of judgement or temper, or disproportion of age, but to her being after all, less affluent than many of her acquaintance, especially than her sister, Lady Stornaway, as is the determined supporter of every thing mercenary and ambitious, provided it be only mercenary and ambitious enough. (285–86)

Fanny and Edmund consider such a philosophy of life *corrupt* (286, 288): for them it represents not an accepted state of affairs, one in which dynastic marriages are the norm, but a falling-off from a chaste ideal. In that sense, Fanny and Edmund, as well as Elinor and Edward Ferrars in *Sense and Sensibility*, may be regarded as forces of progress, while Mary Crawford, who believes her principles to be advanced, is actually a reactionary. Indeed, it was only by the end of the eighteenth century that in the circles of the rural gentry "the ideal of a companionate marriage" had replaced the previous policy of arranged marriages (Waldron 1999: 116), still routinely practiced among the aristocracy. It is in the service of the latter predatory policy that in *Pride and Prejudice* Lady Catherine de Bourgh travels all the way to Elizabeth Bennet's house in order to demand that she decline Darcy's proposal.

The ideal of the companionate marriage is closer to the values of the growing middle class than to those of the Regency ruling upper classes that Mary Crawford emulates.[28] Fanny's and Edmund's belief in a peaceable companionate marriage, with the couple's financial standing beyond the mandatory "competence" (of about £500 per annum) regarded as a bonus rather than a goal, is liberal rather than conservative.[29]

Fanny and Edmund, indeed, seem to strike the golden ratio in the scale of the gentry's attitudes to labor and leisure. On one side of their unhurried occupations is Mrs. Norris's unseemly love of trafficking with her neighbors' housekeepers, gardeners, cooks, and coachmen. At the other extreme is the Crawford siblings' impatience with productive labor and its signs: Henry wishes to shut out the blacksmith's shop so that it might not be seen from Edmund's Thornton Lacey parsonage (166), and Mary is astonished that, contrary to the "London maxim, that every thing is to be got with money" (43), at hay-making time farmers will not spare a cart for transporting her harp. Though Mary's and Henry's urban sophistication should suggest advanced views and freedom from provincial inhibitions,[30] actually the two

28. What Denis de Rougemont writes of the new stability of marriage in seventeenth- and eighteenth-century France was also largely true of England, where upper-class family "alliances" were likewise a matter of negotiation: "If the parties happened to have a real or fancied inclination for one another, this merely added an element of exquisite perfection and of agreeable luxury to the arrangement—an ultimate touch of whimsicality amounting almost to insolence. (In the eighteenth century it quickly came to be considered bad taste.)" (1956: 206).

29. The case of Charlotte Lucas, whose marriage of convenience is not wholly condemned in *Pride and Prejudice,* is an exception that proves the rule. Her knighted father purchased a country estate in lieu of "providing for" the future of his daughters; and Charlotte is shown to be sacrificing part of her own identity and deliberately blunting her senses in becoming Mrs. Collins: she chooses not to hear her husband's tasteless remarks and to have her sitting room in the back part of the house that he frequents least.

30. Modern critics rather enjoy reading Mary's comment on admirals, "Of *Rears,* and *Vices,* I saw enough. Now, do not be suspecting me of a pun, I entreat," as an "indecent [remark] about homosexuality in the Navy" (Hammond 1993: 78), one that most of Austen's target audience would choose not to understand.

display the dated mind-set of the predatory leisure class that, engaged in a Regency antecedent of the modern rat race, rejects the progressive agenda of convergence with the peaceable pursuits of happiness.[31]

When Mary falls in love with Edmund, she considers modifying her expectations while also trying to dissuade him from ordination. Yet even in the context of her jealousy of the Miss Owens in whose brother's house Edmund seems to be spending a long time, she restates, albeit ironically, her maxim that it is "everybody's duty to do as well for themselves as they can" (198). Jealousy, an unwelcome intruder in Fanny's inner life, is a legitimate participant in Mary's psychodrama. One of the reasons why Mary is not transformed by her love for Edmund is her habit of extending invidious emulation to the struggle of all against all in the virtual marriage market. She thrives on invidious sexuality, on competition for sexual power. Unable to imagine that others may be differently disposed, she thinks that Henry's having been coveted by other women should make his offer attractive to Fanny, who would thus triumph over them. At the end of the novel a similar attitude is ascribed to Maria Bertram: when in the course of her adulterous affair she is reproached by Henry "as the ruin of all his happiness in Fanny," she is given "no better consolation in leaving him, than that she had divided them" (314–15). Invidious sexuality is as important a motif in *Mansfield Park* as it is in *Pride and Prejudice* and, through the character of Lucy Steele, in *Sense and Sensibility*.

A touch of voyeurism is sometimes imputed to Fanny (especially in Auerbach 1998 [1983]), but Mary Crawford is actually the more neurotic voyeur of the two. When Crawford's courtship of Fanny is no longer a secret to the Bertram clan, Mary savors the opportunity of writing to Fanny about Maria's jealousy: "'Shall I tell you how Mrs. Rushworth looked when your name was mentioned? I did not use to think her wanting in self-possession, but she had not quite enough for the demands of yesterday'" (267). If Fanny cannot help wishing to watch the rehearsals of "Lovers' Vows," Mary derives a voyeuristic enjoyment from the scenes of other women's defeat in invidious sexuality.[32] This may be the less obvious of the motives for her interest in Fanny, her inferior at any social game, yet the causal plotting of the dénouement suggests that the same feature may ultimately account for Mary's own defeat with Edmund.

31. "Fanny and Edmund, not the Crawfords, are the children of the future, the Victorians. Mary Crawford in particular is an eighteenth-century type, with her exuberance, wit, and Johnsonian preference for the city" (Julia Prewitt Brown 1979: 87).

32. Cf. Daleski 1985: 135 on Mary's and Henry's "predatory" self-indulgence and "need for a constant provision of amusements."

It has not been often noticed that Mary is a link in the causal chain that leads to Maria's elopement with Henry: it is she who detains Henry in London when he is on his mission to Everingham (to adjust property relationships and prepare a world for Fanny). Mary's second letter to Fanny in Portsmouth mentions that Henry "cannot any how be spared till after the 14th, for we have a party that evening. The value of a man like Henry on such an occasion, is what you can have no conception of; so you must take it upon my word, to be inestimable." As Mary's next sentence shows, for her this "value" is not confined to Henry's social skills and ability to enliven gatherings: "He will see the Rushworths, which I own I am not sorry for—having a little curiosity—and so I think has he" (283). Fanny, always willing to see corruption in Mary, translates this into a sign of Mary's "endeavour to secure a meeting between [Henry] and Mrs. Rushworth." Without calling the intrigue by its name, Fanny thinks it in Mary's "worst line of conduct, and grossly unkind and ill-judged" (283). This is the closest she comes to regarding Mary, to whom she owes several minor favors, as "wicked."

In a conversation that Edmund holds with Fanny upon meeting the Crawford siblings, both comment on a flaw in Mary's manners—her harsh remarks, made to new acquaintances, about the uncle to whom she owes a debt of gratitude (46). Manners, according to Veblen, are a sign of conspicuous leisure because a great deal of time has been invested, unproductively, in acquiring them. When in Austen's novels bad manners on one occasion contrast with leisure-class flair on others, a slip in etiquette stands either for advanced liberal principles (subtly explored in Anne Elliot's conduct in Bath in *Persuasion*) or, more frequently, for a moral flaw. Edmund tries to persuade himself that Mary's flaunting of emotional independence from her uncle is not indicative of the latter; her own sense of her conduct is clearly associated with the former.[33] The ending of the novel, in which Mary is not properly horrified by her brother and Maria Bertram's affair, is a reversed replay of the same situation. Though Edmund does not realize that Mary's moral flaw lies not so much in her treating adultery as a social mishap but in her cultivation of invidious sexuality (causally connected with Maria's

33. Mary's indiscreet remarks on her uncle on their first meeting involve, among other things, an implicit expectation of reciprocal frankness and thus constitute an advance that would, at the time, seem too "forward." Yet it is well motivated psychologically—in terms of the trauma of Mary's early experience in her foster home (see Wiltshire 1997: 62).

adultery), he correctly takes her attitude to the debacle not as vicious in itself but as *symptomatic* of values that place her outside his ethos. If for Mary freedom from middle-class lip service to moral appearances is a matter of "improvements" introduced by each generation (along with liberation from family prayers in the chapel), in the novel's system of norms her tactlessness signifies a neglect of moral *realities* and a commitment to the atavistic predatory agenda. Fanny's moral and matrimonial victory over her rival amounts to a local victory of liberal oppositionality over a system of values that is presented as corrupt rather than obsolete.

The tactics of presenting social opportunism as a corruption of positive values is part of Austen's strategies of opposition to authority figures—opposition, for which, as noted above, the conflict with the rival is a "cover story." In *Mansfield Park,* as in *Sense and Sensibility,* Austen critiques the agenda of the expansion of the clan's power through increase of wealth and calculated marriages; however, she presents this agenda not as a norm but as a symptom of deterioration, a fall from the formerly more idealistic principles associated with status and property as trusteeship (see Duckworth 1971: 129).[34] Fanny Price, the mistreated shabby genteel dependant of Sir Thomas Bertram, is shown developing not into a resentful rebel but into an upholder of the very values from which the baronet and his family have been sliding away.[35]

Austen's first novel, *Northanger Abbey,* was written several years after the Jacobin terror in France,[36] during the period of the British political reaction to the French Revolution. As noted above, Austen has long been considered either an apolitical writer or else one associated with the anti-Jacobin trend in the English novel, especially since her novels were read as promoting

34. The view that the holding of old landed estates signified the gentry's undertaking the guardianship of the country's high-cultural tradition (expressed, for instance, in the vast library of the Darcy mansion, which all the generations of the family regarded as their duty to complement with what they considered the best of their contemporary works) is a cultural translation of the medieval understanding that the estates distributed by the kings to their supporters are to be held "in trust" for the king—an understanding subverted by the transformation of these estates into property of the owners.

35. Bernard Paris (1997: 144) contrasts the "education pattern" in nineteenth-century fiction with the "vindication pattern" in terms of which the process of Fanny's gaining recognition is comparable to the stories of *Henry Esmond* and *Jane Eyre.* It is as a guardian of the idealized version of traditional loyalties that Fanny gains her vindication at the end of *Mansfield Park.*

36. The latest known revision dates from 1803; the latest Gothic novel mentioned by the characters is of 1797.

traditional family values. If Edmund Burke presented the French Revolution in terms of a crime against the family, in particular, the family of the King (cf. Hunt 1992), the preservation of the manners and the family morals of the English gentry was regarded as a guarantee of political stability. And though Austen and her present-day readers sympathize with the heroine of her unfinished "Catherine, or the Bower," who wonders, in response to her aunt's scolding, how her having paid more than a standard amount of attention to a young man at a provincial ball could possibly endanger the security of the nation (cf. Claudia Johnson 1988: 1–6), her fiction ultimately points to the method behind the apparent absurdity of conservative positions: the "metatheatre of manners" (Tanner 1986: 27) is mandatory for maintaining the authority of the class whose economic and political status rests on tradition rather than on the power of cash or an armed force.[37]

Austen disapproved, no doubt, of the guillotine, yet she disapproved no less of the axe—especially the one with which Mary, Queen of Scots was beheaded on Queen Elizabeth's orders.[38] She may have carnivalized her own predilection for the mistreated Stuart dynasty,[39] but she was earnestly conservative in not doubting the justice of the general socioeconomic stratification of her society. Her Tory-radical objections were to its excesses as well as to its moral oppressiveness to the disadvantaged members of her own class: the dowryless young women, shabby genteel spinsters, younger sons, victims of the rules of precedence. Authority figures in her novels are judged in terms of their role in this oppression—in *Northanger Abbey,* for instance, the anti-Jacobin General Tilney dampens the spirits of his children, is suspected of psychological violence to his wife, and is guilty of an unpardonable breach of etiquette towards the heroine; moreover, his boast of "burning midnight oil" (172) over pamphlets for the sake of the nation may suggest that he works as a political censor (see Hopkins 1978 and Minma 1996). When the young people are by themselves, on one occasion they slip into a reference to a complex social issue, the enclosures; from enclosures the conversation moves to politics, and from politics it is "an easy step to silence" (100). Silence, an embarrassing lull in a conversation, also follows the question

37. Cf. Worsthorne on an epiphenomenon of British civility: "Anyone who spoke like a gentleman, dressed like a gentleman, carried himself like a gentleman . . . were more than able to overawe, and do so just as authoritatively by carrying a rolled umbrella and wearing a bowler hat as did the boys in blue by wielding truncheons and wearing helmets" (2004: 83).

38. In another piece of juvenilia, her mischievous "History of England," Austen allowed Henry VIII the merit of "not being *quite* so bad as his daughter Elizabeth" (1978: 72).

39. Austen's juvenilia, unlike her mature works, contain numerous carnivalesque touches: "There was humour and absurdity; and every now and then she must have shocked her readers—the members of her own family—by standing morality on its head" (Jarvis 1996: 32).

about slave trade in *Mansfield Park*.[40] In *Northanger Abbey*, however, the step from politics to silence turned out to be prophetically symbolic: this was Austen's only completed novel not to be published in her lifetime.

Austen's later works, though ostensibly apolitical, are characterized by implicit social oppositionality. In her last completed novel, *Persuasion*, the heroine, a baronet's daughter, turns her back on her father's circle and marries a naval officer of humble antecedents. Though this step is facilitated by the co-optation of the successful representatives of this profession into the upper middle class of the time, the values of the social enclave from which Anne Elliot exits are questioned almost openly, even though, as in *Mansfield Park*, invidious emulation is again presented not as the norm but as a corruption of these values. In *Mansfield Park* the oppositional critique of the moral world of the gentry is even more radical than in *Persuasion*, albeit less direct. It consists in the suggestion that there may be life after losing one's niche in the leisure class and that the culture of that class need not be regarded as an absolute standard.

This class culture is challenged—covertly—in the Portsmouth episode of the novel. When, secretly in love with her cousin Edmund Bertram, Fanny rejects the affluent Henry Crawford, Sir Thomas Bertram sends her back to her parents in Portsmouth under the pretext of family feelings but actually

---

40. Fanny's interest in the problem is usually believed to be critical of slavery, but Claudia Johnson calls this into doubt, noting that "Herself a perfectly colonized subject, [Fanny], too, is one of Sir Thomas's slaves, every bit as bound to and constituted by the system that oppresses her as the hero of Edgeworth's appalling story *The Grateful Negro*" (1993: 114). The "dead silence" (136) that follows Fanny's question ostensibly suggests the egotistic Bertram children's lack of interest in their father's concerns (cf. Said 1993: 96), their "indifference and shallowness" (Waldron 1999: 12), yet it may just as well also mean the family's awareness of how much their well-being depends on slave labor (see Southam 1998). The slave trade, much discussed at the beginning of the nineteenth century (see Terry 1995), had been prohibited by a Parliament bill in 1807 but a similar bill was passed again in 1811, to close the loopholes left by the original legislation. Sir Thomas's journey to the West Indies may be dated some time towards the end of the first decade of the century (see the calculations in I. Armstrong 1988: 43–44 and Knox-Shaw 2004: 180–81). John Wilshire, however, calls the possibility of precise dating into doubt because of inconsistencies probably stemming from revisions Jane Austen made at different periods (2005: xliii–xlv; see also the useful overview of debate on Jane Austen's allusions to slavery [lxxiv–lxxvii]). To this one might object by surmising that in the latest revision Austen would have taken care to preempt unwelcome interpretive options. By 1814 many of Austen's readers were likely to know that the ban on the slave trade first led to a deterioration in the conditions of the already owned slaves in West Indian plantations because overseers attempted to maximize the profit from the residual pool of slave labor (see Hammond 1993: 77). This backfired: the resulting unrest among the slaves caused a reduction of revenues. At the same time, in England the returns from country estates dwindled because of the wartime taxation and drain on rural manpower (and eventually the poor harvests of 1811 and 1812—no wonder the farmers cannot spare a cart to transport Mary's harp during haymaking). In any case, G. M. Trevelyan's view that in the mirror that "Miss Austen held up to nature in the drawing room, it is hard to detect any trace of concern or trouble arising from the war" (1942: 582–83) was more representative than right.

as a punishment and a warning. The narrative of the Portsmouth episode promotes our sympathy for Fanny's unhappiness, but it can also smuggle in a disapproval of some of her culture-bound attitudes. Though the account of Fanny's experience in Portsmouth is filtered through her consciousness, it contains clues to a perspective different from her own.[41]

Fanny fails to appreciate the moral reality of her lower-middle-class parents' disorganized, stuffy, unhygienic, noisy, ill-mannered way of life. This attitude seems to legitimate the commentators' near-consensus concerning the incivility, callousness, inefficiency, and confusion in the Portsmouth inner-city dwelling of the Prices, the populous family of the coarse half-pay officer of the Marines.[42] However, Austen's ostensibly negative treatment of the household may also be read as an oppositional maneuver, a decoy: the Portsmouth Prices have a system of values of their own, a *valid* system, though different from that of their landed relations. One of the things that Fanny does not understand is that polished manners, a sign of conspicuous leisure (Veblen 1899: 45–51), are far less important for the status of the Portsmouth family than for that of the Bertrams.

The main trouble with most members of the Price family is lack of consideration for each other's minor everyday needs—this is presented as the result of constant hardships, of Mr. Price's egoism, and of Mrs. Price's well-meaning inefficiency. Ironically, trivial but constant discomforts may be a good seasoning for the Price children, whose prospects are hard work and struggle to keep afloat. Indeed, these children, especially the boys, seem to be doing remarkably well, which suggests that the parents have done something right after all. William, the firstborn, is the most advanced and cultivated, but there are two more grown brothers, one "a clerk in a public office in London" and the other a midshipman (259). There is also Sam,

41. The unreliability of Fanny's ethical perspective is veiled by the third-person narrative. Whereas a first-person narrator can be expected to be ethically unreliable, in the case of the third-person center-of-consciousness technique it is more difficult to distinguish the perspective of the focal character from that of the implied author. In the Portsmouth episode Fanny's perspective is implicitly criticized by the ample supply of meaningful detail that Fanny fails to process.

42. Thus Marvin Mudrick maintains that Portsmouth is "the limbo of the morally unborn" and the Price family is "lost except for the few who by luck and force of purpose have succeeded in tearing themselves away" (1952: 174). Lionel Trilling disapproves of Fanny's family for their indifference to her— "of a piece with the general indecorum of their home"; he sympathizes with her disgust at the "half-clean and the scarcely tidy, of confusion and intrusion" and with the "vulgarity that thrives in these surroundings" (1955: 217). Howard S. Babb perceives the Price household as "dirty and chaotic" and "self-engrossed" (1962: 154). D. D. Devlin (1975), who notes that the novel critiques rural conservatism, still sees the world of Fanny's Portsmouth family as one of economic struggle "that leaves people morally stunted" (1975: 110). Marilyn Butler discusses the Portsmouth episode as Austen's version of the "low-life sequence" common in anti-Jacobin novels (1975: 244–45), eliding the corrections that Austen has introduced into that schema.

who, like his sister Susan, seems to be ready to take the responsibility for whatever needs to be done. The two younger schoolboys are full of healthy animal spirits.

Mr. Price, Fanny's father, is guilty of a less than moderate fondness for alcohol and peer company—compensations of many an impecunious retired officer (especially one who does not have an intellectual disposition and resources such as Captain Harville's in *Persuasion* yet who would have been granted more sympathy by a writer such as D. H. Lawrence). However, in the context of Austen's general sensitivity to family dynamics, the presence of healthy, vigorous, and successful children must suggest that the father is not entirely ineffectual. There is something genuine in Mr. Price's ways, even in his egocentric neglect of Fanny after his first cordial greeting. His interest in his profession is still so keen and aesthetically tinged that it infects almost all his sons. His threat to "be after" the young ones if they continue making noise is disregarded, obviously because the children know that it is not meant in earnest (260); nor is his statement, on Maria Bertram's elopement, that had she been his daughter he would have "taken a rope's end at her" much more than a *façon de parler*. Mr. Price may not have been the one responsible for William's and Susan's manifest commitments to active kindness, but his presence certainly does not create a restraint or cast a gloom on his children's spirits, as does the presence of the tyrannical General Tilney of *Northanger Abbey* or even the courteous Sir Thomas Bertram in their families.

For all the mutual elbowing in everyday affairs, the Prices are knit together by common concerns. When Fanny first arrives at her father's house, the housemaid meets the carriage at the door—not so much to help the travelers as to report the news that "the Thrush is gone out of harbour" (254), and that an officer has been in, looking for William. This servant, however unschooled, is a faithful delegate of the family's anxieties: she has been on the lookout for William, who seems to arrive just in the nick of time. The same piece of news is then repeated, in greater detail, by Fanny's brother Sam, "a fine tall boy of eleven" (255). It is on the Thrush that William is to start his career as an officer rather than midshipman. Young Sam is also to start his seafaring career on this ship, as a cabin boy. Yet Fanny is struck by the lack of attention to herself rather than by the importance of her brothers' not being late to board that ship. As she has not developed an interest in the Thrush[43] equal to her family's, she is pained by the uncouth and noisy ways

---

43. See Chazal 1991 on the symbolism of the ship's name and its connection with another bird, Sterne's starling, alluded to in the Sotherton episode.

of the household and largely oblivious of the urgencies of the situation and the ill timing of her visit. Nor does she understand that her mother's remark to William, "here every thing comes upon me at once" (256), is not banal moaning but a quite accurate reference to the complex rituals of meeting a daughter and parting with two sons at one and the same time.

A hint at the problematic character of Fanny's attitude is given in the ironic inversion in her response to her mother, who meets her with an embrace, "with looks of true kindness, and with features which Fanny loved the more, because they brought her aunt Bertram's before her" (256)—but we almost forget this under the influence of Fanny's hurt when, the first greetings being over, Mrs. Price turns to William, again with the news about the Thrush and with still more details relating to the suddenness of its departure. It is mainly on a repeated reading that we are at leisure to note the effect of gradation—with still more particulars, but of the kind peculiarly interesting to seamen, the same news is then detailed to William by his father,[44] who takes an obvious pleasure in the professional talk and does not even notice Fanny in the twilight. Meanwhile Fanny, tired after the long ride, is concerned not about the brother's gear being packed on time but about her tea not being served.

One of the most insistently recurrent motifs of this episode is haste: not a minute should be wasted before apprising William of the fact that a Mr. Campbell will come for him before six o'clock.[45] William has no time for tea with Fanny because he has to dress and pack; the confusion among his things (their privacy has obviously not been respected in his absence) must be put right in a hurry with the inefficient help of his mother and the servant. Indeed, William seems to get ready just minutes before Mr. Campbell arrives.

The density of the motifs of bustle and haste emphasizes that this family has no leisure to flaunt. They may, however, have a residual hankering after outer signs of leisure: for example, Susan has "the dread of being thought to demean herself" by eventually serving the tea. Indeed, the social circle of the Prices, where, according to Fanny, the men are "coarse," the women "pert" (exempt from Evangelical self-effacing modesty?), and everybody "under-bred," has its own debased version of invidious emulation: the young women

44. There are thus four utterances regarding the Thrush: the servant's (18 words), Sam's (83 words), the mother's (111 words), and the father's (281 words). However neglectful of each other the Prices may be in everyday matters, they are all deeply if inefficiently invested in the career goals of the boys.

45. Mr. Campbell turns out to be a polite young surgeon—what an opportunity for courtship lost!—Dickens will pick it up with Allan Woodcourt and Esther Summerson in *Bleak House*.

there regard Fanny's upper-class manners as false pretense because she exhibits neither the expected signs of upper-class leisure (she does not play the piano) nor the fashionable signs of conspicuous consumption such as "fine pelisses" (268). Susan runs the risk of contamination by such false values, yet her pride in being active and useful (260) augurs well for her development along more advanced ethical lines.

The Prices, indeed, do not really *need* a metatheater of manners in their own house: their sense of self-worth does not depend on displays of conspicuous leisure. But when good manners are needed, the proper front can be put on without much difficulty. Indeed, on meeting Henry Crawford, Mr. Price surprises Fanny by behaving without the crudeness that he shows within the family circle: "His manners now, though not polished, were more than passable; they were graceful, animated, manly; his expressions were those of an attached father, and a sensible man;—his loud tones did very well in the open air, and there was not a single oath to be heard" (274). Fanny, pleased enough with this performance, sees only part of the reason for it: "Such was his instinctive compliment to the good manners of Mr. Crawford" (273–74), forgetting that Crawford is not only her suitor but, more important, the nephew of the Admiral who has secured William's promotion and can perhaps one day do the same for the other brothers. Occasional good manners are here not a matter of conspicuous leisure but a *professional* qualification that an officer father of young seamen cannot forgo. And Mr. Price is an old professional, although Fanny cannot sympathize with the apparent triviality of his "never-failing interest" in the dockyard.

Insofar as the advancement of the Price boys depends on leisure-class connections, they will be likely to treat the acquisition of the appropriate social skills almost as a matter of professional training. William Price provides a study of social expediency when, still an uncommissioned midshipman, he visits the Bertrams in Mansfield Park. His official motive for the visit, to see his beloved sister Fanny, is genuine, but it is not unaccompanied by a practical ulterior motive: to explore the family connections in the hope of getting a commission. William starts by charming his Mansfield audience by tales of his exploits; then, during a dinner party, he proceeds to drop hints about his need for promotion. Advised by Mrs. Norris to visit Maria and her husband, he notes that as a "poor scrubby midshipman" (168) he will hardly be welcome in Mrs. Rushworth's Brighton residence. When his aunt replies that he would find Rushworth "most sincerely disposed to regard all the connections of [their] family as his own," he mutters, in an understated pun, that he would rather find him "private secretary to the first Lord than any thing else" (168). He then complains that Portsmouth girls "turn up their noses at any body who has not a commission," and reinforces the point: "I begin to think I shall never be a lieutenant, Fanny. Every body gets made but me" (171). Elements of this line of conduct are, however, interspersed with accounts of the concerns of other characters, so that we tend to miss their consistency. On the other hand, while making the former two remarks, William is successfully engaged in a card game of "Speculation," during which he sells court cards "at an exorbitant rate" and drives "as hard a bargain" against the others as he can (167).[46] His camouflaged maneuvers meet with success: in a bid for Fanny's affection, Henry Crawford soon applies to his uncle for help in arranging William's promotion. It is interesting that when William engages with his wealthy and ranked relatives on their own grounds, he is presented as displaying signs of the very predaceousness that, according to Veblen, characterizes the leisure classes.

The sphere of life to which William and his Portsmouth family belong, and which extends to Captain Harville and some other characters of *Persuasion,* constitutes the oppositional *room for maneuver* for which Austen's heroines can opt: it is in Portsmouth that Fanny moves from passive principle to active kindness. Austen deploys the motifs of common interests, haste, bustle, noise, and animal spirits in a way that can be distilled in order to build up a consistent system of principles to live by—a system alternative to that of the leisure-class gentry. Austen's target audience, the Fanny Prices and Edmund Bertrams, the Anne Elliots and Elizabeth Bennets of her world,[47] could well be sensitized to this ethos—even though its virtues are camouflaged by its surface inferiority to the idealized standard of the leisure-class manners and morals.

Indeed, though in *Mansfield Park* and *Persuasion* Jane Austen denies the absolute value of this standard, she does idealize it—by, for instance, contrasting Julia Bertram (whose forced but impeccable politeness to Mrs. Rushworth is not based on a genuine considerateness) with Fanny Price,

46. The seemingly aleatic but actually agonistic card game is here a faint reprise of the theatricals, a seemingly mimetic but actually agonistic game during which the players highlight the usually subdued features of their characters. William displays his predatory traits, Fanny her habitual compliance, and Henry Crawford the intriguer's enjoyment of dealing with two ladies' cards as well as his own, and picking up William's hints, all at the same time.

47. Cf. Peter Rabinowitz (1977: 126–27 and 1987: 29–42) on "authorial audience," which can be redescribed as including the mind-set of readers removed from the author in time or cultural space (or both) but seeking intimate understanding of the cultural codes that the author shared with her sociologically specific target audience.

who is constantly trying to live up to the gentle and selfless image that she is taught to project.[48] Manners mark the standard of inner moral refinement that the individual is encouraged to seek—even when they constitute a hypocritical lip service to that standard. This version of everyday civility endeared Austen's novels not only to her target audience but also to her *hurdle* audience (see Toker 2005), the audience that would control the contents of family bookshelves and the subscriptions to circulating libraries—people like General Tilney as well as Sir Thomas Bertram, who, upon his return from his plantation in Antigua, quite symbolically destroys every *unbound* copy of *Lovers' Vows* in Mansfield Park.[49]

Yet even the hurdle audience can be drawn into the mildly oppositional stance through the sheer game of *mimicry:* Jane Austen's emotionally maturing heroines are presented in ways that attract sympathetic imagination—so that even a real-life copy of a Sir Thomas could imaginatively enter the life of an Elinor Dashwood or an Anne Elliott and vicariously reenact her oppositional stance, temporarily abandoning his own. The high-brow scorn for "human-interest" stories was not as widespread in Austen's times as it became (see Carey 1993) in the early twentieth century. Genuine aesthetic experience is sometimes hard to distinguish from sympathetic identification with characters of "human interest" stories. In late-eighteenth- and early-nineteenth-century England, at least judging by Henry Tilney's comments on the novel-reading in *Northanger Abbey,* potential for vicarious experience did not necessarily discredit a narrative even in the eyes of the highly educated. Strictly speaking, even in the twentieth century the Nabokovian scorn for "human interest" narratives has been reserved mainly for works that exploit thrills or sensationalism for marketability, in the absence of less easily attainable claims to distinction. It is in a similar spirit, though with more than a grain of salt, that Fielding explained his prefatory chapters by the need to show a true skill in writing, beyond the imitable spinning of a yarn. Austen, like Fielding and Dickens, can well be read "for the plot," with the aesthetic experience, whether in response to style, humor, *energeia,* or intellectual design, overtaking the reader unawares.

The reasons why Austen's heroines tend to become the Other into whom we readily project ourselves are rooted both in her novels' form of content and in their form of expression. The features of the form of content that

---

48. In an evening prayer composed by Jane Austen, we find the period formula for the relationship between outward conduct and inner reality: "Give us grace almighty father, so to pray, as to deserve to be heard, *to address thee with our hearts, as with our lips.*" (1954: 453; italics added).

49. Sir Thomas's descendant, Thomas Gradgrind, M.P., of Dickens's *Hard Times,* likewise includes censorship of the children's reading matter in his educational practices.

promote sympathetic identification are associated with the heroines' character and condition with their intelligence and integrity as well as agenda
of moral and cultural self-improvement: it is only occasionally (e.g., in the
episode of the Box Hill picnic in *Emma*) that they temporarily repel the
reader, breaking the spell of the vicarious engrossment in their lives. The
prominent feature of their condition is their peculiarly disadvantaged position (not excluding Emma's predicament at the opening of the novel)—the
kind of narrative instability that wins the readers' interest in their welfare;
moreover, in the bulk of the narrative their sorrows are great (bereavement,
expulsion, separation) and their joys small—according to Adam Smith, it
is precisely this asymmetry of grief and joy that facilitates our sympathetic
entering into the situation of another. The narrative techniques (form of
expression) that facilitate this ludic *mimicry* (sympathetic identification is a
game so long as the object of sympathy is a fictional character rather than
a real-life Other) include a gradual attachment of the narrative focus to
the heroines: Austen's novels except *Emma* (and to some extent *Northanger
Abbey*) open with scenes in which the heroines do not participate; they are
introduced gradually; it is by degrees that we are led into their minds, as if in
preference to anyone else around them. This shift in focus is usually supplemented by a suspension of dramatic irony. Incidentally, in the Portsmouth
episode of *Mansfield Park* dramatic irony is replaced by an ample provision
of signals that not only Fanny but also first-time readers fail to decipher; the
readers are thus allowed to remain in denial of the particularly subversive
oppositional contraband in this part of the novel.

If, as the previous chapter has suggested, the experience of reading a
carnivalesque narrative is often, owing to multiple stumbling blocks, agonistic and non-carnivalesque, Austen's novels point to a converse tendency:
the reading of non-carnivalesque oppositional narrative may promote the
kind of *mimicry* that takes us, as readers, out of our own predicament and
in the direction of the mind and feelings of an imaginary other. The mode
of the text and the mode of reading may form a chiasmic relationship, with
some overlap in the intersection. Oppositionality, indeed, shares the festive
carnival's effect of perpetuating the prevailing social structure by making
it more livable. In both, cultural patterns go into remission, and temporary transgressions or relaxation of rules create loopholes in the grim logic
of invidious emulation, struggles for social "consequence," advantageous
marriages, aggressively competitive sexuality, and irreversibility of personal
recklessness. The happy endings of Austen's novels almost invariably constitute witty and well-integrated reprises of the novels' recurrent motifs:
almost as in *Tom Jones,* in the regular course of events, the lives of Austen's

protagonists seem to be headed for grimmer alternatives, but the ludic turns, which we can usually find carefully though unobtrusively prepared, enact a counterlogic. Everything (or almost) may yet be well with the world where the regularities against which Austen's heroines struggle can be presented as errors, corruptions, deviations from the path of ideal integrity rather than the actual order of the day, a massive background for the exceptional. And it may, after all, be true that a society in which even the hurdle audience can be brought to believe that it shares the hedged-in oppositional liberalism of a Jane Austen is one in which the movement of political reform and measured social mobility may be partly accountable for an evolutionary mode of development, eschewing violent convulsions such as the recurrent revolutionary cataclysms of late-eighteenth- and nineteenth-century France.[50]

The most radical of the latter cataclysms is refracted, through the prism of cross-cultural comparison, in Dickens's *A Tale of Two Cities.*

50. I have been glad to discover Jonathan Dollimore's like-minded reading of the so-called poetic justice in Elizabethan and Jacobean plays: "In mid-twentieth century a generation of critics tried to convince themselves that this didactic dénouement effectively discredits or at least neutralizes the subversive questioning and thought which preceded it. Unfortunately for them, from a creative, a theatrical and an intellectual perspective, the didactic dénouement does not so much close off that questioning as enable it: . . . far from foreclosing on it, a conforming framework actually licensed a subversive content" (2003: 41).

CHAPTER FIVE

Checks and Balances

Charles Dickens's *A Tale of Two Cities*

[F]or a gentleman only lost causes should be attractive.

—Borges 1964: 69

SET IN THE HISTORICAL PAST rather than in Dickens's contemporary Victorian society, *A Tale of Two Cities* is, in that respect, less representative of his work. It also differs from Dickens's other novels (with the exception of *Barnaby Rudge*) in the relative prominence of the grimly carnivalesque in its plot and imagery. Yet this difference is quantitative rather than qualitative: like the festive carnival of *The Pickwick Papers,* violent transports are *held in check* in the discourse—though not in the story—of *A Tale of Two Cities.* The novel that revolves against the serial atrocities of the scaffold is, paradoxically, less tearjerking than many of Dickens's other narratives. In comparison with its precursor text—Carlyle's impassioned apostrophe-rich *The French Revolution*—this novel is stylistically reserved almost to formality. The bitter carnivalesque intensities of the plot are distanced by the emotional restraint of the style.

The muffling of the carnival in *A Tale of Two Cities* can be regarded as the form of content aesthetically appropriate to the substance of the idea content—the urgency of the need for cataclysm-preventing social change. According to Bernard Shaw, in the 1850s Charles Dickens converted from a Macaulay-like optimistic complacency to a harsh disapproval of the basics of society, in the spirit of "Karl Marx, Carlyle, Ruskin, Morris and Carpenter," from the opinion that the horrors of contemporary life are a matter of "individual delinquencies, local plaguespots, negligent authorities" to the belief that "it is not our disorder but our order that is horrible; that it is not our criminals but our magnates that are robbing and murdering us; and that it is not merely Tom All Alone's that must be demolished . . . but our entire social system" (41–42).[1] This formula, rather in tune with Shaw's support of Stalinist Russia, disregards Dickens's religiously tinged humanism, "a redemptive view of human possibility, a redemptive view of human destiny, and a redemptive rule of life" (Krook 1959: 8).[2] Before, during, and after the 1850s, Dickens's attitude was not that of a revolutionary but that of a critical reformist who valorizes repair and redemption rather than demolition. In his late novels, as in his early ones, social evils—unsanitary urban slums and parasitic institutions such as the Chancery, the debtors' prison, or the "Circumlocution Office" are presented as a hypertrophy of deficiencies in individual ethical attitudes[3] and personal relationships, much as his critics would wish to argue that their rectification requires social policy rather than moral education (cf. Fitzpatrick 2005). This conjunction of social evils and flaws in character and relationship created the conditions for the traditional motif of conversion in the dénouement of his plots: love, remorse, and gratitude for love are endowed with redemptive power in individual lives. The reverse side of this power is the evil incarnated in Dickens's villains, whether gruesome like Sikes or Rigaut, uncanny like Uriah Heep, or banal like Bitzer.

This high view of human potentiality, shadowed by the admission of the reality of evil, finds its expression in versions of carnivalesque morphology. In Dickens's novels separate carnival features abound in episodes of comic relief and are not limited to such episodes. The *reversals of hierarchies,* for instance, take the shape of the almost mandatory moral and financial

1. Throughout more than half of the twentieth century, it was a catchword of Marxist literary pedagogy that Dickens, a writer of genius, was flawed by misconstruing the roots of evil, that is, not identifying them with the private ownership of the means of production.

2. Krook does not discuss Dickens, but her description of the religious humanist ethical ideology is eminently applicable to Dickens: "there is much in man's nature that is vile, seemingly beyond the hope of redemption," yet a human being "is capable of giving and receiving love; and by believing absolutely in the redeeming power of love, he can redeem—transcend and transform—what is vile in his nature" (5).

3. Cf. Carlyle (1888 [1837]: 30): "As indeed, evils of all sorts are more or less of kin, and do usually go together: especially it is an old truth, that wherever huge physical evil is, there, as the parent and origin of it, has moral evil to a proportionate extent been."

peripeteia—Gradgrind and Dombey face the crumbling of their hopes; Merdle goes bankrupt; the convict Magwitch turns into a rich man and then again into a hunted criminal. As lower-class characters, such as Joe and Biddy (*Great Expectations*), Lizzie Hexam (*Our Mutual Friend*), or Stephen Blackpool and Rachael (*Hard Times*) become the moral mentors of "their betters," the role reversal elicits another carnivalesque phenomenon: the *close contact* and moral equality between people from different walks of life, with its concomitant mutual-friend plots—in most of Dickens's novels each character enters into a personal relationship with every other character. *Scandals* erupt frequently (often in the form of exposure—Pecksniff's, Mrs. Sparsit's, or Bounderby's); and there is a high incidence of melodramatically heightened confession scenes and of almost Dostoevskian self-laceration dialogues: the climax of Louisa Gradgrind's life story, for instance, is the dialogue with her father in which, for once in her life, like an Ibsen heroine, she has her say—even if at the price of a tight-corset swoon and her father's primary-color contrition. The setting of practically all of Dickens's novels includes *slums as well as mansions*. Most of the novels also contain *crowd scenes* (about which later).

Yet in Dickens's major novels these separate features of the carnivalesque mode do not generally converge into the sense of a carnival, either festive or grim—they have, as it were, their separate nonadjacent slots. The spirit of most of these novels (largely in contrast to that of *The Pickwick Papers*) is what Bakhtin termed "biographical" rather than carnivalesque; it is closely associated with Dickens's valorization of domesticity, the carnival's Other. His bitter carnivalesque is distanced from the reader; his festive one is reined in, domesticated, transformed from a cultural remission to "the other thing needful" (*HT* 243)—a necessary and circumscribed part of daily life. It is further sanitized by the notion of the need for public entertainment as part of the civilizing process. Dickens presents the home as a possible site for work and play, fact and fancy, enclosure and permeability. The right measure of each ingredient is not a matter of the middle way but rather that of checks and balances. The individual attainment of a stable identity and of a *modus vivendi* between ethical duties and natural impulses forms a miniature model of civility, of social concession as an alternative to class war.

Accordingly, all forms of the *dissolution of individual identities* are given a negative treatment. Dickens is critical of the statistical perspective from which individuals "are drops in an undemarcated ocean" (Nussbaum 1995: 21).[4] Though in *Hard Times* he refers to workers ironically as Hands, and

---

4. I must, however, put on record a disagreement with Nussbaum's interpretation of the dying

though he mentions Louisa Gradgrind's erstwhile view of them as "something that occasionally rose like a sea, and did some harm and waste (chiefly to itself), and fell again" (187–88), none of the somatic imagery for which his authorial narrator is directly responsible, not even that pertaining to the trade-union meeting, suggests the dissolution of the borderlines of the individual self or its merger with an undifferentiated force. The oil whose smell pervades Coketown on a hot day may "ooze" and "trickle" through the many stories of the mills but it "soils" only the attire of the Hands (146), leaving no metaphoric stain on their identities and causing no metaphoric leaks. It is only Stephen's alcoholic wife who seems to have lost the discreteness of her selfhood. Dickens's satire on the trade-union movement[5] is part of his attack on the forces that refuse to recognize and would zestfully crush the uniqueness and separateness of individual identities.[6] The episode of the workers' meeting in *Hard Times* is emphatically non-carnivalesque—in this sense it bears affinities with Mordecai's philosophical-society meeting in George Eliot's *Daniel Deronda*. Though the meeting ends in Stephen Blackpool's ostracism, it does not degenerate into a baiting session; it leaves individual participants inwardly facing their own conscience.

Writing in a period of legislation for social reform, Dickens seems to have synthesized the attitudes of what Arthur Koestler would eventually call "the Commissar and the Yogi" (1945: 9–20)—the beliefs in the change from without and the change from within. The common denominator of the bulk of social causes that Dickens endorsed as a journalist was the need to create the conditions (the change from without) for a decent domesticity of the lower classes: it was the duty of the social institutions to ensure the sanitary conditions of the poor before expecting them to be godly. Restricted working hours, humane schools, popular entertainment ("people must be amuthed," lisps Sleary in *Hard Times* [82]), and reasonable divorce laws were

---

Mrs. Gradgrind's statement: "I think there's a pain somewhere in the room. . . . But I couldn't positively say that I have got it" (*HT* 224). Nussbaum comments that "Political economy sees only pains and satisfaction and their general location: it does not see persons as bounded centers of satisfaction, far less as agents whose active planning is essential to the humaneness of whatever satisfaction they will achieve. Mrs. Gradgrind has learned her lesson well" (1995: 22–23). Mrs. Gradgrind, however, has been presented as a woman vaguely aware of lessons to be learned but never really learning even the names of the "ologies" involved. Her agony, moreover, makes her see the insufficiency of those lessons. The words quoted above may be interpreted both as reflecting the effect of an opiate distancing one's pain and as voicing her unwanted awareness of the heartache silently endured by her daughter Louisa.

5. Elizabeth Gaskell's *Mary Barton* reflects a similar though milder distrust of trade-union operatives.

6. For Dickens's opposition to utopian thinking as a threat to individual identity see Toker 1996b.

other means to moral improvement. Most of them were goals in their own right, and most called for checks on the self-interest of the capitalists as well as on the complacency of the traditional upper classes: Pope's "'Whatever is is right,'" is, according to the narrator of *A Tale of Two Cities*—"an aphorism that would be as final as it is lazy, did it not include the troublesome consequence, that nothing that ever was, was wrong" (II, 2: 63).

In the second chapter of *Bleak House*, Dickens calls on the upper classes to rise to their obligations, lest the sleeping-beauty spirit of public discontent awake, and all the spits of the kitchen begin to "turn prodigiously" (1977: 11). "To turn" is here synonymous with "to revolve." Indeed, in *A Tale of Two Cities* the French Revolution and the Jacobin Terror are presented as a response to the unchecked tyranny of the upper class: the crimes of corrupt aristocrats against the lower and the middle classes are linked, through a causal plot sequence as well as through the imagery of light and darkness (see Alter 1984: 106–7), with the ensuing crimes of the Jacobin leaders and the revolutionary mob. Dickens's politics can be seen as a critical sequel to Fielding's, Sterne's, and Austen's presentation of the idealized ethical principles of the upper classes as a guarantee for social peace: he indicts the English upper classes not for the viciousness often attributed to their members (in, say, Restoration drama) but for the neglect of their duties to society. Like *Barnaby Rudge*, with its striking presentation of the Gordon riots of 1780, *A Tale of Two Cities* is to a large extent a cautionary tale.

Whereas most of Dickens's narratives begin with an array of arrivals and departures, *A Tale of Two Cities* opens at the point when a certain tendency has reached a precritical stage of development. Like the first paragraphs of Hawthorne's "My Kinsman, Major Molineux," the first chapter of *A Tale of Two Cities* characterizes the historical setting of the ensuing narrative. The topographical setting of chapters 2 and 3 is the liminal space of a moving carriage—the meaning of Mr. Lorry's departure from London, preparatory for Manette's arrival, lies, as we eventually learn, in the degree to which Marquis de St. Evrémond, judging by the cold shoulder he gets at a grandee's *levée* (II, 7), has lost his influence at the French court: a prisoner who had been consigned to the Bastille on his *lettre de cachet* eighteen years previously can now be released. The release appears to have been secured by the lobbying of Tellson's bank, whose importance as a channel of money transfers increases with the growth of the revolutionary situation. Towards the end of Book I, another aspect of this momentum takes the shape of the aggregating Jacquerie in the Quarter of Saint Antoine in Paris.

As can be expected, the French Revolution provides the narrative with all the features of the carnivalesque—the reversal of hierarchies, the merger of the spectators and the participants in crowd experience, and the concomitant breaking of architectural and social partitions, dismemberment of bodies, profanation of the family/domesticity values—by, for instance, a ban on mourning guillotined family members as well as by rough intrusions upon family privacy (Madame Defarge's uninvited calls on Lucie Manette, the nocturnal arrest of Darnay at his family's lodgings in Paris, foreshadowed by the echoes of footsteps in Lucie's house in Soho[7]), the alternation of liminal spaces (the bank, the wineshop, the courthouse, a carriage) and open spaces (streets, village and town squares), the juxtaposition of opposites—"murder and celebration, ritual and anarchy, violence and delicacy" (Hutter 1987: 53), and the burlesque parallelisms between the dramatically heightened metaphors and their profane literalization (as when Manette's "resurrection" finds a parallel in Jerry Cruncher's digging-out of the corpses from their graves). The discreteness of individual identity is endangered by the forces of the bitter carnival—but also willingly surrendered by characters engaged in semimystical spiritual quests; the fragility of personal identity is literalized by the guillotine and emblematized by Manette's tendency to revert to his alternative self as shoemaker in response to new shocks.[8]

The characters of *A Tale* fall into three groups: those swept by the temporarily triumphant sociohistorical forces represented by the crowd, those powerfully attracted by the losing side of the conflict ("drawn to the load-stone rock," II, 24), and those who manage to maintain a psychological distance from both sides in the fray.

Most of the characters of the first group appear as a collective image of sallow faces gathering into a mob. The differences among these faces are largely erased by hunger: we recognize Gaspard, the father of the child crushed by the Marquis's carriage, mainly by his tall lean figure; we identify the road-mender turned woodcutter mainly through references to his profession. As under most dictatorships, members of the endangered group attempt to remain inconspicuous: knowing what the Marquis can do to each of them, all except Madame Defarge and the stultified road-mender avoid looking

7. To many readers this sound of footsteps outside one's door is a reminder of the Gordon Riots. Yet readers who know about the nocturnal arrests in Stalinist Russia appreciate the prophetic character of the details of this episode.

8. For a juxtaposition of Manette's manual labor with the knitting of the women of Paris see Dever 2006: 222–24.

him in the face or attracting his attention. This Lenten tendency of self-effacement is, at the appointed time, transformed into the "oceanic feeling" of discharge within the crowd.[9] The crowd, personified by the toponym Saint Antoine, brings Defarge into the Bastille as on the crest of a wave, rolls through the countryside to destroy the chateaux during the "Great Fear," gives choric responses in the Revolution's courthouses, dismembers the condemned outside La Force prison, whirls around in the Carmagnole, or settles into an appreciative audience around the guillotine.

Dickens presents crowds as extremely suggestible; in the Paris episodes the suggestibility is enhanced by chronic undernourishment—a somatic condition that is known to produce high irritability,[10] deadly when pooled together in crowd experience: corrupt uncircumscribed Lent (see chapter 10) is as lethal as bitter carnival. The *hunger* of the days of the *ancien régime* is not discontinued during the Revolution: after the carnivorous slaughter of their "class enemies," the members of the crowd return to their poor homes and eat their "[s]canty and insufficient suppers," that are "innocent of meat" just outside their thresholds (II, 22: 235). The bitter carnival becomes, literally, the bedfellow of involuntary Lent as the bloodthirsty La Vengeance[11] rests by the side of her starved-grocer husband (II, 22: 235).

The mood swings of the crowd that Dickens portrays in his version of the September massacres, from the butchery of condemned prisoners to the jubilant warm embraces of prisoners who have been acquitted (not without occasional confusion) are also anchored in the reference to its members' "want of sleep" (III, 2: 272). Sleeplessness, like hunger, is known to produce abnormal suggestibility, in which victims come to believe their own fictions or those imposed on them.[12] Sleep, that ultimate form of privacy, the restor-

9. On the "oceanic feeling" see p. 26. "Discharge" is Elias Canetti's term for the moment when all who belong to the crowd get rid of their differences and feel equal (1978: 17). Upon discharge "an immense feeling of relief ensues. It is for the sake of this blessed moment, when no one is greater or better than another, that people become a crowd" (18). John Carey's critical discussion (1993: 29–30) of the ideological confusions in Canetti's attitudes to crowd (the confusions partly caused by the use of the term *masses* in the French title, instead of *foules*, "crowds"—the actual subject of *Crowds and Power*), elides this pivotal point of Canetti's book as well as Canetti's irony regarding this self-delusion. (Yet Carey's *The Intellectual and the Masses* provides helpful links for an understanding of why English classical literature and the atrocities of the twentieth century cannot be seen as belonging to entirely different moral universes).

10. In Gulag literature it is known as "hunger neurosis." It is also attested to by *The Hunger Disease,* based on a research conducted by Jewish doctors (eventually themselves starved or murdered) in the Warsaw ghetto during World War II (see Winick 1979), and by the record of the "starvation experiment" in the United States (see Tucker 2006).

11. Cf. Carlyle on the Menads of the French Revolution, 1888: 195–98.

12. During the Stalinist Great Terror, the use of sleep deprivation helped the interrogators to extract false confessions—not just by forcing the victims to lie in order to avoid torture but, appar-

ative corporeal self-engulfment (cf. Scarry 1985: 167), is politicized during and after revolutions:[13] the artificial insomnia of orchestrated communal transports is an instrument of crowd control.

A further aid in manipulating the crowd is the literalization of its Dionysian spirit, grimly evoked in the scene of the bursting of a wine casket (I, 5). It is in a *wineshop* (rather than in a coffee house or grocery store) that, befittingly, the crowd-crystals of the Revolution are formed; Darnay's escort ranges between sober, half-drunk, and drunk; and the crowds around the guillotine, excited or drugged by drinking and smoking, are further intoxicated with the heady wine-smell of blood.

All three types of somatic states—hunger, sleeplessness, and intoxication—lead to the experience of vertigo, *ilinx,*[14] which is also cultivated for its own sake in the ecstatic whirling of the Carmagnole. *Ilinx*—vertigo—is, indeed, a recurrent motif of the novel.

Crowds aggregate and disperse also in the other of the two cities, London. Here Dickens's images of the rabble divide into what Canetti calls closed and open crowds (1978: 16). A closed crowd is formed in a building; its growth is limited by the capacity of that building. The closed crowd at Darnay's trial for high treason thirsts for the guilty verdict—not despite but because of the horrible dismemberment that it entails: the noises that this audience makes are rendered by the metaphor of the buzzing of flies in search of carrion. Even though the quartering would not be conducted in front of the court audience's eyes, it gives the rabble a thrill to imagine the conversion of the living Darnay into a tortured and dissected body. The potential misrule of the crowd in the courthouse is, however, safely contained by the civilities of the legal game. Such a crowd, rather like the one around the guillotine needs a constant supply of victims; it is controlled by periodic human sacrifice. Unlike an open crowd, however, it can take a disappointment without violent resentment, because the very permanence of the building, in this case the Old Bailey, ensures the repetition of its congregating for the rite.

An open crowd, a foreshadowing of the mob violence of the Gordon Riots that would break out later the same year (1780), moves, in a carnivalesque pageant complete with bear-leader and his bear (II, 14: 161–64), through the streets of London during the funeral of the Bailey spy, Roger Cly, its noise imprinting the (false) news of Cly's death in the minds of the

---

ently, also by helping to persuade some of the victims, at least temporarily, of their guilt.

13. See Amis 2002: 14–20.

14. See pp. 15–16.

population.[15] The crowd does not know that the coffin contains not the body of Cly, who has gone into hiding, but literal clay—sand and stones (on the first reading, we do not know this either). The Bacchanalian dismemberment of a substitute victim is replaced by the tearing-up of the mourning costume; crowd control is exercised through substitutions as well as through the suggestions made by a self-appointed Lord of Misrule:

> the tradesmen hurriedly shut up their shops; for a crowd in those times stopped at nothing, and was a monster much dreaded. They had already got the length of opening the hearse to take the coffin out, when some brighter genius proposes instead, its being escorted to its destination amidst general rejoicing. Practical suggestions being much needed, this suggestion, too, was received with acclamation. (II, 14: 162)

The opening of the hearse could be a prelude to the opening of the coffin, but a "brighter genius," quite probably John Barsad, manages to deflect the energy of the crowd to a dance macabre of a jubilant conveyance of the coffin to the cemetery. But this does not suffice: the dance of death over, the impetus of the crowd has to be given new targets. Anticipating the supply of chance victims to the fans of the guillotine, the mock violence of the London crowd is redirected to substitute victims (cf. Girard 1977: 8):

> *another brighter genius (or perhaps the same)* conceived the humour of impeaching casual passers-by, as Old Bailey spies, and wreaking vengeance on them. Chase was given to some scores of inoffensive persons who had never been near the Old Bailey in their lives, in the realization of this fancy, and they were roughly handled and maltreated. (II, 14: 164; italics added)

Real violence is directed to the traditional enemy of the open crowd—the barrier between the outside and the inside spaces: there is a natural transition to "the sport of window-breaking, and thence to the plundering of public houses" and the tearing down of summer houses, until the impetus is allowed to flag under the pretext of the rumored approach of the Guards, possibly an invention of some inconspicuous Lord of Misrule (II, 14: 164).

15. On the relationship between the political situation of the period when Dickens's *Barnaby Rudge* was written and the riots that it portrays see Michael Goldberg 1972: 100–102. Goldberg (108) also connects the false funeral of Cly with the historical false funeral of Foulon, about which Dickens could have read in Carlyle's *The French Revolution*. For a detailed analysis of Dickens's treatment of the rioting mob in *Barnaby Rudge* and its place in the history of ideas see Magnet 1985: 100–145.

Thus, as in *Barnaby Rudge,* Dickens represents the London mob (as does Hawthorne the Boston mob of "My Kinsman, Major Molineux") as incited and directed by a puppeteer, whether a known leader such as Lord Gordon, a treacherous emissary, or an anonymous "brighter genius" who turns both individuals and the crowd-entity into tools of his trade.

Yet if the London crowd of *A Tale* is in need of spectacles, the one in Paris is also in need of bread. Dickens presents the revolution in France as breaking out when the hunger and the resentment of the population reach a critical degree. When Defarge is losing heart at the seemingly indefinite deferral of the uprising, his wife encourages him by metaphors of aggregated natural forces:

"Vengeance and retribution require a long time; it is the rule."

"It does not take a long time to strike a man with Lightning," said Defarge.

"How long," demanded madame, composedly, "does it take to make and store the lightning. . . . It does not take a long time . . . for an earthquake to swallow a town. Eh well! Tell me how long it takes to prepare the earthquake?"

"A long time, I suppose," said Defarge.

"But when it is ready, it takes place, and grinds to pieces everything before it." (II, 16: 185)

Though in *A Tale of Two Cities,* the recognized leaders of Saint Antoine (the Defarges, La Vengeance) belong to the lower middle class rather than to the working class, the tiger they are riding has arisen from the long decades of deprivation and humiliation endured by the lower classes.[16] It is the emphasis on the forces unleashed during the Revolution that accounts for the novel's cautionary function: the blame is attached to the lack of civil responsibility on the part of the aristocracy, not excluding the emigrant Charles Darnay, who, as his assumed name may hint, had rather ineffectively proposed to mend ("darn"; Eigner 1987: 104) some of the abuses of the *ancien régime* instead of using his power as an aristocratic landowner to seek more wide-ranging improvements (cf. Eigner 1989: 115).[17] The misery of

16. It was not so much the hunger of the masses as the frustrated expectations of the rising Third Estate that toppled the Old Regime. Murray Baumgarten believes that, like Carlyle, Dickens failed to take this process into account. Indeed, the novel's cast of characters does not include the "paper-using notaries and lawyers, merchants dealing in Wemmick's celebrated portable property" (Baumgarten 1983: 166) or Mr. Lorry's French banking colleagues.

17. Cf. Peregrine Worsthorne's (2004) earnest and somewhat idealizing view of the social

the peasants is presented as an evil of oceanic dimensions; hence the meta-phors of the storm, the sea rising without the ebb, to describe the Revolu-tion. These images, along with fire and wind (visualized in the flapping of flags), are also symbols of the carnivalesque merger of discrete identities in the crowd (cf. Canetti 1978: 73–88).

"In seasons of pestilence," comments the narrator of *A Tale of Two Cities,* "some of us will have a secret attraction to the disease—a terrible passing inclination to die of it" (III, 6: 292). In contrast to Defarge or the spy Barsad, Charles Darnay and Sydney Carton are powerfully attracted to "the loadstone rock" of their destruction. The phenomenon of the sweet tempta-tion that leads to death, "a species of fervour or intoxication, known, with-out doubt, to have led some persons to brave the guillotine unnecessarily, and to die by it," is presented not as "mere boastfulness" but as a kind of contagious insanity, "a wild infection of the wildly shaken public mind" (III, 6: 292), a serial crumbling of the inner boundaries between individuals and their psychological environment. This phenomenon is symbolically evoked by the image of the flies in Defarge's wineshop:[18]

> The day was very hot, and heaps of flies, who were extending their inquisi-tive and adventurous perquisitions into all the glutinous little glasses near madame, fell dead at the bottom. Their decease made no impression on the other flies out promenading, who looked at them in the coolest man-ner . . . , until they met the same fate. (II, 16: 186)

Whereas Darnay is brought to terror-ridden Paris by an appeal of a former servant, as well as by his sense of honor and failed responsibility, Carton's motivation for seeking out his friends in Paris and ransoming his rival's life with his own is a latter-day version of courtly love.[19]

---

commitments of the British aristocracy, especially in the nineteenth century. Residues of this view may underlie the widespread critical dissatisfaction with Darnay's character. Lawrence Frank, how-ever, has attempted to redress the imbalance in the scholarly attention paid to Darnay and to Carton by discussing the former as a version of the Romantic parricide (1984: 124–50). The Freudian frame-work of his discussion aligns it with Lynn Hunt's *The Family Romance of the French Revolution* (1992).

18. The image can be read as a link in the chain of the versions of the men-as-flies topos, wedged between Shakespeare's "As flies to wanton boys, are we to th' gods / They kill us for their sport" (*King Lear* IV.i.36–37) and Tennyson's "[a]nd men the flies of latter spring" (*In Memoriam* 50, 1–10).

19. Michael Slater discusses Carton as one of the series of Dickens's biographically inspired hopeless-lover characters, one of the two (the other being Gill Davis in the Christmas Story "The

Carton's love for Lucie Manette is a surface constituent of chivalrous supererogation. In London, amidst his self-destructive dissipation, and in Paris, on the way to his self-immolation, this love has most of the marks of the *cortezzia,* which, if we choose to believe Denis de Rougemont, is associated with the survival of the Manichean heresy in the collective subconscious. Carton's semiconscious avowal of his death drive in a conversation with his antipode Stryver ("I have no business to be, at all, that I know of") is uttered in the same breath as his reference to his own *femme fatale* ("Who is the lady?" 145), *la belle dame sans merci* who is here transformed into her antipode, a tenderly sympathetic Victorian angel of the house. While Carton's self-sacrifice can be seen as *imitatio Christi* (see Alter 1984: 100), he can also be seen as a latter-day gnostic seeking liberation from the prison house of the self, and from the prison house of the world created by an evil demiurge—seeking the otherwordly sublime through an *a priori* unhappy and hence never consummated and unappeasable love.[20] In the Victorian workshop of a Christian humanist writer, mystical courtly love dresses up, paradoxically, as an extension of the utilitarian principle of the greatest happiness for the calculably greatest number of people (a whole family against one unattached person) and is also justified, in a sentimental afterthought, by Carton's desire for posthumous glory that would perpetuate his name in that family's private sphere.[21] One can, however, regard his compensation for his unrequited love for Lucie (thematically linked to the anonymous use of his talents in the service of John Stryver) as a consolation prize, a bonus rather than a direct motive for his self-sacrifice.

A structurally similar unconscious motivation may also transpire through Darnay's challenging death by his return to France. Darnay is a reluctant aristocrat who wishes to lay down his prerogative (along with the responsibilities it should impose) and submerge in the urban professional environment—until he is fatally attracted to the "loadstone rock" that also draws Carton. The latter is a reluctant meritocrat, a brilliant young lawyer whose professional success is impeded by a character- or culture-determined unwillingness to profit by his own actual or potential merit. Carton prefers to submerge

---

Perils of Certain English Prisoners") who are partly compensated by the graciousness of the *"princesses lointaines"* whom they serve (1983: 279).

20. See De Rougemont's (1956: 75–91) discussion of links between courtly love and the Manichean heresy.

21. A dialogue on a legend about similar supererogation in George Eliot's *Daniel Deronda* (see chapter 6) pits the idealization of the heroic act against its reduction to psychological egoism. It may be noted that the surprise which Carton's self-sacrifice occasions to the contemporary reader may have been mitigated by his target audience's memories of similar supererogation in Bulwer Lytton's *Zanoni* or Wilkie Collins's *The Frozen Deep.*

in the alcohol-rich camaraderie of his peers. His "Bacchanalian propensities" (II, 5: 90) are described through the metaphor of flowing water, akin to the metaphor of the tide without the ebb that Dickens applies to the surge of the revolutionary forces in Paris: "What the two drank together, between Hilary Term and Michaelmas, might have floated a king's ship" (II, 5: 90).

Whether due to a deep-seated neurosis, a mystical unrest, unrequited love, or plain alcohol dependence, Carton is unable to change his way of life despite Lucie's appeals. However, in the terror-ridden Paris he functions with flawless efficiency *unaided* by alcohol: the *ilinx*, the sensation of vertigo that he is addicted to, comes from other sources. Carton's addiction therefore emerges not as substance dependence[22] but as *a passion for vertigo*, a model of the dissolution of identity boundaries in a transcendent spiritual whole.[23] Though this passion may bear structural similarities to the thirst for the carnivalesque blending with the crowd, it is actually a spiritual antithesis to the psychological discharge in crowd experience.

Carton is the most dramatic representative of the need to break out of the hermetic discreteness of identity; and Darnay is not the only other character to become, to a smaller extent, an exponent of this topos. The puzzling first-person passage about the privacy of the individual soul in the third chapter[24] laments not only the secrecy of the minds and stories of the people around one but also the tomblike self-enclosure of one's own emotional life: "In any of the burial-places of this city through which I pass, is there a sleeper more inscrutable than its busy inhabitants are, in their innermost personality, to me, or than I am to them?" (I, 3: 15). In *A Tale of Two Cities* most characters need to overcome their self-enclosure,[25] at least temporarily, in the crisis scenes that give shape or direction to the further flow of their emotional lives. Some achieve this transient opening of the borders of personality through drink, others through crowd experience or ideological identification with a cause, still others (Lucie, Jarvis Lorry) through compassion, given or received. By contrast, in the bitter carnival (cf.

---

22. According to de Rougemont, passion itself is an intoxicating drug (1956: 142).

23. In another frame of reference, this tendency has been described as the need for breaking out of the prison house of bourgeois individualism (Baldridge 1998). But for the new-Marxist epithet "bourgeois" almost automatically attached to "individualism," this reading of Carton's motivation goes a long way towards describing the thematic continuity between his dissipation in London and his death in Paris.

24. An earnest version of Sterne's Tristam Shandy's ironic reflections on the absence of the Momus's glass in human anatomy (I, 23: 65).

25. Thermodynamics teaches us that in the absence of external sources of refueling, closed systems are bound to run down; indeed, nineteenth-century versions of entropy form one of the most insistent recurrent motifs of Dickens's fiction, particularly prominent in *Bleak House, Our Mutual Friend,* and, in the image of Miss Havisham, in *Great Expectations.*

Bernstein 1992) of revolutionary terror, the need to transcend the boundaries of the self is also translated into the spilling of the blood of another, violence to the bodies that seem to bar the flow of the immanent will just as architectural barriers impede the crowd's drive for expansion.

The culture of the carnival recognizes this profound human need and institutionalizes the regulated occasions on which self-enclosure is allowed to relax. Affects are pooled; the self ventures upon a temporary loss of discreteness and a communion with the emotional life of its environment—not to vent the inner pressures but, on the contrary, to recharge inner energy by the contact with an external source: one loses oneself in the magma of communal desire in order to find oneself again. The venerable institution of the Lord of Misrule and its various analogues, such as the conventions of popular entertainment, legislation of the closing time of bars, and the fine art of crowd control, limit these cultural remissions in order not to ban them. The carnivalesque osmosis between discrete selves and larger social forces provides a necessary balance to the entropy-breeding emotional and social compartmentalization of human life, but the legal and conventional checks on the scope and time span of this osmosis (suspended during the revolutionary terror) keep it from lethal irreversibility.

In Carton, in contrast to the other characters, though not to Darnay, the need for a relaxation of the hold on his own ego, the well-endowed identity that might have led him to professional eminence, is presented as suicide by inches.[26] Hence the leitmotif of water, and death by water, that accompanies his progress through the novel.[27] In the Paris episode leading up to Carton's death, this motif is associated with the presentation of the revolutionary forces as a storm, the sea rising, and, on the other hand, with the *ilinx,* the vertigo evoked by the image of an eddy, a miniature whirlpool, that Carton watches from the bridge:

> The strong tide, so swift, so deep, and certain, was like a congenial friend, in the morning stillness. [Carton] walked by the stream, far from the houses, and in the light and warmth of the sun fell asleep on the bank. When he awoke and was afoot again, he lingered there yet a little longer, watching an eddy that turned and turned purposeless, until the stream absorbed it, and carried it on to the sea.—"Like me!" (III, 9: 327)

26. Cf. Schor's comment on Carton's self-description as "self-flung away, wasted, drunken, poor creature of misuse" (II, 13: 156): "The work of the novel is to remake that self-flinging into the heroic self-sacrifice Carton effects at the end" (1991: 91).

27. In a different conceptual framework, the motif of death by water in *A Tale of Two Cities* is discussed by Garrett Stewart (1987).

If we move from the mimetic to the thematic model of character analysis (Phelan 1986, 2005: 20ff.), Carton's self-immolation emerges not only as an ultimate realization of his character but also as a part of the strand of motifs peculiar to this novel.[28] In "Narrative Art and Magic" (1972), where "magic" is not just a metaphor for the spell cast by narrative art but is, quite literally, sympathetic magic, Jorge Luis Borges suggests that narrative details may have a life of their own: an image attracts images like it, and so the fate of the character may be ruled not by causal determinacy but by the life of a motif. Carton's self-sacrifice is the climax of the motif of the submergence of the self; and he is made to work hard on practical particulars in order to make such closure seem plausible. The foresight, energy, and manipulativeness that Carton displays in arranging the details of his replacement of Darnay in the Conciergerie, that is, in arranging his own execution, accord with what we know of his talents. The highest exertion of his organizational powers is, appropriately, accompanied by the total stunting of Darnay: Carton drugs Darnay and then pretends that Darnay is a visitor who has fainted at the thought of his friend's impending death. This turn of the plot, prepared by Carton's visit to a chemist (who, symbolically, warns him against *mixing* the ingredients), exonerates Darnay of consciously accepting Carton's self-sacrifice while constructing a redistributionary seesaw: Darnay gets the prolonged emotional ordeal of the helpless condemned man, while Carton gets the execution.[29]

The third group of the novel's characters keep away from the forces of history, whether by maintaining a show of neutrality or by outward conformity and cooperation. When Jerry Cruncher joins the crowd of the revelers at Cly's funeral, he only pretends to have become a part of it: his agenda is to

28. In terms of Phelan's classification of components of characterization, this interconnection of Carton's portrayal as a "possible person" (the mimetic model) with the dependence of this portrayal on a broader narrative structure constitutes a "synthetic" model (2005: 20) also marked in Fielding's creation of Jenny Jones (see chapter 2).

29. At each stage in the novel, the passivity of one of these two characters has been balanced by the exertions of the other. This can be classified as one of the uses of "splitting" in this novel—as Albert D. Hutter notes, one of the prominent uses of the splitting of a personality into different constituents (some of them in the shape of "doubles") is a defense-mechanism distancing of emotion (1987: 50–55); cf. also Harold Bloom 1987: 11. Incidentally, one of the reasons for the reader's frequently recorded dislike of Darnay may be associated with the way in which, in their second interview (II, 20: 214–16), Darnay parries Carton's emotional boundary-crossing offers of communion by perfectly benevolent arms'-length politeness (it is only after Lucie's rebuke [II, 20: 216–17] that Darnay ceases to treat Carton with condescension).

find out the burial place of the corpse, which he can later "resurrect" for sale to medical students. Throughout the novel, Jerry of the spiky hair rising from his head like a hedgehog's spines (don't touch me!) is submissive to employers but truculent with his family: his very occupation, violating the last privacy of human beings, poisons his domestic life. Yet Jerry's camouflaged estrangement from the London mobs prepares the reader for his change of heart on watching the crowds in Paris: on seeing the great number of "Subjects without heads" (III: 9, 320), he vows to convert from a grave robber to a grave digger, a bona fide agent of the privacy of the ultimate dissolution.

In contrast to Jerry, the spy Solomon Pross, alias John Barsad, is forced into Carton's service by threats of disclosure. Barsad's character is a somewhat awkward vehicle of the coincidences in the novel's plot: in *A Tale of Two Cities,* and throughout Dickens's work, the density of uncanny surprises is enhanced by the principle of avoiding anonymity that often draws the interpreter into the game of making connections—who, indeed, is the "bright spirit" who manipulates the London crowd at Cly's funeral? Yet his character also serves at least one topical issue and one recurrent theme. The former, the semantic facet of the subplot, illustrates a bitter regularity in the external field of reference: the service of the post–Revolutionary Terror regime provides an asylum for the otherwise socially and morally disgraced individuals.[30] The latter, part of the novel's internal field of reference (the "syntactics" of the semiological triad; see pp. 18–19 above) is the theme of containing, controlling, distancing the outflow of emotion—as, for instance, in Barsard's unexpected meeting with his sister Miss Pross.

The need to control the expansion of the affect (the purpose of the wet towel around Sydney's drunken head) links Barsad with one more character who evades both the attraction of historical forces and victimization by them—the benevolent and sensitive bank clerk Jarvis Lorry. Discreetness and discreteness are his twin principles; they are also the principles according to which his bank avoids ostentatious display, thus contrasting with the showy premises of the fake insurance company in *Martin Chuzzlewit* and with its own luxurious office in the corrupt old-regime Paris.[31]

It is not because of bourgeois acquisitiveness that Lorry's leitmotif is "business"; this is also his refrain in the emotion-fraught first dialogue with

---

30. Cf. Carlyle (1888: 220): "The Spoilers these; for Patriotism is always infected so, with a proportion of mere thieves and scoundrels."

31. Cf. Carlyle (1888: 24): "If when the oak stands proudliest flourishing to the eye, you know that its heart is sound, it is not so with the man; how much less with the Society, with the Nation of men!"

Lucie Manette: by trying to persuade himself and her that his role in the story is strictly that of an agent of the bank, Lorry struggles to distance himself from the emotion that threatens to engulf him. In the later parts of the story, it is again his loyal service that helps him to resist emotional involvement. He shrewdly withholds full hospitality from Dr. Manette's family in London: he places them, literally, at a distance (a walking distance) from Tellson Bank's Paris branch, where he is quartered. Lorry deftly contains the intrusion of the self-important Stryver into Lucie's life; he practically tames Miss Pross. In his dialogue with Manette, Lorry discusses the latter's mental condition after Lucie's wedding not in the second but in the third person, with the transparent pretense of consulting a doctor about an anonymous friend, distancing and thus anaesthetizing the pain of the doctor's predicament.

The novel's three significant shifts in the use of personal pronouns are associated with Lorry. The famous first-person-singular passage about the secrecy of the human soul—in the coach-ride episode at the beginning of the third chapter of the novel—can be read as free indirect speech that reflects Lorry's thoughts in the carriage, among wrapped-up fellow passengers ("No more can I look into the depths of this unfathomable water, wherein, as momentary lights glanced into it, I have had glimpses of buried treasure and other things submerged," I, 3: 15); this is echoed in the use of the first-person plural in the coach-ride episode of the escape from Paris at the end of the third to the last chapter ("The wind is rushing after us, and the clouds are flying after us, and the moon is plunging after us, and the whole wild night is in pursuit of us," III, 13: 372). In accordance with the principle of avoiding anonymity, one might be tempted to connect his bank's early involvement in Manette's affairs with the sentence "my love, the darling of my soul, is dead" in chapter 3: Lorry might have been in love with Manette's bride the way Carton is in love with Darnay's. Yet Lorry's past remains hidden not only from his friends but also from the reader.

Throughout the novel the reader is likewise kept at a distance, through style or structure, from the emotional heightening of even the most intense situations in the novel.[32] Stylistic distancing techniques may be observed in the episode of Lucie's appeal to her unresponsive, deranged father during their first meeting. She calls on Manette to break out from the armor of his madness, his identity as a stunted shoemaker, and to allow himself a free expression of his pain:

32. Cf. Mullan 1988: 178–88 on Sterne's technique of distancing the reader from the emotions presented in *Tristram Shandy.*

"If you hear in my voice any resemblance to a voice that once was sweet music in your ears, weep for it, weep for it! If you touch, in touching my hair, anything that recalls a beloved head that lay on your breast when you were young and free, weep for it, weep for it! If, when I hint to you of a Home that is before us, where I will be true to you with all my duty and with all my faithful service, I bring back the remembrance of a Home long desolated, while your poor heart pined away, weep for it, weep for it!" (I, 6: 48)

The strategic use of the double refrain "weep for it, weep for it!" adds a formal rhetorical finish to this appeal, thereby cushioning its emotional intensity for the reader while heightening it for its addressee.[33]

The reader's sympathetic involvement in the moral ordeals of this novel is alleviated by effects of surprise: the *alea* impedes *mimicry*. The pain of the condemned to death is cushioned first by the emphasis not on Darnay's self-mourning but on his attempts to control his thoughts on the eve of his expected execution; later the reader's attention is diverted by the uncanny surprise at Carton's taking his place in the Conciergerie. On the first reading, the night that Carton spends sleepless in Paris before this exchange is not recognized as the last night of the condemned, since the inside views of Carton's experience carefully avoid direct reference to his intentions. Like Darnay, Carton attempts to control his psychic flow, carefully avoiding thoughts of the guillotine, but on the first reading we do not know this. At work in the episode is the technique that Genette calls "paralipsis" (1980: 195)—presenting less information than is available to the focal character. The suppression of this detail is here not signaled to the reader, thereby creating a "surprise gap" (Sternberg 1978: 244–45) and leading the reader to the hypothesis which, when eventually withdrawn, divides our attention between the plot development and our own experience of forming and correcting motivational schemata. When the exchange takes place in the prison, we can recognize that it has been well prepared by a series of hints that now, in retrospect, fall into place. On a repeated reading—as on a repeated reading of Fielding's *Tom Jones,* the formerly underread deployment of the textual details that set the stage for the surprise reversal competes for our attention with vicarious experience.

Even when we are almost led up to the scaffold from the tumbril of the condemned, Carton's suffering is further distanced by his heroic determina-

33. In his analysis of repetition, cumulative vocabulary, and the tension between rhetoric and exuberance in *A Tale of Two Cities,* Sylvère Monod likewise notes Dickens's "deliberate attempt at stylization" and his restraining of exuberance in this novel (1970: 185–86).

tion to give loving support to another—the young seamstress who functions as a stand-in for Lucie of the "Golden Thread,"[34] and by the narrative's shift to the issue of the memory of the dead.

Thus in *A Tale of Two Cities* Dickens seems to be taking measures to reduce the reader's emotional empathy with the characters. In comparison with, for example, *The Old Curiosity Shop,* or *Bleak House,* or *Great Expectations,* and despite the ample references to extreme violence (and in the case of the death of the governor of the Bastille, a graphical representation of it), here the effect of the melodramatic heightening is considerably reduced. It has been noted that "the public executions, especially when accompanied by torture, can be seen as a nightmare of transparency, of publicly displaying what is hidden, intimate, secret, in the interests of creating social order and cohesion," and that the evocation of such events in *A Tale of Two Cities* may read as an indirectly self-reflective comment on the novel's own (intrusive?) revelation of private lives (Gallagher 1987: 128, 125). Yet the novel's leaving gaps in some parts of its plot, its recurrent motif of secrecy (sub rosa: cf. Madame Defarge's use of the rose to signal the presence of spies), and its dramatization of emotional distance through the behavior of such characters as Lorry on the one hand and Barsad on the other, likewise stand in a self-reflective relationship: the cautiousness of the character thematizes the cautiousness of the narrative. The novel that stages the dire need for control of the dangerous pooling of affects, along with the need for social justice and private morality that might preempt the rise of that danger, is also engaged in controlling and rationing readerly compassion. D. A. Miller's suggestion (1988) that the role of the novel may complement the function of the police in disseminating civil self-restraint should perhaps be modified by a milder analogy—between the effect of some narratives, *A Tale of Two Cities* among them, and the function of the Lord of Misrule, presiding over limited conditions for emotional release.

The representation of the bitter carnival in *A Tale of Two Cities* and this novel's muffling of the carnivalesque response on the part of the reader are associated with the ethics of individualism that accompanies Dickens's humanist religiosity. Individualism as ethical ideology (not to be confused with a disparaging appellation for the socioeconomic forms of egoism)

---

34. This may be seen as a case of typically Dickensian oneiric transference, as in the case of the incrimination of the maid Hortense rather than her mistress Honoria Dedlock in *Bleak House.*

means that moral values are derived not from a vision of the collective good but from respect and concern for the rights of every single individual—so long as that individual's aims do not encroach on the rights of the individuals around him. One of the most basic rights of the individual is to preserve his or her identity; one of the most basic obligations is to recognize this right for others. As Frances Ferguson (2005) has demonstrated, Dickens's novel presents terror as based on the dissolution of individualities in the minds of others: a modern terrorist, like a Paris Jacobin (like, for that matter, a Stalinist or a Nazi), refuses to act on the basis of the distinction between collective affiliation and individuality; Ferguson draws an aesthetic link between this idea and *A Tale*'s recurrent pattern of the social ineffectiveness of purely individual action, especially in terror-ridden France. By contrast, it has been asserted that Dickens had "no patience with the institutions of government" (Sicher 2003: 331). Indeed, Dickens called for the same attention to the individual in benevolent activities as in punitive justice; he negotiated reforms and institutionalized care of the needy yet was critical of the unimaginative workings of the system, and on the use of statistics (Sissy Jupe's "stutterings") to obfuscate the realities of the human predicament.[35] The slow rate of institutionalized change had to be compensated for by the corrective of individual philanthropy. If, across the Atlantic, Ralph Waldo Emerson regarded a dollar given away in charity as an "evil dollar," which scattered his strength and diverted him from the real work he had to do in the public sphere,[36] Dickens sent the most admirable of his characters on fact-finding missions followed by philanthropic acts focused on particular individuals. He was not impeded by the fear that personal charity might exempt the government from care for the welfare of the citizens:[37] the scope of these individual efforts could only be limited (and hence socially ineffective)—for one orphan adopted by a benevolent family, hundreds remain in the streets, for one Jo dying sheltered there are hundreds who die, as he had

35. On December 30, 1854, in a letter to the statistician Charles Knight, Dickens wrote that the satire in *Hard Times* was "against those who see figures and averages, and nothing else—the representatives of the wickedest and most enormous vice of this time—the men who, through long years to come, will do more to damage the real useful truths of political economy than I could do (if I tried) in my whole life—the addled heads who would take the average of cold in the Crimea during twelve months as a reason for clothing a soldier in nankeen on a night when he would be frozen to death in fur—and who would comfort the labourer in travelling twelve miles a day to and from his work, by telling him that the average distance of one inhabited place from another in the whole area of England, is not more than four miles" (1993, VII: 492–93).

36. This could be regarded as a rhetorical refraction of Bentham's position on the matter; see Stokes 2001: 712 on the difference between Bentham's and Dickens's views of individual charity.

37. Cf. de Graef's 2004 tracing of this dilemma to the attitudes of the speaker of Wordsworth's early poems.

lived, spurned and neglected—which would not mean, for Dickens, that the one Jo should not be rescued because others like him would still be left in the lurch. A suffering individual has no time to wait for changes in legislation or economy: individual charity is, for Dickens, a partial compensation for the slow rate of social change: "Do it at once," as, in totally different contexts, Josiah Bounderby would say in *Hard Times* (63).[38] Whereas in Austen and Eliot individual charities take place mainly offstage, Dickens places them in the limelight, bravely engaging side issues such as the embarrassments of gratitude, humiliation, belatedness, futility, intrusiveness—not without reminding us that behind the lucky recipients of charitable assistance there are thousands whose plight is not alleviated. Acts of charity, such as a Scarlet Pimpernel rescue, are remissions in otherwise inexorable social processes, sometimes remissions that foreshadow cure. Dickens associated the notion of charity, in the practical and the religious senses, with that of love;[39] his focus on the pains and pleasures of personal philanthropy emphasized the need for institutional remedies while rendering the presentation of human suffering bearable because balanced by its palliatives: the attention of Dickens's target audience would be drawn, all the more effectively, to the misery of many if the relieved suffering of a few left the many in the background.

Thus Dickens's cautious treatment of sociocultural remissions relates to his stand on social policies as well as on the psychic economy of the individual self. The erasure of individuality in the imagination of another characterizes terrorism; but such erasure also underlies the purely institutional benevolence unhelped by private philanthropy. Yet an individual's own yearning to dissolve in the transcendent other is as dangerous to the self as the yearning for "discharge" in a crowd is dangerous to others. Dickens's awareness of the attraction of the "loadstone rocks" of Scylla and the whirlpool of Charybdis energizes the carnival elements in *A Tale of Two Cities;* yet his carnivalesque is hedged in by ethical individualism and balanced by the

38. The contemporary principle mentioned by Bulwer Lytton, "When abuses arise to a certain pitch, they must be remedied" (see Belcher 1982), assumes that no social remedies are called for so long as there is no statistical information about a social problem: the individual affected would fall between bureaucratic chairs. In *Hard Times,* the teacher who asks Sissy to evaluate a case of "only five-and-twenty" people starving to death in the streets of a city with a million inhabitants (97) is not indifferent to the problem of destitution but seems to regard the statistical size of this problem as insufficient for institutional intervention, as, that is, an isolated phenomenon rather than a typifying epiphenomenon of the socioeconomic structure. Sissy, however, wants the suffering of the destitute to be addressed immediately and irrespective of statistics: "it must be hard upon those who were starved," she says, "whether the others were a million or a million million" (97).

39. Cf. Barbara Hardy on Dickens's "combination of social despair and personal faith, his capacity to distrust both society and social reform while retaining and perhaps deepening a faith in the power of human love" (1970: 3).

techniques that activate the reader's intellectual engagement with the text at the expense of participative emotion.

As noted in chapters 3 and 4, the self-forgetfulness under the spell of the novel and the emotional sway of vicarious experience—the carnivalesque elements of reader response—are the effect of specific narrative techniques, that is, of the form of expression, rather than of the form of content, carnivalesque or other. However, the specific ethical significance of the narrative conditions for the tide or the ebb of such a response depends largely on the substance of the content—here the position that the narrative evolves on the issues of the discreteness of the individual self and the measure and manner of the self's blending with, or into, its communal environment. Whereas sympathetic identification (the game of *mimicry*) creates a model of sharing affects, the effect of surprise (when not simultaneous with that of the protagonist[40]) highlights the difference between the intellectual and emotional trajectories of the characters and those of the reader; it returns us to a more detached, analytic type of reading.[41] *A Tale of Two Cities* is a landmark in Dickens's narrative reflection on the need for balance between natural impulses, whether positive or negative, on the one hand, and the self-restraint or, conversely, the glorified barbarism of civilization on the other. The pulsations in the reader's distance from the characters and empathy with them form an ethically and aesthetically congruent pragmatic facet of this exploration.

40. See Toker 1993a: 73 and 97–97 on "isochronic experience"—in Dickens's *Bleak House* and Austen's *Emma*. In *A Tale of Two Cities*, the reader's surprise at the announcement that Dr. Manette is the main witness for the prosecution of Darnay is isochronic with the surprise of the protagonists and enhances the reader's identification with them. By contrast, the surprise at discovering Carton's self-sacrificial intentions distances the reader from this character, and thus lightens the sympathetic pain of his destiny.

41. Cf. Gumbrecht's justaposition of "communion" and "analysis" in the sports fans' observation of a ball game or an athletic competition (2006: 205).

CHAPTER SIX

Across the Boundaries of Self

George Eliot's *Daniel Deronda*

> [T]he situation of the exile is essentially a situation of permanent crisis.
>
> —Nathan Rotenstreich, *Zionism: Past and Present*, 54

IF THE MAIN FEATURES OF THE FORM of content in the carnivalesque mode are the horizontal erasure of boundaries and the vertical reversals of social stratification, narratives in which only one of these two topoi is manifest may be regarded as intermediate. One example is George Eliot's *Daniel Deronda*, which thematizes the blurring of identity boundaries.

The phenomenology of imagination that characterizes this novel corresponds to its halfway modal status. Its topography includes a variety of outdoor scenes, but in most of them—the circumscribed archery grounds (admission by ticket), the river, the Chase, the Park, the *Judengasse*—confinement within bounds dominates over openness. Conversely, most of the indoor areas are either vast (the parlors and dining halls of the great houses) or liminal (the house in Gadsmere and the Meyrics' house in Chelsea opening up, respectively, on the garden and the river). The most meaningful engagements between the characters, their self-protective armor giving way or being reasserted and repaired, are played out against such a spatially ambivalent background.

The form of expression likewise straddles the line between the carnivalesque and the "biographical" modes. The narrative begins *in medias res*: the opening scene around the gambling tables in Leubronn follows Grandcourt's initial courtship of Gwendolen and Deronda's rescue of Mirah in the plot but is presented before these events. Yet this scene does not represent the inevitable outcome of a growing tendency; it is presented as a chance collision that creates new instabilities.[1] On the other hand, an element of thematic determinism is also at work: the paths of Deronda and Gwendolen converge in the same tourist resort as a result of the swelling of tendencies on each side: both these characters have translated the sense of displacement from the center of their being into a geographical distance from home, and both are uneasily deferring conjugal commitments. The opening of the novel is thus a hybrid form in which the convention of a chance encounter combines with the carnivalesque pattern of tendencies swelling to a point of crisis. The eye contact between the two protagonists opens up their identities to each other, creating a narrow but deep channel of communication from which others will remain excluded.

Carnivalesque events are not a prominent part of the substance of the novel's content. Only two such events are referred to, and only very briefly. One of them is mentioned in a discussion of political expediency: the Archbishop of Naples is said to have sanctioned, in what would now be called a populist gesture, the St. Januarius procession against the plague (1993: 384). The other is embedded in a simile: the attitude of British mainstream society to Jews is compared with the attitude of the matrons of Delphi to the tired Maenads who had wandered into their city: the matrons "tenderly" minister to the Bacchae and take them "safely to their own borders" (195).[2] Both the events thus serve local rhetorical purposes. Both also serve as instances of the motif of horizontal osmosis: in such *pageants without footlights* the spectators touch the participants, and the borderlines of states, bodies, minds, groups, or classes are temporarily transgressed (see Bakhtin 1968: 7; 1984: 108–47). In contrast to the novels of Dostoevsky, George Eliot's contemporary, *Daniel Deronda* seldom gives this topos a melodramatic heightening, yet it explores a spectrum of its thematic permutations.

In particular, it is largely through the representation of blurring boundaries—between the participants and the spectators, the individual and his or her immediate physical or psychological environment, the self and the other, the self and a larger whole—that the novel negotiates an ethical compromise between supererogation at one extreme and nihilism at the other. The

1. Cf. Phelan 2006 on the role of instability in narrative and D. A. Miller (1981: 3–106) on "narratable" and "non-narratable" states of affairs.

2. Susan Meyer (1993) discusses this simile as associated with the British proto-Zionism that promoted the Jews' seeking of their homeland with the idea of seeing them safely away from their own midst; I see it also as a part of the novel's analysis of the boundaries of sympathy.

ideological stance thus evolved is one that has moved, somewhat hesitantly, from an Austen-like middle-way model in the direction of the Dickensian model of checks and balances. The images and motifs pertaining to the blurring of boundaries are, in *Daniel Deronda,* associated with the dialectics of self-loss and self-transcendence: the extreme of self-transcendence may amount to self-loss but an insufficiency of self-transcendence can be equally self-destructive. This deployment of possibilities is carried out via the twin themes of vocation and sympathy.[3]

George Eliot is one of the first major nineteenth-century novelists of vocation. As Alan Mintz has shown (1976, 1978), the birth of the romance of vocation (as opposed to the romance of love) is associated with the ideological changes and the work ethics of the Victorian period. Prior to the Industrial Revolution and the nineteenth-century spread of scientific ideas, a person's self-definition would rest on religious identity and affiliations in terms of family, community, geographical region, and nationality, whereas profession was regarded mainly as a way of making a living and thus securing one's place in the above frameworks. With the weakening of religious beliefs and the intensification of economic pressures on the upper classes, profession, idealized as "vocation," stepped in to fill the void, redefining the options of self-realization available to the individual.[4] In *Daniel Deronda,* indeed, the concern with vocation reconciles the pursuit of social, national, or communal progress with the agenda of self-perfection: the Commissar and the Yogi, the change from without and the change from within, enter into a somewhat uneasy alliance.

The proto-Zionist plot of *Daniel Deronda* emphasizes the change from without, the need for a radical restructuring of the life of the Jewish nation. The novel's prophet of this change, Ezra Mordecai Cohen, is, however, represented as a version of the Yogi, a mystic whose spirit transcends and, as it were, consumes his fragile body, and who therefore stands in need of the "executive self" in the shape of the healthy, handsome, puritanical Daniel Deronda. The reader is partly prepared for Daniel's ultimate endorsement of Mordecai's vision by the narrator's explanations of his inability to commit himself to British politics, the field that in her previous novel, *Middlemarch,*

3. See Rimmon-Kenan 1985 on theme as the meaning of a recurrence of narrative details.
4. In the twentieth century the romance of vocation, persisting mainly in the field of popular fiction and film, developed into a more somber subgenre, the romance of career (e.g., Klaus Mann's *Mephisto*).

George Eliot presented as a sufficiently grateful sphere for the application of idealistic individual energies. The reference to the St. Januarius procession is made in the context of Daniel's reluctance to opt for party politics, his fear of a conflict between loyalty to the narrower and the broader frameworks—much like the quandary of the Archbishop of Naples who must have made a compromise with his conscience by allowing a carnivalesque event to raise the spirits of the population during an epidemic. The most significant of obstacles preventing the wholehearted dedication of Daniel's energies to the liberal politics and the reform movement of the time is his sympathy with the potential opponents: although, as an apprentice to Sir Hugo Mallinger, Daniel shares the ideology of the Whigs, he is strongly drawn to the valorization of traditions represented by the Tories. He is "fervently democratic in his feeling for the multitude," yet "through his affections and imagination, intensely conservative; voracious of speculation on government and religion, yet loath to part with long-sanctioned forms which, for him, [are] quick with memories and sentiments" (364). As a secret outsider, sensitive to the insecurity of his position, Daniel is drawn to the ethical aspects of the traditional forms of life just as much as, in the novel's other plotline, Grandcourt, the legal heir to estates and rank, is obsessed with the aesthetic externals of his status.[5] Moreover, Daniel's painful misapprehension of his place in Sir Hugo's household at the symbolic (Bar Mitzvah) age of thirteen promotes his responsiveness to the suffering of others and sympathy for the predicament of the losing side of each struggle.[6] Therefore, "as soon as he took up any antagonism, though only in thought, he seemed to himself like the Sabine warriors in the memorable story—with nothing to meet his spear but flesh of his flesh, and objects he loved" (364). Deronda is, a century ahead of his time, what Richard Rorty (1989: xv) has called "a liberal ironist"—one who resists a complete surrender of his identity to the imperiousness of a larger ideological frame.

Daniel refrains from placing himself in the British political arena not only because he is reluctant to commit himself to a consistent party platform but also because he fears loss of self. The expression of this fear is couched in terms of compromises with his personal integrity into which politics might force him: "I don't want to make a living out of opinions. . . . I can't see any

5. For a discussion of a network of similar thematic links between different episodes and subplots of *Daniel Deronda,* see Daleski 1985: 27–38.

6. I agree with Susan Ostrov Weisser (1990: 6) that "Deronda's ego boundaries are markedly permeable" and that his sympathies are broad, yet calling these sympathies "chameleon-like" is one of the cavalier sound bites that mar Weisser's valuable comments on the desireless sexual power play in the novel.

real public expediency that does not keep an ideal before it which makes a limit of deviation from the direct path. But if I were to set up for a public man I might mistake my own success for public expediency" (384). This is Daniel's secret meeting point with Gwendolen, who dreads her liability to impulsive wrongdoing and whom he advises to turn her dread into a safeguard. He himself acts in the spirit of his advice: aware of the danger of confusing the personal and the public, he seeks, and eventually finds, a vocation in which the need for distinguishing between his self-actualization and the public good would be much less insistent.[7] Meantime, however, he objects to political "humbug." Sir Hugo's reference to a possible "good style" of humbug as opposed to a "bad style" does not suffice to overcome Daniel's ethical fastidiousness on the issues of party politics.

Ironically, this attitude is an ethical counterpart of Grandcourt's aesthetical squeamishness that attracts Gwendolen's interest. Grandcourt and Gwendolen meet in their shared intolerant awareness of "what brutes his fellow creatures were, both masculine and feminine; what odious familiarities they had, what smirks, what modes of flourishing their handkerchiefs, what costume, what lavender water, what bulging eyes, and what foolish notions of making themselves agreeable by remarks which were not wanted" (670–71). In his early (eventually surmounted) disgust with the pawnbroker Ezra Cohen and his family, Daniel displays his own tendency to share the leisure-class aesthetics epitomized by Grandcourt. Gwendolen eventually tries to train herself in Deronda's preference for ethical rather than aesthetic discriminations, though her aesthetic fastidiousness in human relations remains deeply ingrained.

The sense of physical disgust in George Eliot's presentations of the pawnbroker's family has given rise to some readers' suspicions that underneath the proto-Zionist ideas in the novel lies the kind of residual anti-Semitism that makes exceptions for those Jews who, like Mirah, Daniel, and his mother, do not display any would-be typical "Jewish peculiarities" (225)[8] or whose

7. Andrew Miller regards the portrayal of Daniel Deronda (a version of "*Waverly,* sixty years hence," 2008: 74) as an instance of George Eliot's characteristic dramatization of "the tension between a theory of morality that stresses the importance of perspective (a theory furthered by the genre in which she is working) and an unflagging belief in the duty of choice" (70).

8. Such suspicions are particularly clearly articulated in Meyer 1993: 747. For many years, the pressures of political correctness (genuine or otherwise) made it almost a relief to read the product of responses that have not been self-censored and that do not avoid words such as "lurk," "repugnant,"

uncouth racially marked physique is either refined and transcended (by Mordecai's combination of disease and spirituality) or redeemed (by Klesmer's "genius"). It may, however, be argued that the unattractive Jewish "specimen[s]" (206) in the novel are offered as a challenge to the expansion of sympathy that George Eliot called for in her essay "The Natural History of German Life" (1901: 360). In *Daniel Deronda* the treatment of sympathy is significantly more complex and ambivalent (see During 1998) than in George Eliot's previous works.

Indeed, several types of sympathy can be distinguished in the novel. One of them is ideological, and it consists in the acceptance, or toleration, of alien, unshared affects of the cultural other. Mordecai, for instance, is practically resigned to the vulgarity, false claims, and intellectual limitations of the Cohens. His tolerant, self-disciplining attitude to the cultural inferiority they represent is an *ideological* commitment: their mild misrule is accommodated by a slot in his fixed conceptual network. In an effort to win Daniel to his messianic cause, Mordecai attempts to turn the Cohens into objects of Daniel's sympathy by suggesting that it is the diaspora condition that causes the "spiritual poverty of the Jewish millions" (571).[9] And yet this sympathetic condescension is shown to be misplaced and to shrink its objects in the eyes of the observer: Mordecai, it turns out, underestimates the Cohens when he expects them to be unhappy on meeting Mirah because they have lost the daughter of the family: to everyone's surprise the Cohens are not resentful—they transcend their hidden sorrow and extend to Mirah a wholehearted welcome. Daniel is, of course, even less of a fair judge than Mordecai: his early exposure to "ugly stories of Jewish characteristics and occupations" (206) and his superficial early observation of Jews in London streets have lowered the threshold of his attention to whatever might further feed his prejudice. Behind his back, however, the implied author sends different signals to the reader. For example, whereas Gwendolen has to lock her knife in a box and a drawer for fear of her own violence, the Cohens make their little scion Jacob a gift of a knife and allow him to play with it,

---

"hateful and contaminating," or "unpleasant fact" that one might wish to "fumigate and becloud" (206–7), especially when they come from an author who is ideologically opposed to anti-Semitism (these days, however, untrammeled anti-Semitism has made it back into the media, again calling into question the point where gut-feeling frankness of speech turns into abusive incitation to violence). Bernard Harrison believes that the aesthetically tinged "social" anti-Semitism, amply present throughout the history of English literature, is less dangerous than the political anti-Semitism that purports to struggle against what it sees as pan-Jewish political conspiracy (2006: 12–13).

9. Ortwin de Graef (2010) notes a dialectics between Mordecai's movement towards transnational humanism through the restitution of national selfhood to the Jews and the sense of emotional leaning towards one's own ethnicity expressed in George Eliot's *Impressions of Theophrastus Such*.

evaluate it, boast of it, compare it with other knives: apparently, they have no reason to fear any violent impulses that the knife may bring out.

Even after having moved towards Mordecai's attitude of *ideological* sympathy for the stunted Jewish population that he comes to see as awaiting a Zionist redemption, Daniel does not develop the *resonating* type of sympathy with the Jewish environment. This, however, is part of a more general pattern: hardly ever, in the course of the novel, is the emotion of any one character shown to enter into a synergetic unison with that of another. All the symbolic and literal ingredients of Dickensian resonating sympathy are evoked in different episodes of *Daniel Deronda* but never really combined to produce this boundary-crossing phenomenon itself. When Klesmer sits down to observe and evaluate Mirah's singing, the hearts of the four Meyrick ladies are "beating fast in anxiety" (483), but this resonant pulsation is not publicly expressed and therefore not transformed into a carnivalesque pooling of affects. As this example shows, the object of the resonant sympathy is not the person who also feels it but the one towards whom an attitude is shared. It is not so much the drunken Marmeladov whom Dostoevsky's Raskolnikov pities—together with Marmeladov he grieves for his wife and for his daughter Sonia, enhancing the emotion of the reader by the sense of synergetic resonance.

By contrast, Mordecai's Zionist speech in the club does not arouse the interest of more than a few of his listeners. The narrative refers to the imperious "chord" (503) in Mordecai's voice when he claims Daniel's allegiance, but Daniel's ultimate endorsement of Mordecai's goals is caused not by psychological contagion, not by a resonating string, and not even by a consent to extend a dying man's life by his own;[10] it is a matter of a rational persuasion on a subject in which—as during his eventide boating trips—his own "thinking and desiring melt together" (188). Vibrating chords, music, synchronized heartbeats, contagion, sympathy, cooperation—all these potential constituents of resonant Dionysian sympathy, of the horizontal blending of individual selves and the dissolution of boundaries between them, are referred to but held in check in the novel. With the one telling exception of the three Cohen children crying in cacophonous unison (574), individuals' affects are insulated from each other, as if to preempt the type of carnivalesque crowd experience against which, a century later, the poetically heightened phenomenology of Elias Canetti's *Crowds and Power* would sound a warning.

10. David Marshall suggests that at a certain point in their relationship Daniel "seems ready to take another for a larger self, enclosing his self in another" (1986: 224). Actually, Daniel tactfully yet consistently resists the temptation of the loss of self in the merger with another.

Unlike resonating sympathy, which is allowed to remain only in remoter backgrounds of the novel's action, a third kind of sympathy is rather massively staged, namely the *redistributive* variety that consists not of pooling but of rationing the affect. The mechanism is described by the eighteenth-century economist and philosopher Adam Smith, who bases his understanding of sympathy on one's ability to "enter" into the situation of the other: detailing the causes of one's grief to others allays part of the pain by transferring a diluted portion of it to the listeners while also entering into their experience of listening to oneself:

> [A]s nature teaches the spectators to assume the circumstances of the person principally concerned, so she teaches this last in some measure to assume those of the spectators. As they are continually placing themselves in his situation, and thence conceiving emotions similar to what he feels; so he is as constantly placing himself in theirs, and thence conceiving some degree of that coolness about his own fortune, with which he is sensible that they will view it. As they are constantly considering what they themselves would feel, if they actually were the sufferers, so he is constantly led to imagine in what manner he would be affected if he was only one of the spectators of his own situation. As their sympathy makes them look at it in some measure with his eyes, so his sympathy makes him look at it, in some measure, with theirs, especially when in their presence, and acting under their observation: and, as the reflected passion which he thus conceives is much weaker than the original one, it necessarily abates the violence of what he felt before he came into their presence. (23–24)

As if to prove that there is a considerable measure of economics in morality and, conversely, of ethics in economics,[11] Adam Smith's view suggests that the sum total of suffering does not change within an encapsulated situation. Rather, its amount is redistributed: the listener shoulders part of it, relieving the speaker of the onus. As in Bakhtin's pageant without footlights, the boundary between the spectator (listener) and the performer (speaker, sufferer) is permeable: part of the affect moves from the latter to the former. In contrast to carnivalesque affects, while there is an element of interchangeability in this traffic across the borderlines of the self, there is no pooling of emotion, no blending: each subject steps in and out of the other's position in a move to imagine what he or she would feel in the other's footgear.[12]

11. For this observation I am indebted to Michael Benedikt, in conversation.

12. This kind of offering of the self as a container for the suffering of another can actually be more readily described in terms of Lent (see chapter 10).

Such choreographic sympathy is what characterizes Gwendolen's need for Deronda, and it is what has prompted Lisabeth During, for instance, to point to the major problem with this need: in the process of sympathy, part of the individual emotional life, ambitions, goals, loyalties, and beliefs of the sympathetic listener may be erased.[13] When the listener takes over some of the speaker's burden of pain, part of the listener's own personality shrinks. Such a self-mortification can, in principle, be salutary for both sides, but in *Daniel Deronda* the danger of excessive sympathy to its donor is emphasized at least as strongly as its positive effects on its recipient.

The theme of the reduction, cancellation, suppression, surrender of one's own self under the sway of sympathy is given striking expression when Daniel neglects his own studies at Cambridge in order to save Hans Meyrick's; he thus forfeits his own possible alternative vocation, that of mathematician. Incidentally, the choice of mathematics as the subject for which Daniel is gifted has a double effect: mathematics notoriously represents an abstract sphere of intellectual labor that sharply contrasts with the warm-hearted practical commitments that he will undertake at the end of the novel; yet it is also a thematic complement to Klesmer's music as a possible vocation for Gentile or Jew.[14]

Another example of the theme of the self-immolating effect of sympathy is provided by Hans Meyrick himself—in his story of "Bouddha giving himself to a famished tigress to save her and her little ones from starving" (465). Mab Meyrick's response to this parable of supererogation is a utilitarian irony: as a result of such actions, "[t]he world would get full of fat tigers" (466)—if sympathy is not hedged in, its object may end up consuming its source.

Daniel Deronda effects a double *tour de force:* it links sympathy with

13. "The action of sympathy fills up all the empty spaces where a private subjectivity might come to exist. The object enjoying the sympathy is encouraged to think that the sympathizer truly 'lives' in them. And this has the effect of making it very difficult for the dynamic of sympathy to be reciprocal. The more you respond to and indeed uncover my needs, the less likely I am to imagine your life and needs apart from me. In this sense sympathy acts as an incentive to egoism, rather than as its corrective" (During 1998: 77). Moreover, contrary to the common belief that sympathy expands one's world, its immediate effect may be, like that of physical pain, the contraction of the subject's own consciousness—not just of the reflection of this consciousness in the mind of the recipient. Which is not to deny that this askesis may have long-term redemptive effects.

14. William Myers associates Klesmer's vocation with politics, suggesting that, like art and ritual, political, philosophical, and ethical theories "work on the affective life independently of their purely intellectual value" (1971: 115). Unfortunately, Myers's disapproval of George Eliot's belief in the personal human agency in the direction of these forces leads him into untenable statements such as "the central characters, cut off from society, are thereby turned into mere puppets. The conviction that personality determines history has paradoxically deprived George Eliot's major characters of distinctive personalities in their own right" (1971: 121).

the metaphor of anthropophagy and yet exonerates Mordecai Cohen of consuming another human being. Mordecai's terminal tuberculosis generates his desire to extend his life through blending with another, yet on meeting Daniel he does not try to appeal for personal sympathy. Unlike Gwendolen, Mordecai seeks not so much to appropriate Daniel's attention, his self, his life, but to elicit his resonating sympathy with the cause. Insofar as he wishes to erase the boundaries between himself and Daniel through what he misnames "the marriage of our souls," it is not through consuming but through being consumed. He wishes to be internalized by Daniel, in the "blent transmission" (751) of ideas and yearnings—a likely effect of mourning[15] as well as ideological consent. If there is a morbid side to this desire to feed the spirit of another by his own, it is symbolized by his offer that his writings should be published under Daniel's name. It can, of course, be argued that in this craving to blend with another, the wish to be consumed is tantamount to the wish to consume.[16] In the novel, however, the theme of cannibalism is diverted from Mordecai to the mentally sadistic Grandcourt, who is compared to an alligator (157), a stalking predator (412), a lizard (137, 587).[17] Grandcourt becomes a decoy for a motif that might have marred the portrayal of the novel's main exponent of idealistic supererogation.

Whereas the final part of the novel tells the story of Daniel's accepting his new vocation, it also tells the story of his gently resisting the personal demands of Gwendolen and Mordecai alike, since Gwendolen might present an obstacle to his ideological agenda and Mordecai might signify the wrong reason for its pursuit. It is out of conviction born through the questioning of the principles of others while putting his own assumptions at stake, rather than in surrender to an ideologist's charisma or in a Buddha-like compassion, that Daniel chooses his course of action. This is not to deny the role

15. Cf. Borg 2003 for a discussion of mourning in Joyce's *Finnegans Wake* in terms of the concepts of incorporation and introjection developed by Abraham and Torok (1994).

16. See the development of a similar theme in Montaigne's "On Cannibals" (1958: 105–19). On cannibalism and the carnival (in the early representations of Native American communities), see Klarer 1999.

17. This figurative language actually conflicts with the psychology of sadism—at least in its Schopenhauerian interpretation (see 1969, I: 364)—that seems to underlie George Eliot's presentation of this phenomenon: the precondition of the perpetrator's sadistic enjoyment is his (misguided, Schopenhauer would say) sense of total separateness between himself and his victim (cf. also McCobb 1985).

of feeling, especially love for Mirah, in Daniel's choices. Though, as noted above, *Daniel Deronda* is not a carnivalesque novel, it shares a key modal feature with the genre of the Socratic dialogues (which Bakhtin regarded as proto-carnivalesque): its protagonist is engaged in ideological maieutics. In most of the episodes where he appears, Daniel is presented as an active and often tone-setting party to charged conversations with exponents of a variety of ethical principles. Unlike Socrates in Plato's dialogues, he seldom seeks to persuade interlocutors; instead, through tactful argument, he attempts to construct his own aims and principles. His ultimate choice of the proto-Zionist course in which generalizable intellectual conclusions blend with his love for a particular woman may be regarded as a refraction of the *ad hominem* twists to which Socrates occasionally takes recourse in the process of philosophical argument.

Mordecai is but one in the series of spokesmen for Daniel's ideological options; the sway of his personality is, emphatically, not the sole reason for Daniel's making this particular choice. George Eliot mildly subverts Mordecai's stature by the end of the novel, in particular in the ethical argument which he holds with Mirah and which pertains to the fine-tuning of the ethical stance of the novel as a whole.

In order to emphasize his point about personal sacrifice ("Burn, burn indiscernibly into that which shall be, which is my love and not me"), Mordecai tells his sister what he believes to be a Midrashic story of "a Jewish maiden who loved a Gentile king so well, that this is what she did:—She entered into prison and changed clothes with the woman who was beloved by the king, that she might deliver that woman from death by dying in her stead, and leave the king to be happy in his love which was not for her" (735). For Mordecai, this is "the surpassing love, that loses self in the object of love," but Mirah sees it not as a case of supererogation but as one of psychological egoism: the Jewish maiden "wanted the king when she was dead to know what she had done, and feel that she was better than the other. It was her strong self, wanting to conquer, that made her die." She goes on to argue that the maiden "must have had jealousy in her heart, and she wanted somehow to have the first place in the king's mind. That is what she would die for."[18] Mordecai has nothing but an unfair *ad hominem* argument against this position:

> "My sister, thou hast read too many plays, where the writers delight in
> showing the human passions as in dwelling demons, unmixed with the

18. On Kantian supererogation and the place of uncommon virtue in the Aristotelian view of character, see the dialogue between Baron 1987 and Sherman 1988.

relenting and devout elements of the soul. Thou judgest by the plays, and not by thy own heart, which is like our mother's."

Mirah made no answer. (735)

Mirah's tactful silence in response to her brother's patronizing rejoinder[19] is, under the influence of his allusion to her heart, all too easily read as referring to the nature of her jealous love for Daniel. This is another decoy, since at issue is not Mirah's but Mordecai's supererogation. By presenting the self-sacrificing Jewish maiden as a kind of Henry Jamesian Milly Theale, who succeeds, after her death, in taking precedence over Kate Croy in Densher's heart (or else as the case of Dickens's Carton translated into a version of psychological egoism), Mirah demystifies Mordecai's idealistic exegesis. Her undermining of the parable of supererogation may send the reader back to the remarks on St. Theresa of Avila in the Prelude of George Eliot's *Middlemarch,* where the traditional concerns of the Spanish lady are presented as "light fuel" to a brilliant girl, whereas a demanding spiritual or ideological cause is expected to provide a more sustaining nourishment: "Her flame quickly burned up that light fuel; and, fed from within, soared after some illimitable satisfaction, some object which would never justify weariness, which would reconcile self-despair with the rapturous consciousness of life beyond self" (1977: xiii). The figurative language, the metaphors of consuming and being consumed that align Dorothea Brook of *Middlemarch* as an avatar of St. Theresa with the prophet of Zionism in *Daniel Deronda,* pit the belief in supererogation against skepticism about the motives for self-sacrifice—as possibly originating in the pursuit of exalted or triumphant states of the soul.

This hesitation about the moral credit of idealism if fuelled by personal *need* is consistent with the novel's cautious bracketing of the transgression of boundaries between the self and the other or the self and the larger whole. As I have been trying to show, carnivalesque narratives generally tend to explore and develop the higher view of human possibility, a nonutilitarian ethics of a predominantly deontological kind, which posits human capacity for totally disinterested action, idealistic self-sacrifice, and a yearning for good for its own sake while also recognizing the profundity of the evil of which a human

19. As this episode strongly suggests, Mordecai is not the spokesman for the author. Though Edward Said critiques Mordecai's formulation of his Zionist vision as if it reflected George Eliot's own mental patterns (1980: 62–66), the fact that at the end of the novel Daniel embarks on a mission of fact-finding rather than immediate implementation of Mordecai's thoughts confirms the distance between the implied author of the novel and its ideologist character. For an important critical processing of Said's views see also Henry 2002: 113–23.

being is capable. By contrast, the non-carnivalesque narratives lean towards utilitarian ethics and the Aristotelian golden mean, towards skepticism about altruistic service of ideals yet also towards a denial of the existence of radical evil, towards a moderate pitch of legitimate ethical expectations. The uneasy modal affiliation of *Daniel Deronda,* a non-carnivalesque narrative that provides a testing ground for different forms of the carnivalesque blurring of boundaries, especially in its treatment of the issues of vocation or of sympathy, is associated with a hesitancy in the novel's ultimately middle-ground moral vision. Narratives in which the carnivalesque flights and lapses of the human spirit are present in a limited or selective way often tend to negotiate the relationship between utilitarian and deontological criteria for attributing moral credit. Whereas the plots of both *Middlemarch* and *Daniel Deronda* trace possibilities of the convergence of individual integrity and self-interest, sacrifices made to personal integrity in these novels do not coincide with supererogatory impulses. Yet the novel's caution about idealistic supererogation is not characterized by an Aristotelian preference for the middle way in the practice of virtue. Rather, it stages a dialectics between a commitment to future-oriented social goals and emotionally alert sympathy for individual human beings. The here-and-now workings of sympathy may impede the service of those goals and, if unhedged, may produce an alternative form of Buddha-like supererogation for the sake of fat tigers. In its absence, however (as is amply demonstrated in Dostoevsky's novels, especially *The Possessed*), supererogation threatens to transform into nihilism (cf. Wolf 1982).[20]

In *Daniel Deronda,* despite the rationalist individualism suggested by the balance between the agenda of self-perfection and that of service to causes outside the self, idealistic supererogation is nevertheless not devoid of glamour. Boundaries of the self are repeatedly transcended or transgressed— eventually to be redrawn, but redrawn in order to be opened up again—for a sympathetic seepage of affect in interpersonal relationships and for an exchange of creative energy between the self and a larger whole. The types of cultural remission evoked in *Daniel Deronda* (as in most of George Eliot's novels) emerge not so much as pauses in self-perpetuating deterministic regularity but as new lines of development, best appreciated with the benefit of hindsight.

---

20. The issue of nihilism as involving the service of a vision of the future at the expense of emotional response to one's human environment in the present is analyzed in Tzachi Zamir's 2000 essay on *Macbeth.*

In terms of legitimating an ethical ideology alternative to the dominant system of values, *Daniel Deronda* is more radically oppositional than Austen's *Mansfield Park* or *Persuasion*, yet the cultural remission that it may represent for its mainstream audience is still circumscribed. The novel creates a path towards liberal irony: the readers are assisted in entering the minds and conditions of the people who make ideological choices different from their own. The resulting tolerant sympathy for the politics and ethics of another highlights the contingency of one's own ideological stance without necessarily proposing to alter this stance. The textual conditions for allowing the reader this freedom of commitment lie in the comparatively low degree of resonating sympathy with the main characters: the element of vicarious experience in the reader response to the Deronda plotline (in contrast to the Gwendolen plotline) tends to be of the cognitive, ethical, intellectual, rather than of the emotional, kind.

The response of the reader is also affected by the recurrent staging of redistributive sympathy: by "sharing" their suffering with others Mirah or Gwendolen or Mrs. Davilow actually transfer a part of it to their listeners. Redistributive sympathy cannot be simulated by the reader in relation to a fictional character; it can take effect only in an actual deictic situation. We cannot alleviate the suffering of the fictional character by reading about it any more than we can prevent the murder of Desdemona or the drowning of Melville's *Pequod.* Yet on reading about the acute unattested individual suffering caused by social injustice or political atrocity we often respond to the sense of our own helplessness by an extratextual political commitment: generations of Russian revolutionaries grew up on the diet of literary refractions of brutal social oppression. Conversely, the topos of deathbed comfort—dying Jo sheltered by Dr. Woodcourt's semireligious care in Dickens's *Bleak House,* Pip attending on the dying Magwitch in *Great Expectations* and Abel Whittle on Henchard in Hardy's *The Mayor of Casterbridge,* the heroine's father and aunt coming home to die surrounded by sympathetic friends in Gaskell's *Mary Barton*—stages the redistributive sympathy that can mitigate the effect of the characters' pain. In contrast, for instance, to the solitary death of Jude in Hardy's *Jude the Obscure* or the unwitnessed murders of K. in Kafka's *The Trial* or of Winston Smith in Orwell's *Nineteen Eighty Four,* this topos (at times debased to a sentimental convention[21]) suggests that the given social order is not irredeemable. It may also be noted that in such episodes of redistributive sympathy it is usually the surviving

---

21. This convention is not to be confused with the topos of the dying person's last words, whose ethical phenomenology is usually of a totally different kind.

carer rather than the dying sufferer who attracts the participative emotion of the reader. Both the latter effects are brilliantly yet disturbingly explored in Kazuo Ishiguro's *Never Let Me Go*.

The subliminal ethical effects of narrative form can, of course, be trumped by special sensitivities. For great numbers of Jewish readers, who have been responding resonantly to Mordecai's sympathy for diaspora Jews in the context of their own life experience, the novel has been a prophesy and a call to Zionist action. Yet this virtual interpretive community was not George Eliot's target audience.

CHAPTER SEVEN

Carnival Reversals

Thomas Hardy's *The Mayor of Casterbridge*

[H]e could actually feel between them the insuperable barrier of that very strength which could handle alone a log which would have taken any two other men to handle, of the blood and bones and flesh too strong, invincible for life, having learned at least once with his own eyes how tough . . . not a young man's bones and flesh perhaps but the will of that bone and flesh to remain alive, actually was.

—Faulkner, "Pantaloon in Black" (1960 [1940]): 111

WHEREAS GEORGE ELIOT'S *DANIEL DERONDA* can be regarded as intermediate between the carnivalesque and the non-carnivalesque modes because it is dominated by only one of the two main carnivalesque topoi— that of permeable boundaries between the self and the other, Thomas Hardy's *The Mayor of Casterbridge* displays both the morphology of horizontal osmosis, with its attendant hesitations, and that of the radical reversals of vertical hierarchies. The latter topos is, however, preponderant in the plot of Hardy's novel.

The carnival intensities of *The Mayor of Casterbridge* are rooted in the portrayal of the protagonist, Michael Henchard; in less energetic forms they also unfold in the world around him. Unlike *Daniel Deronda*, this novel prominently includes carnivalesque occasions in the *substance* of its content. Yet the versions of the carnival that figure in its social setting are presented as worn-out, diminished, bitter, or corrupt: the substance and the form of the content intersect in the recurrence of this feature. The first episode, for instance, takes place at a country fair that has reached a sad stage of deterioration (5, 15)—not only because it is drawing to an end and is first seen in the evening but also because fairs such as this, cyclic business-and-festive carnivalesque occasions, are losing in the competition with the weekly market in towns like Casterbridge. The novel depicts the period when the process of domesticating, taming, and officially endorsing potentially disruptive Dionysian remissions reached an advanced state owing to the spread of new business procedures, especially in agriculture. At the time represented in the novel, the carnival has become an intrinsic part of a market town's regular life:[1] its *agôn* and cross-class shoulder-rubbing have been transferred to the *carrefour* of the market, its *ilinx* and choric intoxication confined to the weekly Sunday-afternoon half-pint in The Three Mariners, and its transgressiveness taken over, on a perpetual basis, by the appropriately named Mixen Lane (194–96).

The Mayor of Casterbridge starts with a carnivalesque version of *in medias res:* the first major drama of Henchard's life, his falling in love with Susan, is in the past (J. Hillis Miller 1970: 102), and there is already a sense of "stale familiarity" (4) in his attitude to her, enhanced by the family's weariness as they are walking into the fairgrounds. It is not the first time that Henchard indulges in loud drunken fantasies about the sale of his wife: the tendency has been swelling and has reached the point of crisis. This crisis is, indeed, played out in the furmity tent, conflating a pagan refutation of Christian marriage with a mercantile replacement of personal relationships by a business deal (cf. Bruce Johnson 1983: 76–83). The tenuousness of threadbare man-made structures—whether a marriage or a tent—is placed in contrast with the endurance of basic natural patterns, such as the loving intimacy of horses huddling together at the fair (11).

As has been noted (see J. Hillis Miller 1970: 96–102; Tandon 2003), *The Mayor of Casterbridge* is pointedly concerned with the submerged continuity of the past in the present. Traces of the carnival survive in the world of the novel—in its hierarchy reversals, unsolicited confessions, the residue of the local *corrida* that nearly maims Lucetta and Elizabeth-Jane, and the skimmington ride (213–14) that leads to Lucetta's death. These corrupt excesses are followed by Lent (Henchard's self-starvation in exile), likewise corrupt because not limited in time.

---

1. Cf. Stallybrass and White's 1986 discussion of carnivalesque transgression as a constant endemic part of culture rather than cyclically recurring license.

Against such relics of the carnival in the general sociocultural setting, the novel stages a number of striking cases of peripeteia. Its misrule is of the topsy-turvy kind; its crownings and uncrownings take the shape of the making and loss of fortunes and prestige characteristic of the early period of market economy. The characters' rolling up and sliding down the wheel of fortune, typical of Hardy's novels in general, is here thematized most systematically: "'Tis turn and turn about, isn't it! . . . Up and down! I'm used to it," says Henchard to Farfrae, for whom this is "the way o' the warrld" (173). From the homeless hay-trusser Henchard has moved on to become a rich merchant and Mayor of the town, eventually to fall from grace, go bankrupt, turn into a buffoon (on the occasion of Prince Albert's visit), lose every hope of family affection, and die in solitude and destitution. His wife Susan's position moves from that of a desired woman in the remoter fictional past to a burdensome chattel in the novel's first episode, from a beloved companion to a deserted single parent, and then up again from a poor relative to the Mayor's wife. The fortunes of Elizabeth-Jane, Lucetta, and Farfrae likewise fluctuate throughout the novel, almost like stock prices on the Exchange. Different rural professions lend their poetics to the Hardy novels set against them: in *The Mayor of Casterbridge* the corn and hay trade of the period prior to the 1848 repeal of the Corn Laws is largely responsible not only for the novel's sociohistorical setting but also for the symbolism of its internal topography.

In keeping with the incidence of carnivalesque episodes in the plot, the topography of the novel is dominated by open spaces—the fairgrounds, the market square, the Heath, and the Ring in which transgressive privacy combines with agoraphobia—and liminal spaces, such as the bridge, the inn, the yard, the doorway, a door disguised by wallpaper. The shifts of perspective in these two kinds of *mise-en-scène* suggest a restrained interpenetration. It is on the virtual threshold of the transgressive furmity tent that we first see Newson; on his second appearance he crosses the town's threshold river with the help of a removable plank; it is from the threshold of the King's Arms that we first see Henchard when Susan comes to seek him in Casterbridge. A stone bridge is the setting for Henchard's aborted suicide. Thin partitions allow for theatrical eavesdropping scenes that enhance the motif of communication gone awry. This motif also includes uncalled-for confessional outpourings (Henchard's to Farfrae, Lucetta's to Elizabeth-Jane), the recidivistic suppression of needful information (whether about the quality of merchandise or about people's identity and fate), and the characters' "selective deafness and blindness," their denial of "headroom" to each other's messages (Adamson 1991: 56).

The heart of the town of Casterbridge is its *agora,* the market square, in which people from various walks of life come into close contact, engage in exchanges, and provide entertainment for themselves and others. Lucetta and Elizabeth-Jane watch this arena from a doubly liminal space, an upstairs window of a house facing this square. The participants and the spectators seldom merge but can sometimes exchange places: after watching a heart-breaking scene of the imminent parting of a laboring couple, Farfrae walks down into the market and, admiringly observed by Lucetta, hires the man who would otherwise have been separated from his sweetheart. Lucetta and Elizabeth-Jane are themselves, metaphorically speaking, in the marriage market while they are watching the literal market from the window. During the "skimmity ride" Lucetta suddenly—and fatally—realizes that from her secure place in the audience she has been pushed into the center of the show.[2]

Carnival settings come in pairs and threesomes in the novel, with a licensed carnival usually shaded by a darker counterpart. The photonegative of the institutionalized market square of Casterbridge is the Roman amphitheatre, with its memories of bloody spectacles: surreptitious meetings for shady deals take place on these spacious yet detached and haunted grounds. However, a spectacle of cruelty makes inroads into the town square, which is complete with a bull stake—the place where bulls used to be baited with dogs in order to increase their blood circulation and thus soften their flesh before they are slaughtered—a fit allegory on the larger-than-life Henchard being "baited by little people" (Paul Turner 1998: 98; cf. Showalter 1979 on Henchard's "unmanning").[3] As entertainment, the market square vies with the competing playgrounds set up by Henchard and Farfrae during a festival. At the Weydon-Prior's fair a licensed vendor of alcoholic drinks has its rival in the smuggler's furmity tent, the one that draws Henchard into its "maelstrom depths" (6). Finally, the stately procession down the main streets during the royal visit (temporarily disrupted by Henchard's carnivalesque intrusion), is shadowed by the skimmity ride (an "inn-joke," cf. Longstaffe 1998: 21) that exhibits the effigies of Henchard and Lucetta.

Whereas in *Daniel Deronda* the reversal of fortunes is an auxiliary motif, a catalyst rather than a consequence of psychological developments, in *The Mayor of Casterbridge* it is the motif of the horizontal transgression of boundaries that is relegated from the foreplane to the background. The topography

2. The carnivalesque elements, including the public or open-air setting of most of the pivotal scenes in the novel, are also discussed in Michael Valdez Moses 2000: 175ff.

3. On critical discussions of the motif of the bull in relation to Henchard see Daleski 1997: 199n10.

of this background is a storehouse of carnival semiotics. Though Caster-bridge has no suburbs (21, 70) and is separated from the countryside by the remains of an ancient moat and earthwork fortifications, it is invaded by field butterflies and dust, and, as a market town, hosts and traffics in stocks of agricultural implements and produce. Its boundaries are also crossed in the other direction—the citizens occasionally descend into the surround-ing villages to help with the harvest. Inside, the carnivalesque tendency of "individual unrestraint as to boundaries" (46) is held, but only just, in check. Doors and windows are open (46), making the ground floor transparent from the street to the back gardens, but one usually enters Henchard's house by a tunnel-like passage leading to the yard; the entrance to the hospitable Three Mariner's Inn is through a narrow dark passage; the front door of Peter's Finger Inn is usually bolted, and one enters through a slit in a side wall.[4] In the daytime, shopkeepers' wares encroach on the sidewalks outside the shops, to the unhappiness of constables. The motif of expansion also involves the dough that is made from Henchard's grown wheat and that overflows the ovens and swells the consumers' stomachs (cf. Garson 2000: 87). The dinner at the King's Arms, where the hecklers from behind the thin partition reproach Henchard for his "unprincipled bread" (24), is presented as Henchard's Austerlitz (103), a Pyrrhic victory of Napoleonic overreach-ing—and perhaps a Napoleonic disrespect for the lives, or in this case, the health, of the multitudes: instead of retracting the bad grain and absorbing the loss, as principle would require, Henchard brazens it out in public while desperately seeking help in private. In a dogged fight for his own dignity, Henchard tramples the dignity of others, "meddling with yer eternal soul and all that," as Abel Whittle explains to Elizabeth-Jane (170). No wonder the laborers prefer the better informed and civilized Farfrae as an employer even if it means longer hours and smaller wages.

Images and motifs tend to acquire a life of their own in Hardy's narra-tives. In *The Mayor of Casterbridge* the carnival morphology seems to have drawn out and domesticated a small repertoire of appropriate motifs, for example, public entertainment with or without a small fee (81), Elizabeth whirling vertiginously in a dance with Farfrae, a vicious mask on the back wall of High Place Hall (108–9). The topos of anthropophagy creeps in through Christopher Coney's digging up of the pennies that had covered Susan Henchard's eyes and spending them on drink—the townspeople regard this as "a cannibal deed" (92), and Solomon Longways, who defends

---

4. As Marjorie Garson notes, on the basis of such imagery as well as the catalogue of flowers next to Casterbridge houses, the town is "eroticized" (2000: 84).

Coney, is moved to collocate the reference to this act with the "resurrection-ist" digging-up of corpses for sale to anatomists. The motif of dismember-ment is likewise brought in by a member of the choric townspeople, who, confusing the ancient Romans with the Roman Catholic James II, tells Far-frae that "Casterbridge is a old, hoary place o' wickedness. . . . [W]e rebelled againt the King one or two hundred years ago, in the time of the Romans, and . . . lots of us was hanged on Gallows Hill, and quartered, and our dif-ferent jints sent about the country like butcher's meat" (40): the execution for high treason is turned into a *sparagmos*.

The Euripedean motif of dismemberment, the destruction of the whole-ness and discreteness of bodily identity suggested by the latter utterance, also characterizes the tension between the conscious motives and the sub-conscious drives of the protagonist, Michael Henchard. The motivation of this "Man of Character," as he is called in the novel's subtitle, is associated with his peripeteia; the unconscious drives with his uncanny attraction to the lodestone rock of identity-erasure. The former are a prominent feature of his life story, and the main core of the novel's plot. The latter—the tense dialectics of self-fashioning and self-erasure, building up of a power-ful self and the impulse to surrender its discreteness—are a hermeneutic challenge. The contradictions by which Henchard is riven have been inter-preted in a variety of ways—for example, as a conflict between the desire to achieve eminence and the desire to love, seen as stronger than the need to be loved (Gatrell 2000; Rivinus 1992); as the syndrome of alcohol depen-dence (a "commonplace and tragic malady of the human spirit," Rivinus 249) temporarily replaced by an addiction to work; or as a clash between career and ethical commitments (Moses 2000). But the contrasting phases of Henchard's characters can also be read as oscillations between the life drive and the death drive—in keeping with the full title of the novel, *The Life and Death of the Mayor of Casterbridge*. Within the conceptual structure of carnival topoi, the death drive signifies an individual's unrestrained sur-render of the *principium individuationis,* an unchecked release of one's hold on one's own separate self.

A larger-than-life personality impatient with middle-ground compro-mise, Henchard is presented as liable to extreme self-abnegation. Though strong, healthy, imposing, and well versed in country things, he harbors a version of the "universal wish not to live" (Hardy 1981: 411), which he tends to misperceive as anger at himself or others.[5] A less mysterious (because temporary) form of this death wish is displaced onto his estranged wife, Susan, whose response when on arriving to Casterbridge she sees him in his new splendor is "I want to go, pass away" (26). After Susan's death, during the wake, even the young Elizabeth-Jane thinks of life as "terrestrial constraint" (91). Soon after that point, the motif of reaching out to one's own death shifts back to Henchard and grows in intensity. In the tumult of misery on learning that Elizabeth-Jane is not his daughter, Henchard wends his way, symbolically, to the former site of executions (97); after the skimmington ride he goes to the river with a suicidal purpose and is stopped by the surprise of seeing his effigy in the water: in effigy, at least, he is already dead. On leaving Casterbridge at the end of the novel, Henchard compares himself to Cain, whom none can slay ("I—Cain—go alone as I deserve"; 239). He interprets the deferral of death as Cain's punishment: "folk dying before their time like frosted leaves, though wanted by their families, the country, and the world; while I, an outcast, an encumberer of the ground, wanted by nobody, and despised by all, live on against my will!" (244). The burden of this simile is the wish to die; the author subverts the connotations of fratricide by sending *Abel* Whittle to be at Henchard's side (cf. Raine 1994: 162). Abel, whom Henchard had brutally exposed for oversleeping, is then put in charge of the privacy of Henchard's last sleep.[6]

Henchard's death of self-starvation (which Schopenhauer would call a saint's death[7]), with his last will and testament calling for the obliteration of the communal memory of the self which, over the past twenty-two years, he has been struggling to impose on the social structure around him, is a confluence of penance and fulfillment. A fictional character's mode of punishment

5. Henchard's sense of life has been described as one of "perpetual soreness within" (Raine 1994: 168), a "constitutional" gloom (Moynahan 1956: 121), occasionally palliated by music and compensatory feelings.

6. J. B. Thompson's 2001 analysis of Henchard's forcing Whittle to appear at work without his breeches demonstrates that even in that episode, the balance of our sympathies is tipped in favor of Henchard rather than Farfrae even though the latter comes to Whittle's rescue.

7. A Schopenhauerian saint starves himself to death in order to dissolve his identity as an objectification of the Will (Schopenhauer 1969, I: 352, 380). Though a number of articles and one book-length study (J. Hillis Miller 1970) have been devoted to Hardy's relationship to Schopenhauer, it seems that the issue of the overlap between their systems of value is still not exhausted. The coda of *The Mayor of Casterbridge*, on Elizabeth-Jane's learning "that happiness was but an occasional episode in a general drama of pain" (256; cf. also 43), has a clearly Schopenhauerian ring, whereas the Manichean coda of Schopenhauer's *The World as Will and Representation* would probably have resonated with Hardy's own sense of existence on what his Tess Durbeyfield regards as a "blighted" star (Hardy 1991: 21).

may often be seen not as a weak deterrent but as a deep-seated motive for his transgressions: King Lear might have, secretly from himself, wished to be closed up from the world with Cordelia, and for a moment before the end he may have found "a way to have what he has wanted from the beginning" (Cavell 1987: 69); Coleridge's Ancient Mariner might have sought the radical solitude that becomes his Nemesis (cf. Cavell 1988: 56–65).

Even Henchard's loves may be seen not as expressions of the life drive but as forms of a partial self-surrender alternative to death. His affair with Lucetta in Jersey began during "one of those gloomy fits" when, he says to Farfrae, "the world seems to have the blackness of hell, and, like Job, I could curse the day that gave me birth" (60). His need for love is diagnosed in an ambiguous vocabulary: "He was the kind of man for whom some human object for pouring out his heat upon—were it emotive or were it choleric—was almost a necessity" (95): "human object" here connotes his tendency to treat a human being as property, the pronoun "some" suggesting that such "objects" are interchangeable; the phrase "pouring out" (like Keats's nightingale "pouring out its soul abroad") trails in the topos of surrendering the discreteness of the self. Since absence of familial bonds—the bonds that he himself periodically shakes off—gives him a sense of "an emotional void" within (113; cf. Daleski 1997: 116), beloved "human objects" may seem to be instrumental in filling that void. But that would mean a consolidation of the self rather than its surrender. Henchard's loves are not of this constructive companionate kind.

Rather, they may be described as relics of the Manicheanism that in older times had gained expression in courtly love. Henchard's is a gnostical temperament unaided by Manichean beliefs. His inner void lurks where the gnostic's sense of an inner spark, a fragment of a transcendent spiritual realm, could have been—but he tends to displace this spark onto others and then jealously seek it again—in brother or wife or daughter: at the end of his life it is Elizabeth-Jane, who "in the midst of his gloom" seems to him "as a pin-point of light" (220). His passion needs distance and denial in order to last because it replaces, and replicates, a reaching-out to a realm beyond the self.[8] He displaces his own inner beacon onto other human beings and loses interest in them as soon as they prove unable to sustain it. The blow that Elizabeth-Jane deals him by venting her resentment of him at her wedding

---

8. This is not to deny other interpretations of Henchard's self-defeat: he may, indeed, be seen also as a misogynist, a latent homosexual, an after-ripple of the "Wild Man" incapable of humble adulation (cf. Bernheimer 1952: 121), or a single-minded capitalist climber. By itself, however, none of these readings suffices for the sense of the tragic grandeur that is accorded to this character in the novel.

is not analyzed in the narrative; one may read it as caused by, among other things, the transformation of another icon into a small-souled accuser who scapegoats him for all the deceits among which she has lived her life. Thus Henchard's last idol may be shattered. At this point, however, the narrative focus shifts to Elizabeth-Jane,[9] and her belated remorse prevents us from reenacting this revulsion.

Whereas for Henchard close personal relationships link up with the death drive, his rags-to-riches power drive emerges as a version of the life drive—in twentieth-century novels of career this distribution of significance will be reversed. Henchard's stint of prideful vitality demands practical self-realization in socioeconomic activity; his commercial success crowns his attempts to be "separate, unbeholden, emotionally and economically autonomous" (Adamson 1991: 53), socially and sexually independent.[10] This agenda is eventually deenergized by the opposite pull, the lodestone rock of resentful and jealous emotional dependence. His worldly success begins soon after he takes an oath to abstain from alcohol for twenty-one years after he sells his wife.[11] The success is thus an epiphenomenon of this self-imposed sobriety, that is, of his suppression of his own self-destructing Dionysian flow; yet he seems to perceive this self-refashioning as penance for which his rise in the world is a bonus palliative.[12] His triumphs cease, not when he starts drinking again, but earlier—when he recoils from his love for Farfrae. His passions subvert the constructive channeling of his energy. His economic downfall begins with his starting to make business decisions not for reasonable profit but in order to underbid Farfrae, who has become his competitor.

---

9. Jane Adamson notes that the indefinite articles in the novel's subtitle, "A Story of a Man of Character," suggest the "unfinality of the narrative itself, its status as a story about a man of character about whom different stories might be told" (1991: 57). This effect is also achieved by the absence of inside views that would specify the composition of Henchard's attitudes at various points in the novel, especially when he leaves Casterbridge at the end. Adamson analyzes the vast variety of metaphors through which Henchard is represented as one of the measures against "mind-shutting" on the reader's part—that is, against a flaw in the cultural attitudes similar to a flaw that endangers interpersonal communication in the world of the novel.

10. H. M. Daleski sees in Henchard a masculine version of "the Diana complex" (1997: 111) that keeps some of Hardy's heroines, such as Batsheva Everdene of *Far from the Madding Crowd* or Sue Bridehead of *Jude the Obscure,* struggling against the threat of losing autonomy and self-enclosure, a threat, implicit in sexual union, of the permeability of the boundaries of the self.

11. Hardy's copy for this oath as well as for the sale of the wife came from news items in the *Dorset County Chronicle* (see Paul Turner 1998: 92); attributing both these acts to the same agent may have been a challenge for the construction of overdetermined psychological causality.

12. But see Lance St John Butler 1994: 108–15 for the place of the doctrine of compensation in Hardy's worldview.

The reading of Henchard's passions in terms reminiscent of Sidney Carton's Manichean self-immolation (see chapter 5) can gain support from his name, which is strikingly different from the plain-folk names in the novel, such as Grower or Newson. He seems to be one of the characters who exemplify Hardy's belief that submerged among the English rural lower classes are descendants of old upper-class families, such as the aristocratic D'Urbervilles, whose name, a combination of the Latin and French roots meaning "town," is symbolically countrified in Durbey*field,* the name assumed by Tess's great-grandfather. The very sound of the name "Henchard" suggests that the origins of the protagonist of *The Mayor of Casterbridge* go back to the Norman side of the Battle of Hastings; an ancestor of his would have been rewarded with a landholding that could have slipped out of the hands of ensuing generations, leaving young Michael Henchard in the predicament of a parish-supported apprentice (64).[13] The combination of Henchard's name and distinguished Roman profile with his position as a job-seeking hay-trusser at the beginning of the novel hints at a reversal of hierarchies before the main action of the novel has even started. The contrasting connotations of a drop of poison (antiar) in his last name and of the angelic valor in his first name (Michael) suggest a tragic conflict of values and drives. Even his heathen divorce is not merely an echo of old rural ways; it is a reductive replica of annulments of dynastic/mercantile marriages that would have been widely practiced by his upper-class ancestors, usually under the pretext of incestuous bonds. Susan, indeed, is more of a sister than a wife to Henchard. She is presented as an uneducated countrywoman, yet one of "true cultivation" (8) that seems to be somehow mysteriously innate and that prepares the reader for her daughter Elizabeth's conscious agenda of self-perfection. If Susan appealed to the humanely peaceable part of Henchard's self, also represented by his brother who died at an early age and who at one point seems to be reincarnated in Farfrae, then her and Farfrae's simultaneous arrival in Casterbridge effects a double return of the repressed.

A further paradox lies in the feudal coloring of Henchard's capitalist business dealings, his forceful, outwardly ruthless, rule-of-thumb procedures with employer-employee relationships based, as it were, on expectations of loyal vassalage.[14] Farfrae, on the other hand, represents the rise of the peace-

13. Joe Fisher's (2000: 135ff.) associating Henchard's image with motifs that would make up the medieval "Wild Man" may get further support from this reading in view of the belief that the status of that grotesque figure used to be imagined not in terms of "a gradual ascent from the brute, but by a descent" (Bernheimer 1952: 8).

14. At the top of his power Henchard, indeed, exhibits most forms of behavior characteristic of what Veblen sees as the predatory upper class, claiming not only the labor but also the leisure of his dependents.

able lower-middle-class forces in the civilizing process that seeks to create new meritocratic hierarchies.[15] Farfrae is quintessentially a middle-way moral agent, satisfied with building his fortune—and his happiness—on "small profits frequently repeated" (122). Elizabeth-Jane exemplifies a more feminine spiritualized form of the same ethical ideology when she discovers the secret "of making limited opportunities endurable" by "cunning enlargement, by a species of microscopic treatment, of those minute forms of satisfaction that offer themselves to everybody not in positive pain" (255). Like George Eliot, Hardy sees his contemporary society as unfavorable breeding grounds for heroic grandeur. His novels present the splendor sought by the discrete individual self as a doomed atavistic relic, a self-defeating aesthetic self-fashioning at great cost. The sober utilitarian attitude to moral practice is in his novels a more assured way to survival, but though his evolutionary meliorism thus valorizes the extra effort needed for adaptation to the changing conditions, such an effort invariably emerges as diminishing a character's moral stature and flattening his or her aesthetic appeal. The vertical axis of Hardy's carnivalesque is associated with the rise of an extraordinary personality, inexorably followed by decline and fall. Such personalities (Tess, Eustacia, Henchard, Jude) are not harbingers, not premature specimens of the spiritual future of humanity; on the contrary, they are the belated blossoming of old-time private heroica in which the moral supererogations of the feudal past have been translated into an aestheticized integrity. If in George Eliot's fiction cultural remissions can be seen as incipient strands of development, in Hardy's novels they tend to be represented as brief and belated flare-ups of energies that have run down.

In the worlds that Hardy conjures up, the petty, well-regulated, quotidian social ethos is victorious and in no need of artistic redemption. In a sense, Hardy prefigures the late-twentieth-century shift from admiration of the heroism of self-sacrifice to the valorization of survival, everyday care, and endurance. What he does not rise up to is the challenge of finding the perspective that would grant ordinary sociality its own active aesthetic appeal.

⸺

The struggle between the life and the death drives in Henchard's character are an instance of the carnivalesque seesaw reversal in the novel's thematic

---

15. With reference to Derrida's notion of writing as *pharmakon*, medicine and oblivion-inducing poison in one (1981 [1968]), Earl Ingersoll (1990) links Farfrae's modern business practices, complete with notes and accurate ledgers, to the tendency of personal and cultural forgetfulness, whereas Henchard's obsolete oral business practices emerge as a lingering cultural memory.

structure. A case can be made for a causal relationship between the rise and fall of his fortunes and the victories and defeats of the energies that maintain the discreteness of his identity. It seems, however, that the relationship between the oscillation of the order and anarchy in his character and the deployment of the carnival topoi in the novel's setting are a matter of congruence rather than of cause.

An insight into this congruence of the syntactics of motifs in the setting, plot, and character psychology can be gained from Jorge Luis Borges's essay "Narrative Art and Magic" (1972). Borges considers mechanical causality and psychoanalytic determinism unsatisfactory aesthetic principles in the construction of the narrative plot; instead, he suggests that narrative details are linked to each other by magic. Here "magic," as noted above, is not a metaphor for aesthetic charm, a "grace beyond the reach of art," but a literal reference to sympathetic magic of the kind discussed in Frazer's *The Golden Bough:* like attracts like—and though *post hoc* is not *propter hoc,* Eustacia Vye in Hardy's *The Return of the Native* dies after an ill-wisher pierces her doll-effigy with a pin. It is therefore not the experience of a character that dictates the choice of images, but the life of the image that may determine the character's fate: Tess's murder of Alec at the end of *Tess of the d'Urbervilles* may seem to be as much a development of the motif of red on white (Alec's blood on the whitewash) as it is a consequence of her emotional turmoil;[16] Henchard's self-starvation likewise puts a finishing touch to the dialectics of the magma of immanent will and the *principium individuationis* that underlies the carnivalesque strands of the novel's motifs. Demystified, this statement may lead us back to the thematic model of character construction (Phelan 1987; see also p. 108 above). Reversed, it may also lead us to redescribe sympathetic magic (along with its relics in our quotidian pet superstitions) as the workings of the aesthetic impulse in the patterning of human life.

16. Cf. Hardy's journal entry for June 3, 1882: "As, in looking at a carpet, by following one colour a certain pattern is suggested, by following another colour, another; so in life the seer should watch that pattern among general things which his idiosyncrasy moves him to observe, and describe that alone. This is, quite accurately, a going to Nature; yet the result is no mere photograph, but purely the product of the writer's own mind" (F. E. Hardy 1928: 198).

CHAPTER EIGHT

Morphology of the Test

Non-Contact Measurement of Self in Conrad's "The Secret Sharer"

> In this breathless pause at the threshold of a long passage we seemed to be measuring our fitness for a long and arduous enterprise, the appointed task of both our existences to be carried out, far from all human eyes.
>
> —Conrad, "The Secret Sharer," 180

WHEREAS A LARGELY CARNIVALESQUE WORK such as Hardy's *The Mayor of Casterbridge* can stage interpersonal communication gone awry, Conrad's corpus—most of it belonging, like Austen's novels, to the non-carnivalesque mode—contains a novella, "The Secret Sharer,"[1] whose action isolates, names, and dramatizes (and whose title may provide a generic name for) a non-carnivalesque yet no less profound human communication.

"Secret sharing" is self-recognition in another, a nonparticipative actual or virtual reenactment of another person's experience, during which, in contrast to carnivalesque fusion, individual identities remain separate and affects are not pooled. This phenomenon crystallizes primarily in literary discourse, though in ways that can reach back into extratextual reality.

---

1. In an early version, published in 1910 in *Harper's Monthly Magazine*, the title of the novella was "The Secret-Sharer," with the hyphen, which weighted the reading of the syntactic ambiguity in the direction of "sharing a secret" rather than having a secret double (see also Dazey 1986). It is usually very important what changes the authors make for the more definitive editions: Conrad seems to have opted to tip the scales of ambiguity in favor of the motif of the double.

There is some overlap between narratives—or episodes—of "secret sharing" and carnivalesque narratives. It consists in the sense of an extraordinary span of time, dominated by an unusual kind of human relationship. However, these narratives stage a non-carnivalesque restraint: the characters refrain from merging with the environment. Resisting the lure of osmosis, they struggle for self-possession as well as for definiteness and separateness of identity.

The protagonist of Conrad's novella discovers—or imagines—an unexpected affinity or "mysterious communication" (185) with a stranger who crosses his path. At the outset, the protagonist, a young, newly appointed captain of an English ship in the Gulf of Siam, feels alien to his ship and crew as well as "somewhat of a stranger to [him]self" (181). After a real stranger comes aboard, the captain turns him, whether by projection or introjection,[2] into a mirror of his own self—"It was, in the night, as though I had been faced by my own reflection in the depths of a somber and immense mirror" (186). Without touching that reflected image, he seeks in it a recognition of the veiled aspects or potentialities of his own self: to borrow the language of Wolfgang Iser (1993: 281–303), this *secret sharer* helps to make "the self present to itself." In the end, as the dramatic encounter is concluded, the captain gains self-assurance and a sense of the "perfect communion of a seaman with his first command" (217).

Whereas a multitude of narratives merely *include* stories of missed contacts with accidentally encountered striking individuals, unexpected and unaccountably profound relationships, flashes of reciprocal understanding between totally different personalities—Waverley and MacIvor in Walter Scott's *Waverley*, Louisa and Sissy in *Hard Times*, Pierre Bezukhov and Platon Karateyev in Tolstoy's *War and Peace*, Margaret Schlegel and Mrs. Wilcox in E. M. Forster's *Howard's End*, Timofey and Victor in Nabokov's *Pnin*—Conrad's story is *wholly devoted* to such an issue and explores the borderline experience in its purest form. Its shipboard setting isolates a segment of reality and purges it of the complications of the lee shore, thus creating laboratory conditions for an experiment in non-contact measurement of self.

As noted above, the story time in which the secret sharing is played out is usually short—a matter of a few days, one long conversation, or several extraordinary encounters amidst the quotidian wear and tear. The encounters

2. A paradigm of possible psychoanalytic readings of the story is presented, somewhat ironically, in Johnson and Garber 1987. See also Wexler 1991.

are so densely fraught with meaning that in retrospect they may seem to occupy a greater number of memory cells than years of regular "untempted" (183) life. This phenomenon is reflected in various blow-up techniques in the texture of the narrative, mainly a slow dramatic "showing" that contrasts with the surrounding narrative compression.

Whereas the circumscribed character of the liminal time span is reminiscent of the carnivalesque version of the unity of time in narratives of crisis, Conrad seems to have resented and resisted carnivalesque impulses. "The Secret Sharer," like most of his tales, dramatizes the situation of the test[3] rather than that of the crisis. As noted in chapter 1, one of the main structural features of the narratives of crisis is the *refus de commencement,* which consists in the absence of specific events accountable for triggering the action: the action starts when a certain tendency that has long been fermenting finally swells to a breaking point. In test situations, by contrast, the protagonist has to face trials for which he is not ripe; the action is triggered by an unexpected and largely random occurrence (the sudden appearance of Leggatt, as though from the depths of the sea, in "The Secret Sharer") without which the familiar routine of the protagonist's life might have remained undisturbed.

Yet the randomness of the trigger is relative. In Conrad's fiction, *the unexpected event that brings the protagonist to face his major test is usually produced by the growth and the culmination of a crisis situation elsewhere.* It is not by accident that Leggatt has killed a rebellious sailor on his own ship, the *Sephora.* In telling his story to the protagonist, Leggatt mentions the "simmering" wickedness of his victim throughout his, Leggatt's, service on that ship. The sailor's maliciousness reached a violent boiling point during a long storm—significantly, not at the outbreak of the storm but after the storm had been raging for several days. Like the protagonist, Leggatt had been but recently appointed chief mate of the *Sephora* and was still a stranger to his ship. Like the protagonist, he had also been involved in an agonistic relationship with a father figure, the elderly red-whiskered captain Archbold, the chiasmic counterpart of the protagonist's chief mate (see Johnson and Garber 1987: 632–35). Leggatt's aggression (he admits "boiling" with rage at Archbold, 203) may have been transferred from the captain to the disgruntled sailor; the protagonist's suppressed hostility has likewise been directed not so much at the intimidating chief mate as at the young second mate, whom he suspects of being a "sneering" (180) clandestine frondeur.

3. For a detailed discussion of the test-of-character plot in "The Secret Sharer" see Ressler 1984.

Yet the orchestrated circumstances of the murder may be but a surface expression of Leggatt's inner crisis of self-possession.[4] Leggatt, whose name evokes associations with "messenger" and who almost becomes an uncanny harbinger of blight in the protagonist's career, is the protagonist's scout into the ripening of a crisis to which he himself is liable: "He appealed to me as if our experiences had been as identical as our clothes. . . . I saw it all going on as though I were myself inside that other sleeping-suit" (187). The onstage test is thus triggered by an offstage crisis, and the protagonist's success in the test cuts short his inchoate movement towards a crisis of a similar kind.

Whereas the narrative of the "secret sharing" usually involves a test situation, not every story of the test of character is also one of "secret sharing." The pattern of one person's crisis leading to another person's test (and perhaps, vaccinationlike, preempting a similar crisis), does not, for instance, apply to Conrad's "Typhoon." Yet "Typhoon" has stronger carnivalesque elements than "The Secret Sharer": here the test is less like that of a litmus-paper revelation of the hidden ingredients of the character and more like a situation in which it is up to one's will and action to determine which ingredients of one's character, and hence fate, will become dominant. This kind of test, in contrast to the one in "The Secret Sharer," bears a closer affinity to a rite-of-passage crisis: indeed, in "Typhoon" it is young Jukes's tendency to submit to a poorly restrained imagination that is brought to a head by a storm.

The main body of a narrative of crisis is usually the exploration of the ways in which the discreteness of individual identity is subverted. By contrast, the main body of "The Secret Sharer" is a story of self-knowledge, and of self-possession achieved at the risk of losing it—in the span of a cultural remission carried up to the brink of disaster. Yet whereas in carnivalesque narratives the self loses its separateness and begins to merge (emotionally, intellectually, or even physically) with its human or natural environment, the experience of the "secret sharing" is more one of reenactment than of participation in the experience of another. Here there is no pooling or blending of different peoples' emotions, anxieties, or hysterias; the self does not *wish* to lose itself even in order to find itself again. Rather, the individual is engaged in a self-study that amounts to specular processing of images.

Though the appearance of Leggatt subverts the captain's illusory confidence in "an elementary moral beauty" of a seaman's "untempted life"

4. H. M. Daleski regards the vivid image of Leggatt's tight ten-minute grip of the sailor's throat as a symbol of "a holding on that is simultaneously a letting go" (1977: 175). Whereas Conrad's works explore the necessity of abandon at crisis moments in order to reassert one's self-possession, the convergence of the two impulses in Leggatt's case is highly ambivalent in moral terms; see ibid., pp. 174–77.

(183), his narrative does not suggest any immediate wish to get Leggatt out of his way: he is not like Razumov, who wishes to get Haldin out of his life in Conrad's *Under Western Eyes*. In "The Secret Sharer," indeed, it is not the protagonist but Captain Archbold of the *Sephora* who shows a "spiritless tenacity" (197) in trying to get Leggatt not only off his ship but also off his hitherto immaculate career record (199). By contrast, the protagonist of "The Secret Sharer" seems to be not unpleasurably spellbound by the presence of his "double" despite the anxiety caused by the need to conceal it from his shipmates. He is drawn to Leggatt like a schoolgirl to an unfinished novel, her homework left undone. Away from Leggatt, he feels that he is in two places at the same time and hastens to return to him as if, among other things, to heal the split. Sharing Leggatt's cultural affiliations and codes (they had gone to the same school), he seems to be fully receptive to his verbalized and implied sentiments—as if he felt that Leggatt's crime was of a kind that, under parallel circumstances, he himself might have been tempted to commit, Leggatt's experience being a virtual phase shift of his own. Like a writer who endows his characters with tendencies consciously or unconsciously suppressed in himself, the protagonist seems to be watching himself in a forking world.

The two men almost never touch each other, except at parting; yet they coordinate their positions in space and often stand in postures that suggest a mirror reflection ("He rested a hand on the end of the skylight to steady himself with. . . . One of my hands, too, rested on the end of the skylight," 188; "we, the two strangers in the ship, faced each other in identical attitudes," 193). Conrad seems to have taken deliberate care to fend off suggestions of a homosexual attraction: the two men talk by the "bed-place" (189) rather than by "the bed."[5] However that may be, their body language is emblematic of the danger of touching one's specular double—one may, like Narcissus, lose one's balance. The double exists, as it were, in a world separated from one's own by a looking-glass pane. Sometimes, however, one of the two worlds begins to leak: the captain's inability to draw the curtains across the bed where Leggatt is lying hints at a breach in the hermetic wholeness of his identity (cf. Guerard 1950: 11).

With the help of the conventions of the first-person narrative, Conrad makes Leggatt's conscious attitude to the relationship with the captain (the protagonist) unavailable to the reader. Leggatt does suggest that having been

---

5. The same vocabulary is used also in "The Shadow-Line," whose material is based on the same period of Conrad's own seafaring career. The verbal choice that impedes the interpretation of the relationship between the Captain and Leggatt as homosexual need not entirely rule out the connotations of homoerotic romance (see Casarino 2002: 218–20)—it may have been called for precisely by the pressure of such connotations.

addressed quietly and in English by the captain was a most welcome relief after weeks of loneliness and hours of solitary swimming (193), but it is not clear whether he recognizes in the captain a secret sharer (as Coleridge's Ancient Mariner recognizes the man to whom he must "teach" his tale) or whether he plainly maneuvers the vulnerable psyche of the officer whom he has a chance to turn into a coconspirator. In any case, other elements in the story suggest that both secret sympathy and unconscious reenactment of affects may exist where least expected. There is, for instance, a weird analogy between the conduct of the steward of the *Sephora* (leaving Leggatt's door unlocked and thus enabling him to escape) and the conduct of the steward of the ship where the action is set. Having noticed "the growing wretchedness" of his steward's expression, the captain attributes it to his hectoring the inoffensive man, exposing him to unpredictable orders and eccentricities (206). But it is quite as probable that the steward may have noticed more than the captain suspects and may have become a tacit sharer of the captain's secret. It is, perhaps, not accidental that when the steward has to hang the captain's drying coat in the bathroom, he does so by merely stretching his hand with the coat through the doorway towards the hook, without looking inside—as if to maintain an alibi. In addition to acting on the impulse of secret sympathy with a man close to himself, whether Leggatt or the captain, each of the stewards may thus, unbeknownst to himself, reenact the experience of his counterpart on the other ship.

The story thus presents a cross-section of types of nonparticipative sharing. The sharing may be conscious and take place in the actual bodily proximity of one's "double": one may recognize in the other one's own latent tendencies, or else one may recognize in the other the latency of the tendencies that have been dramatically actualized in one's own experience—or one may reenact the experience of another without even knowing that the other exists, on the basis of general psychological regularities.

In all the above cases, the reenactment of the experience is not a matter of carnivalesque psychological contagion. Contagion is a participative experience—in the best case one individual is swept along by the ennobling emotion of another; in the worst, he is swept along into the violence of the crowd: the invisible partitions between the individual and the environment are punctured, and the body language literalizes different kinds of tactile connection. The borderline area between "secret sharing" and psychological contagion is the sphere of the influence of *a role model,* a partial embodiment of "that ideal conception of one's own personality every man sets up for himself secretly" (181). Individuals' choices of role models are based on their recognition of shared anthropological or psychological grounds; the effect of the role model may take the shape of self-perfecting emulation or it may become corrupted in the carnivalesque transport of hero worship. In a number of his works, and, in particular, in "Typhoon," Conrad explored the reassuring influence of the role model: the courage of the other boosts one's own spirits not by downplaying the danger but by showing that it is possible to brave it against the odds. Significantly, in "Typhoon" the transmission of one individual's courage and confidence to another takes place through the medium of touch, which in "The Secret Sharer" is held back.

At the end of the story the captain thinks about Leggatt as "a free man, a proud swimmer striking out for a new destiny" (217). This image has been generally interpreted as associated with the captain's liberation of Leggatt from the specular doubling framework by acknowledging his individuality and independence: the freedom of the swimmer is his escape not only from the hand of maritime law but also from the psychological entanglements with the narrator. Yet the narrator's momentary identification with Leggatt at their leave-taking, his imaginative placing of himself in Leggatt's predicament, may be extrapolated to suggest that Leggatt's courage in embracing a new and unknown destiny shows the captain a way out of the careerist paranoia that he reluctantly shares with Archbold. It is a reassuring oppositional thought that there is life after forfeiting one's career—in Austen's *Mansfield Park* and *Persuasion* it is analogously half-suggested that there is life after dropping out of one's class. For a person such as Archbold there is no life beyond his career; his anxiety about his three-decades-long record is certainly justified—yet, having turned into an *idée fixe* it makes him regard Leggatt not as a human being but as a disastrous obstacle to be removed in the legalistically most appropriate way: in that sense Archbold is almost a caricature on Razumov in *Under Western Eyes* (and an antipode of Melville's Captain Vere). By contrast, the protagonist of "The Secret Sharer" does not merely choose to acquit himself in a dilemma by offering Leggatt perfunctory help: he not only manages to help Leggatt leave the ship unobserved but, by moving as close as possible to Leggatt's *faute-de-mieux* destination, the Koh-ring Island, he consciously puts the ship, not to mention his career, at risk. The rise of his confidence in his command as a result of this adventure is analogous to the pattern that H. M. Daleski (1977) traces through most of Conrad's fiction: occasionally one must let go of the object of one's desire in order to retain one's hold on it. The example of Leggatt's courage enables the captain to endanger his command so that he can eventually reassert it. If Leggatt has started by demonstrating to the captain the realized liabilities of their shared tendencies, he ends by enacting an alternative of identity control that can liberate the captain from the petty worries about his authority and success with the main chance that he has prematurely received. We are not told whether henceforth the mates stop doubting his competence or undermining his authority: it is as if, by leaving the informational gap in place, the narrative emphasizes that what matters most is the captain's being freed from his former morbid attentiveness to their gestures, tone, facial expressions, and *sotto voce* remarks—that is, from the pervasive paranoia that haunted him at the outset of the passage, when even the "multitude of celestial bodies staring down at one" marred the comfort of his "quiet communion" with his vessel (180). At the end of the story "the stars ahead" are perceived not as a panopticon but as fixed objects that, by "gliding from right to left," serve as reassuring extra indicators of the changing position of the ship (217).

It likewise remains unknown whether Leggatt loses the captain's hat in the water or leaves it there deliberately to help the captain navigate his ship away from the shore[6] (the visually measurable change of distance between the ship and this single floating object shows the captain, just in time, that the ship has "gathered sternway," 216). Indeed, such a thought occurring to Leggatt could likewise be a matter of lucky chance: it is thus a contingency that lays the ground for the poetic justice of the ending.[7] One could say that the captain is rewarded for his genuine sympathy with the body of the other, a sympathy based on solidarity rather than on a psychological compulsion. On the other hand, he risks the bodily welfare of his whole crew by endangering the ship for the sake of pursuing his idiosyncratic personal goal. It speaks, of course, in his favor that the goal in question is saving a life and not, as in the case of Melville's Ahab, vengeful destruction. The moral complexity of the story is enhanced by the ambivalence of the captain's motives for his unconventionally egalitarian volunteering for a five-hour anchor watch (182) at the outset—this solitary watch, a remission in the functioning of the hierarchies, is what enables Leggatt to board the ship in secret: the captain's undertaking that watch may have stemmed from a considerate attitude to the crew members fatigued by the embarkation or else from an apologetic sense of insecurity.

The measure of the carnivalesque or non-carnivalesque elements in a text may be taken on the basis of the dominant text-play.[8] As noted above, the

---

6. Cf. Facknitz 1987: 123: "[Leggatt] takes the money to placate the captain; whether he intends to leave the hat in the water remains one of the principal invigorating mysteries of the story."

7. See also Daleski 1977: 183.

8. See pp. 15–16.

type of play dominant in the experience of the characters may or may not coincide with the type of play in which the rhetoric of the text involves the implied reader.

The deadly serious game-type that dominates the experience of the protagonist-narrator of "The Secret Sharer" is *alea*, or fate as dice. It is not on merit, through fair agonistic emulation, but owing to an *aleatic* constellation of special circumstances ("in consequence of certain events of no particular significance, except to myself," 180[9]) that the captain has got his command. Leggatt, a Conway graduate like himself, had got his position on the *Sephora* not strictly on merit but through connections; that is, through the *alea* of hereditary social membership. The convergence of the twain off a Far Eastern shore is a statistical miracle. But the main feature of the *aleatic* spirit in the substance of the story's content lies in the captain's striking passivity on Leggatt's arrival. Like Mr. Dick in Dickens's *David Copperfield*, he immediately sees that the newcomer must be clothed and sheltered, but, unlike Betsy Trotwood in the same predicament, he never asks "What shall we do with the boy?"—he makes no plans for Leggatt's future. "[I]t is only the young who are ever confronted by such clear issues," he ironically comments on Leggatt's early definition of alternatives as either coming on board or swimming till he sinks, just before retrospectively admitting that at the time of the events he was young himself (185). It is only a few days later, when Leggatt himself gauges the situation and asks to be marooned, that the captain takes responsibility for the course of events.

It is at this point that the element of the *agôn* begins to take the upper hand in his experience. Contrary to *alea*, which involves a relegation of responsibility (and initiative) to others, *agôn* is a deliberate contest of skill, strength, or prowess, a competition in which one seeks to assert one's control over self and circumstance. So long as the captain merely makes the kind of effort necessary to keep Leggatt concealed, his rising to minor emergencies, such as the steward's walking into his cabin at an unexpected time, are self-protective aleatic responses to unforeseen contingencies. Had the captain agreed to let Leggatt leave the ship in just any location, his conduct would have continued this aleatic pattern. However, at this point, the captain takes over the initiative. To Leggatt's request to be marooned he responds by a supererogatory effort of bringing the ship close to the shore, entering, in the process, into a struggle not only against natural perils but also against the resistance of the officers of his crew. Whereas the emergence of a test situation is an aleatic event, the transition from *alea* to *agôn* is a necessary condition for a successful passing of the test.

9. A variation on such a sequence of events is developed in Conrad's "The Shadow-Line."

Elements of the other two kinds of play distinguished by Caillois (1961), *mimicry* and *ilinx,* are only marginally present in the captain's experience. His identification with Leggatt, to the extent of regarding him as his double, is a corrupted form of mimesis—corrupted because occurring not as make-believe. The only touch of purely make-believe mimicry in the captain's experience is his consciously imagining himself in Leggatt's physical predicament and therefore giving him his hat: the captain's one truly redeeming, spontaneous yet responsible action thus comes as a result of a ludic move—pointing to one of the areas in which the borderline between ludic and practical imagination is erased. By contrast, the aleatic submission to Leggatt's spell and to the overwhelming spell of his own fantasy of having a double leads the captain to the edge of madness: not only does his behavior towards the crew become eccentric to the point of insanity, but for one moment he is even ready to believe that his "double" is invisible to other people and literally haunts only himself (207).[10] Here he is close to intellectual vertigo, a corrupted form of Caillois's *ilinx.* The test of the captain's character involves such critical moments, when the discreteness of psychic identity almost gives way.

Whereas in the captain's experience a subdued element of *ilinx* combines with *alea,* Leggatt's experience on the *Sephora* involves the combination of the vertigo, actually caused by the storm, with agonistic engagements—the storm, Archbold, and the rebellious sailor, all at once. Caillois notes that *agôn* and *ilinx* are incompatible in the process of the game (1961: 72–73); apparently, however, the two can converge, all too dangerously, in the corruptions of the game, that is, under circumstances when the corresponding relationships are played out in earnest or under constraint. Braving storms at sea is mastery of a vertigo similar to that of mountain climbing and parachuting, but in the seaman's life it is an inevitable occupational hazard rather than a desired play. (The name of the unimaginative, prosaic, and highly professional captain in Conrad's "Typhoon," McWhirr, includes a truncated whirlwind.) *Ilinx* may have been dominant in the *Sephora* episode, where Leggatt's insane violence to the sailor stemmed from his treatment of the latter as a complication in his struggle for the mastery of the vertiginous chaos in which the ship and the sailors were caught. In "Typhoon" such a struggle is played out in the foreplane; in "The Secret Sharer" it is relegated to the fictional past.

The dominant games in which "The Secret Sharer" involves the reader are *alea* and *mimicry.* Whereas in *A Tale of Two Cities* the aleatic ingredient in

10. "The captain gives [Leggatt] a sleeping-suit like his own, proper clothing for one who must live as in a dream" (Guerard 1950: 11).

the reader's experience is enhanced by suspense and by astonishing reversals, in "The Secret Sharer" it is mainly associated with the narrative's avoidance of creating concrete expectations. None of the events are anticipated; at the beginning there is only a general sense that something extraordinary is going to happen. The twists of the plot, such as Leggatt's appearance, his addressing the captain in Standard English, the steward's near-discovery of Leggatt in the captain's cabin, and the floating of the hat, come to us as surprises— but surprises that do not conflict with any previously formed impressions. The narrative technique that accounts for this *aleatic* deactivization of the reader consists in the textual proximity of cause and effect: for instance, it is immediately after the captain notices that the rope ladder had been left hanging over the board of the ship that he also becomes aware of someone holding onto that ladder—the reader has too little time to form conscious expectations concerning the ladder before such potential expectations are realized.[11] Likewise, the narrative does not mention the captain's wet coat left on the deck separately from the scene in which the steward is seen carrying that coat into the captain's cabin: Conrad, as it were, does not subscribe to Chekhov's principle that the gun that hangs on the wall in the first act will shoot in the third—in "The Secret Sharer" the gun, metaphorically speaking, is noticed only a second before it shoots. The only exceptions from this regularity are an early reference to the *Sephora* spotted in the distance, the reference to the captain's being a stranger on his ship, and the character sketches of the captain's two mates. These details are, however, tantamount to the setting of the territory on which the game of chance is to be played out.

The *aleatic* nature of the reader's experience is a reenactment of the captain's own submission to the force of outside events. Yet, likewise reenacting the experience of the captain, we may find ourselves caught up in a sort of *mimicry,* namely identification with a character and a vicarious participation in his experience rather than parallel reenactment of it.[12] Not only do

11. A page and a half earlier, on the nocturnal watch the captain perceives his ship as "very roomy for her size, and very inviting" (182); yet at that point the reader has no way of perceiving the "invitation" as extended to anyone but the captain himself.

12. Cf. Caillois: "For nonparticipants, every *agôn* is a spectacle. Only it is a spectacle which, to be valid, excludes simulation. Great sports events are nevertheless special occasions for *mimicry,* but it must be recalled that the simulation is now transferred from the participants to the audience. It is not the athletes who mimic, but the spectators. Identification with the champion in itself constitutes *mimicry* related to that of the reader with the hero of the novel and that of the moviegoer with the film star. . . . The audience are not content to encourage the efforts of the athletes or horses of their choice merely by voice and gesture. A physical contagion leads them to assume the position of the men or animals in order to help them, just as the bowler is known to unconsciously incline his body in the direction that he would like the bowling ball to take at the end of its course" (1961: 22). Callois's latter remarks pertain, indirectly, to vicarious experience in the reading of narrative.

we share the captain's surprise at discovering Leggatt but, like the captain, we may find ourselves sympathizing with Leggatt as the first-person direct-speech narrator of his escape from the *Sephora*. The reader generally tends to identify with a character engaged in a difficult and risky project or pursuing a far-off goal; this tendency to feel concern for the protagonist's success is so strong that it may lead to a temporary disregard of the nature of the goal and sundry attendant circumstances—witness *Moby Dick, Lolita, Bonnie and Clyde*. And it is only towards the end of the story that a similar vicarious desire for success is elicited by the captain himself, when he manipulates his ship and crew in order to improve Leggatt's chances of reaching the shore. Here, however, in the framework of utilitarian calculations his conduct is so problematic that, with some readers at least, mimetic response may yield to agonistic doubts as to the reliability of the narrator's perspective. The reader's identification with the protagonist is restrained, mainly by the constant sense of the difference between the tangled knot of the retrospective narrator's often ineffable attitudes and the incremental linearity of the reader's ludic cognition. Moreover, the multiple ambiguities of the narrative and the gap between Archbold's and Leggatt's versions of the events[13] (which of them, for instance, could take the credit for saving the *Sephora* by setting her reefed foresail?—it is one man's word against the other's[14]) are eventually bound to provoke the reader's agonistic challenging of the protagonist-narrator's version of the events of his story. Significantly, a number of commentators have questioned the narrator's reliability, as if having liberated themselves from the sway of his ethical confidence and from the spell of sympathetic identification.

Roger Caillois regards the reader's identification with a character and, implicitly, a vicarious living of the character's life as an instance of *mimicry*. Yet vicarious experience may also have the marks of vertigo. It is in the case of this type of experience that the footlights of the pageant disappear and the boundaries of intellectual identity are blurred. Insofar as the reading of fiction is a ludic activity, the reader's vertiginous surrender to the spell of the yarn is associated with a combination of *alea* and intense *mimicry*. Conrad's narratives do not encourage intense identification with the characters; their audience actually tends to reenact that resistance to *ilinx* which is a recurrent feature of his fictional worlds: those characters of Conrad's who give in to

---

13. In "If Everything Else Fails, Read the Instructions" (Toker 1994/1995), I insisted on the difference between informational gaps as a narratological concept and the epistemological gaps crucial for Wolfgang Iser's approach to reader response (see also Harrison 1993/1994). Yet in the case of the first-person narrative stance of "The Secret Sharer," the two kinds of gaps practically coincide.

14. This point is forcefully argued by Michael Murphy (1986).

the whirlwind of drives and suffer the consequences (Jim, Kurz, Almayer) are outnumbered by those who resist self-surrender and those who, at moments of crisis, are incapable of letting go (Axel Heyst in *Victory* or Charles Gould and Gian' Battista in *Nostromo*). In *Under Western Eyes,* the possibility of an emotional abandon, of an ecstatic confession, of a brotherhood of souls with Haldin is contemplated by Razumov at one point but then eclipsed by the illusive prospect of the "secret sharing" with Prince K. In "The Secret Sharer" the captain may receive Leggatt's confessions (if this is what his narratives are) but he reciprocates them only with the most relevant factual informa-tion about himself (193), the confessional element being reserved, in both senses of the word, for the reader. The secret sharing remains a non-contact reenactment of the actual or virtual experience of another, on a larger or a smaller scale. It is a similar kind of secret sharing that characterizes the implied reader's nonvicarious reenactment of the captain's experience—the reader's passage from *alea* (with a small and sporadic stint of *mimicry*) to interpretive *agôn,* maintaining an emotional detachment from the experi-ence of the characters and engaged in its intellectual processing.

Emotional detachment, however, does not preclude the kind of sympathy for the protagonist, and even for his criminal double, that can itself be described as oppositional "secret sharing"—the metadescriptive connotation of the novella's title extends to the experience of the target audience. The story was written at the period of an ideological crisis, which led to the spread of particularist ethics, a nominalism that voided abstract notions—such as patriotism, naval discipline, or party fidelity—of their meaning when they conflicted with the responsiveness to the human Other. Conrad's fiction, especially his *Lord Jim* and *Under Western Eyes,* is oppositional in the sense of placing particularist personal relationships above the demands of rigid social frameworks—the law, the codes, the social contracts. The failings of a variety of Conrad's protagonists are usually caused by their betrayal of human beings by their side, whether for the sake of abstract ideas or, rather, for the sake of misguided personal interests or desires. In "The Secret Sharer" the response to the other clashes not only with the protagonist's personal career-oriented prudence but also with obedience to the general and naval laws. The captain's cabin, in which the fugitive is harbored, is turned, liter-ally, into room for oppositional maneuvering. The reader's sympathy for this maneuvering is, strictly speaking, a cultural remission, privileging the protagonist's unorthodox choices over the legal regulations of an officer's conduct. As a part of the reader's experience, the "secret sharing" emerges as an exploration of that facet of the reader's self that endorses the character's transgressiveness, in opposition to the hegemonic system of norms. In a sense, however, "The Secret Sharer" is not an optimal example of oppositionality, since, at the time of its composition (1910), the official conduct regulations that the protagonist subverts were already perceived as obsolete. Oppositional particularism was well on the way to becoming a mainstream principle in intellectual circles—the transgressiveness of the protagonist's ethical experiment may well be regarded not as a prophetic anticipation of counterhegemonic shifts but as a species of conformism to nonconformism, toeing an already emergent ethical line.

CHAPTER NINE

Carnivalization

Throwaways in Joyce's *Ulysses*

> Loud, heap miseries upon us yet entwine our arts with laughters low.
>
> —Joyce, *Finnegans Wake*, 259

A GREAT WORK OF LITERARY ART may have the power to impose new determinacies while subverting old ones; it can disseminate a counterculture just as works that toe the line of the dominant ideology may disseminate official culture. Elsewhere (Toker 2000: 158) I have argued that the multiple contradictions in Varlam Shalamov's stories, especially contradictions between narrative commentary and plot situations, allow the author to eschew this authority-predicament, to state his opinions as a free individual, and yet to keep from imposing them on the reader. In *Ulysses* Joyce accomplishes a similar feat on a grand scale, by systematic self-carnivalization.

Some errors, or error look-alikes, in great works are destined to remain uncorrected. It may have been on July 14, 1798, that William Wordsworth and his sister Dorothy stood on the spot he remembered a few miles above Tintern Abbey—not on July 13, as the subtitle of the poem records (Johnston 1983: 13[1]). The symbolic ambergris that spreads an exquisite odor amidst the stench of a whale's carcass in *Moby Dick* is actually an odorless substance used in the traditional perfume industry as a fixative. "Come in" in

---

1. The issue is, of course, complicated by the fact that the Bastille Day was not yet celebrated in 1798.

Finnegans Wake was Joyce's response to the knock on the door, which Samuel Beckett faithfully wrote down as part of the novel's text that the master was dictating; Joyce later decided not to remove the intrusion of this extratextual contingency (Ellmann 1983: 662). In the wrapping-stuff of the butcher's shop in Joyce's *Ulysses*, Leopold Bloom reads a note about a model farm on Lake Kinnereth, advertised by a planters' company, "Agendath Netaim." The Hebrew is inaccurate—it should have been "Ag*u*dath Netaim"—but, if we believe Stephen Dedalus, a genius does not make mistakes: "his errors are volitional and are the portals of discovery" (255). "Agendath" is a play on "agenda": indeed, both Stephen Dedalus and Leopold Bloom have different but complementary *agenda,* unspoken in the novel but quite distinctly described in a book whose French original Joyce acquired in 1913, the year before he began work on *Ulysses*—Bergson's *Creative Evolution* (see Gillespie 1983: 46; Ellmann 1983: 779n30).[2] The Bergsonian subtext may help define the two types of creativity represented by the novel's two male protagonists—and also exemplify the kind of liberating carnivalization that serious philosophical thought tends to undergo in *Ulysses.* Joyce's cultural remission means not only asserting his freedom from literary conventions (by, among other things, turning the adultery topos upside down in *Ulysses* and "A Painful Case" or reversing the seduction plot in "Eveline") but also preventing his own philosophical vision from gelling into a "great, useful, and uncommon Doctrine" (Fielding 1995: XII, 8: 422) that might end up turning into a new convention, a new automatic-pilot habit of thought.

The fourth episode of *Ulysses,* the so-called "Calypso," opens with a carnivalesque fleshpots-of-Egypt reprise of the milk-and-honey breakfast scene of "Telemachus":

> Mr Leopold Bloom ate with relish the inner organs of beasts and fowls. He liked thick giblet soup, nutty gizzards, a stuffed roast heart, liver slices fried with crustcrumbs, fried hencod's roes. Most of all he liked grilled mutton kidneys which gave to his palate a fine tang of faintly scented urine. (65)

The scene also carnivalizes the Lenten intake referred to in the first paragraph of episode 3, "Proteus": "Ineluctable modality of the visible: at least

---

2. It is not clear whether this book, among others bought the same year, was paid for in full—typical of the everyday carnivalesque of Joyce's unsettled life.

that if no more, thought through my eyes" (45).[3] It would be too neat to say that Stephen, the artist, processes sense impression, literary reminiscences, and philosophical thought, while Bloom, *homme moyen sensuel,* processes scientific, practical, and emotional realities. The difference between them lies not so much in the kind of materials marshaled as in the *division of labor* in confronting the flow of reality.

It is this division of labor that can be defined in terms of Bergson's *élan vital,* the vital impetus, which is the main subject of *L'Évolution creatrice.*[4] In this book (*Creative Evolution*) Bergson describes life, whose origin, for him, is consciousness, or "supra-consciousness" (1944: 284), as "a movement" in the direction opposite to that of materiality.[5] Indeed, "materiality is the inverse movement, . . . the matter which forms a world being an undivided flux, and undivided also the life that runs through it, cutting out in it living beings all along its track. Of these two currents the second runs counter to the first, but the first obtains, all the same, something from the second. There results between them a *modus vivendi,* which is organization" (272). The idea of the "undivided" flux of life is balanced by the thought about the scission that takes place in that flux: the stream branches when it meets obstacles produced by the counterflux of matter. But then it confronts matter not only up front but also laterally, recuperating (in a version of osmosis) parts of life from flowing towards oblivion.

It is the task of the artist to engage the flow of reality up front, to cut into the unknown so as to create—that is, in the language of *A Portrait of the Artist,* "to encounter for the millionth time the reality of experience and to forge in the smithy of [his] soul the uncreated conscience of [his] race" (1960: 253). It is the province of the average sensual human being to pick up the debris cast off in the process and to reabsorb them into discourse, collective memory, moral-intellectual life. The latter process of salvaging throwaway fragments of the main line of progress is what may be called "economy," which, in the Gilbert schema (see Gilbert 1952: 41), is the "Art" of the "Calypso" episode.

3. In the third paragraph of *Creative Evolution,* Bergson, a kindred soul, refers to the deceptive stability of visual perception as one of the earliest examples of constant variation of states of consciousness (4).

4. Most commentators on Joyce's affinities with Bergson concentrate on other works by the philosopher, such as *Time and Free Will, Matter and Memory,* and "Laughter"; recently, however, John S. Rickart (1989: 33) noted the analogy between Bergson's *élan vital* (which makes its way into *Finnegans Wake* in the guise of "Elanio Vitale"—*FW* 221.22), and Aristotle's *entelechy* on which Stephen bases his view of identity.

5. "[T]he *élan vital* at every instant separates into two movements, one of relaxation (*détente*) that descends into matter, the other of tension that ascends into duration" (Deleuze 1991: 95). On Joyce's place in the history of ideas between Bergson on the one hand and Deleuze and Derrida on the other, see Borg 2007.

Part of this "Art" of economy is economics: Bloom thinks about the price of the goods he consumes,[6] his daughter's salary, the honorarium for the prize essay, and the real estate value of the businesses he passes on the way. His does not like to let things go to waste: the blood-soaked wrapping paper of his breakfast kidney goes not into the trash bin but to his cat; the diet includes both choice cuts and those "inner organs of beasts and fowls" that would be discarded in many a kitchen: in addition to the kidney of "Calypso" and the steak-and-liver that he dines on in "Sirens," it also includes giblets and gizzards, and the crubeen and pig's feet that end up going to a hungry dog in "Circe." Yet the main agenda of his economy is that of reassembling items—lost, cut away, passed by—back into consciousness: imperfectly remembered Bouvard-and-Pecuchet-style bits and pieces of high school curriculum, media information, music, personal memories, residue of emotions, and carnivalesque desires mixed with sober knowledge of the world. In addition to returning the fragments of material life into the life of emotion and memory, toilet-paper-less Bloom also makes practical use of discredited literary production, the prize story (85)—one example of the way in which, throughout *Ulysses,* any attempt to conceptualize the novel's material is subjected to parody and profanation, whether by Mulligan or by the book itself:[7] if everything that rises must converge, it must also be carnivalized.[8] "Laughters low" (*FW* 259) help us to rise above the miseries heaped upon us and lighten the intellectual armor we devise against them.[9]

6. Even his bowel movement is thought of as "costive one tabloid of cascara sagrada," 84; where "costive" ("constipated") plays on the "cost" of the physic.

7. One of the central theses of Robert Bell's *Jocoserious Joyce* (1991) is that Mulligan recedes from the narrative of *Ulysses* at the point where the novel itself undertakes his carnivalizing role. For some of the earlier comments on elements of carnival in *Ulysses* see Ivanov 1976: 27; Lodge 1982; and Parrinder 1984: 16.

8. Robert Klawitter discusses the relationship between Joyce and Bergson as that of friendly parody—not Joyce's parody of Bergson but as Joyce's "parodic representation of unreality as Bergson describes it, a parody of the inevitable unreality of the human world." Klawitter tends to ascribe to Bergson a vision of a radical gap rather than a flowing continuity between verbal art and human reality: "reality for Bergson is always falsified by representation" (435)—a case could, however, be made for seeing in Bergson's philosophy a Moebius-strip continuum in which language and reality flow into each other. When Bergson writes that language renders merely the impersonal or interpersonal aspect of sentiments, he may actually be understood as presenting a challenge to which Joyce responds by exploring—and exploding—the deautomatizing effects of counterconventional use of all the aspects of language: phonetics (and acoustics), morphology, semantics, lexis, and syntax.

9. The relevance of Bergson's essay "Laughter" to Joyce's work has been much commented upon, often with more justice to Joyce than to Bergson. William T. Noon writes, for instance, that "Joyce would have been prepared to concede to Bergson that comedy is an appeal to the intelligence, and to the social intelligence at that, but he would not have agreed with Bergson that you must therefore anaesthetize your heart in order to laugh" (1957: 87). The causal relationship in Bergson's view is, rather, the reverse; laughter, called out by the conjoining of the mechanical and the living, is a cause rather than the effect of a (temporary) anesthetizing of the heart.

The above difference between Stephen's and Bloom's labors is no exception from this rule of carnivalization. Nor is it tidily polarized. Bloom's lateral reabsorption of experience is not alien to Stephen; Stephen's forward thrust of creative energy is not alien to Bloom. Indeed, Stephen also processes and reshapes odd scraps of academic disciplines and extracurricular literary and philosophical data. Yet warmth and conscious care for this lateral flow are lacking in the first three episodes, those about Stephen's morning. The contact with Bloom, an unlikely spiritual father, can well be expected to let this principle of care rub off on the younger man, to bring the need for it from Stephen's subconscious to his consciousness. Stephen's stormy search for new horizons in forging the conscience of his race must also prominently involve the acceptance of the rejected.

Here a gap between Bergson's thought and his figurative language is bridged by Joyce—as if the novelist were trying on a philosopher's thought, finding it narrow in some places and worn in others, loosening the seams, repairing the ruptures, and adding motley at the fringes.[10] The problem with figurative language is this: for Bergson, the vital impetus is *not* the "march of the mind"; and yet it is for the march of the intellect that the semantics of the forward thrust is used. The evolving human consciousness, writes Bergson, "not only abandoned cumbersome baggage on the way; it has also had to give up valuable goods" (1944: 291). These "goods," the debris, include intuition. And yet it is intuition, creative intuition, that runs *with* the vital impetus,[11] whereas intellect adapts itself to the flow of matter: "intuition goes in the very direction of life, intellect goes in the inverse direction, and this finds itself naturally in accordance with the movement of matter. A complete and perfect humanity would be that in which these two forms of conscious activity should attain their full development" (291). At the beginning of the novel Stephen distributes the roles of intellect and intuition in a different way. He seems to be waiting for his intellect rather than intuition to forge his creativity—Bergson would have recommended reserving the intellect mainly for processing the by-products of the creative process.

10. Wyndham Lewis's essay on Joyce in *Time and the Western Man* (1957) suggests that Joyce's adaptation of Bergson's worldview was all too wholesale; cf. Klein 1994: 2. This is one of Lewis's multiple misrepresentations.

11. It must be noted that Deleuze's reading of Bergson denies the distinction between intuition and rigorous philosophical thinking: "Intuition is neither a feeling, an inspiration, nor a disorderly sympathy, but a fully developed method, one of the most fully developed methods in philosophy" (1991: 13).

The much-expected meeting between Stephen and Bloom in *Ulysses* may enact the mutual complementation in this as in other senses. Indeed, June 16, 1904, contains ample material for a full-fledged *Künstlerroman*. At the break of that day, Stephen Dedalus is rather sterile as an artist. He does not yet seem to have produced anything apart from brief epiphanies. The leitmotifs of Stephen and Bloom form a chiasmus: if in "Telemachus" we are introduced to an artist who does not—*so far*—seem to achieve creative self-transcendence, in "Calypso" we meet an ordinary sensual man who *no longer* procreates, failing to transcend his psychological arrest: for a decade since the death of his infant son, Bloom has not had full sexual intercourse with his wife and is wasting his potential for procreation and true human intimacy on autoerotic pleasures. However, both Stephen and Bloom seem to be getting ready to make a move towards overcoming the impasse, each by adopting some of the agenda of the other.

In both the episodes, breaking the nocturnal fast is symbolically promising. According to Bergson, creative evolution involves two stages: "(1) a gradual accumulation of energy (through food, actual or metaphoric), and (2) an elastic canalization of this energy in variable and indeterminable directions, at the end of which are free acts" (278). Food, a mandatory constituent of the carnival, is treated ambivalently in *Ulysses:* the carnivorous Bloom is disgusted by the uncouth gluttony at Burton's and will not flow with the novel's turbid stream of alcohol, whereas Steven, who has gone without dinner for several days, combines a temporary Lenten vegetarianism with carnivalesque Bacchanalian excess.

The intake of literal food in "Telemachus" and of spiritual nourishment in "Proteus" ("thought through my eyes") is, indeed, followed by the composition of a poem in the latter episode. At this point we are not told what it is that, writing-paper-less, Stephen scribbles on the torn-off blank end ("My tablets," 60) of Deasy's letter to the newspaper. What we are given is the mental process that leads to the composition of the quatrain while Stephen is looking at the sea and at a vagrant woman on the shore:

> She trudges, schlepps, trains, drags, trascines her load. A tide westering, moondrawn, in her wake. Tides, myriadislanded, within her, blood not mine, *oinopa ponton,* a winedark sea. Behold the handmaid of the moon. In sleep the wet sign calls her hour, bids her rise. Bridebed, childbed, bed of death, ghostcandled. *Omnis caro ad te veniet.* He comes, pale vampire, through storm his eyes, his bat sails bloodying the sea, mouth to her mouth's kiss.
>
> Here. Put a pin in that chap, will you? My tablets. Mouth to her kiss. No. Must be two of em. Glue 'em well. Mouth to her mouth's kiss. (60)

The last sentence is an allusion to the last stanza of "My Grief on the Sea," a poem translated from the Irish by Douglas Hyde (1860–1949) in his *Love Songs of Connacht* (McCarthy 2007: 3763).[12] Hyde's stanza runs as follows:

And my love came behind me—
He came from the South;
His breast to my bosom,
His mouth to my mouth.

A stimulus coming from Hyde is pinned down, like Homer's Proteus, or a collector's butterfly. In Hyde's "lean unlovely English" Stephen appreciates the idea of the reciprocity of love ("Glue 'em well" for a kiss of true love) and the alliteration—"must be two of em"—is a pun on the two cases of the sound m in "His mouth to my mouth."[13] Instead of Hyde's alliterating "b" ("his breast to my bosom"), Stephen's poem plays on the repeated "s" sound, the sibilant of the wind, in tune with the dominant image of the episode in which this poem is finally given us—"Aeolus":

On swift sail flaming
From storm and south
He comes, pale vampire,
Mouth to my mouth. (168)

Stephen's poem departs from Hyde's pre-text almost as a new organism does, by way of scission. Acoustic play is the necessary stimulus in the *actual* division of what has been "potentially manifold" (Bergson 282). In the language of *Creative Evolution,* "a poetic sentiment, which bursts into distinct verses, lines and words, may be said to have already contained this multiplicity of individuated elements, and yet, in fact, it is the materiality of language that creates it" (ibid). The keen attention to the materiality of language is one of the points at which Joyce may have recognized an affinity with Bergson.

Whatever erotic connotations the "mouth" of the last line may carry, it also links up to the motif of the foot-and-mouth disease that Deasy's letter is about—and hence with the motifs of all flesh (*omnis caro*) and the butcher's meat. Incidentally, Bloom will opt for a vegetarian lunch in the next episode

12. Gifford and Seidman (1988: 62) regard Stephen's poem as "a souped-up (Canting Academy)" version of Hyde's.

13. Other aspects of Joyce's reworking of Hyde's poem, in relation to Bram Stoker, Yeats, and Blake, are discussed by Robert Adams Day (1980).

(Davy Byrne's pub, where he has his cheese sandwich, is still one of the most popular Bloomsday destinations).

Thus, in "Proteus" there occurs a sudden discharge of part of the accumulated energy. When later, in "Aeolus," Stephen produces Deasy's letter, Editor Crawford, noticing that a part has been torn off, inquires, "Was he short taken?"—bringing back the memory of the ignominious end of the prize story in Bloom's jakes. The quatrain is presented as Stephen's tacit answer—yes, he, not Deasy, was short-taken, in a different sense.

Yet it is in more than one way that, in "Aeolus," Stephen's credentials as an artist improve. When Crawford challenges Stephen to write a significant work, "something with a bite" (171), Stephen, that "toothless Kinch," rises to the occasion, like the bards of old, with a piece of oral epic: "The Pisgah Sight of Palestine, or the Parable of Plums." The piece, marking a new stage in the *Künstlerroman,* is an exquisite exercise in an artistic recycling, a sort of lateral reabsorption, of his recent observations: the two midwives whom he sees, or imagines, in "Proteus," their diet, their Irishtown language and little ways, Nelson's pillar which he has just passed, the plum stalls beneath it, the parody of the Pisgah sight of Palestine, the promised land inaccessible to Moses (used typologically in a speech quoted earlier in the chapter), and finally the pits of the plums, the seeds, dropped from the top of the pillar onto the paved street—a waste!

The symbolic intake of nourishment that follows this discharge is a drink with the newspapermen in the pub. This is followed by the next episode in the *Künstlerroman*—Stephen's discourse on Shakespeare in the National Library. The rhythm of storing physical energy and discharging it in different genres of discourse continues when Stephen drinks again, this time with medical students in "Oxen of the Sun," where his and Bloom's mental and physical paths reconverge.

This convergence, carnivalized and particularized with due "validational modesty" (Grabes 2007: 160–61), can be read as a literalization of Bergson's treatment of memory as "virtual coexistence" (see Deleuze 1991: 51–72), not necessarily rooted in an individual mind. As early as in *Time and Free Will* Bergson discusses, among other things, the interpenetration of successive states of consciousness (see also Mackey 1999: 125)—an idea that underlies much of the stream-of-consciousness technique and other treatment of recurrent motifs in modernist fiction, including Joyce's own. Joyce takes a further step—he represents the interpenetrating states of consciousness as intersubjective: whereas his protagonists' physical and affective identities remain discrete, the interplay between the motion of their heterogeneous new experience, their conscious memories, and subconscious drives traverses the boundaries of identity. In "Scylla and Charybdis" and "Sirens" Stephen and Bloom, respectively (259 and 362), seem to be thinking, in near-identical vocabulary, about Shakespeare walking in Fetter Lane—though this motif in "Sirens" may read as a musical variation on a sentence from the earlier episode, irrespective of focalization. In fact, however, the latter technique anticipates the conflation, in the "Circe" episode, of the contents of two different subconscious stores of images and motifs—Virag "rubs shoulders with Philip Drunk and Philip Sober" (Daleski 1987: 158), and the rules of focalization are not just subverted but oneirically carnivalized.

> In one sequence, for example, in which Bloom is the focus, Molly appears as "a handsome woman in Turkish constume," . . . with a camel in attendance. When the camel ambles near her "with disgruntled hindquarters," she "slaps his haunch" fiercely, "her goldcurn wristbangles angriling, scolding him in Moorish," and says: "Nebrakada! Femininum!" . . . Molly's word could pass well enough in nighttown, for "Moorish," but they are not only beyond her ken but Bloom's too, for they come out of a book by "the most blessed abbot Peter Salanka," which earlier in the day Stephen has seen on a book-cart and idly paged through, finding in it that a woman's love may be won by saying "the following talisman three times with hands folded: '*Se el yilo nebrakada femininum! Amor me solo! Sanktus! Amen.*'" . . . Bloom himself, in a later sequence with the nymph, seizes her hand and says: "Hoy! Nebrakada!" . . . Similarly, when Stephen falls foul of the English soldiers, Private Carr and Private Compton, at the end of the chapter, he figures as the focus in a sequence in which there appear, among others, the Citizen, who calls for the death "Of the English dogs / That hanged our Irish leaders," and Rumbold, Master Barber, who proceeds to hang the Croppy boy. . . . but it is Bloom who met the Citizen at Barney Kiernan's pub and argued with him, not Stephen; and Rumbold is no more than a name on a letter that is read out aloud when Bloom first enters the pub on the same occasion. (Daleski 1987: 158–59)

Vladimir Nabokov's diagnosis of such conflations is that the Nighttown episode does not present the nightmares of either Stephen or Bloom; rather "the book itself is dreaming" (1980: 350).[14] Perhaps what it sees in its dream

---

14. For Joyce, "thoughts, like matter, are indestructible and persist in some 'repository' out of

is some of Bergson's virtual Whole in which the images of the past and the present coexist across individual subjectivities.

The Bakhtinian "word of another" is, in Joyce's text, a word, a phrase, or a motif with an intersubjective status. Intertextual links are, for instance, not merely text-enriching allusions which often affect our readings of the precursor texts to which they refer—they are also instances of intersubjectivity. In the shared images of "Proteus" and "Aeolus," the processing of canonical motifs (Psalms 65:101, Luke 1:38, Homer, and Shakespeare) intertwines with the friendly pastiche of a contemporary (Hyde) and co-opts other scraps.

Such scraps include the fringe echoes of the vampire lore, realizing its potential to function as a metadescriptive somatic literalization of the carnivalesque metaphor of boundary-crossing. In *Dracula* by Bram Stoker (another Dubliner), the pale, black-clad vampire comes to England by sea from the southeast (from Hungary, Bloom's grandfather's birthplace). His arrival is heralded by a bat, which cruises into Stephen's thoughts just before he composes his poem in "Proteus." The name of Dracula's English victim, Lucy Westenra, may be heard in Stephen's "tide westering"; in her grave, in her sleep, "undead," she will rise to seek her prey. Stoker's female protagonist is, however, another woman, rescued from the pale vampire at the last moment, a woman who gives birth to a boy in the end. Her name is Mina, short for Wilhelmina, which connects her not only with the anthropophagical bar-siren Mina Kennedy but also with Wilhelmina (Mina) Purefoy, who, after three days of painful labor, gives birth in "Oxen of the Sun." The motif of ghouls, vampires, chewers of corpses in *Ulysses* (a thriller version of the Joycean recurrent theme of the Eucharist carnivalized as anthropophagia) connects, in its turn, with the theme of ghosts, another version of the "undead" ("bed of death, ghostcandled"), causes for remorse. Both of these strands of motifs may be shown to have firm conceptual nuclei in the novel and to fade diffusively at the fringes, making the reader wary of overinterpreting ("open your mouth and put your foot in it," 752). What seems important at the present juncture is that, unlike Mark Twain's Huck Finn, who "don't take no stock in dead people" (1994: 12), Joyce's protagonists trail their personal and cultural ghosts, undead, in the flux of their consciousness, effecting an emotional version of prālāyā (389), the reabsorption of the deceased back into creative consciousness (see Gifford and Seidman 1998: 333): "Never know whose thoughts you are chewing" (217)—the thought one is thinking and the sensation one is taking in are not always solely one's own.

---

space and out of time, yet accessible in certain privileged moments to the 'subliminal self'" (Gilbert 1957: 30).

This possibility, dramatized in the appearance of intersubjective motifs in both Bloom's and Stephen's conscious and subconscious registers, is also raised by the reference to Akasic records (182), that is, communal memory not lodged in any individual brain—Bergson, it may be noted, viewed the individual brain not as a repository of memories but as an obstacle, a sieve that filters data to protect the ego (cf. Mackey 1999: 139).

The distribution of labor between "Oxen of the Sun" (episode 14) and "Circe" (episode 15) is similar to that between "Blephen" and "Stoom" (798). "Oxen of the Sun" stages the motif of development, progress, gestation, birth—the many forms of the forward thrust of the vital impetus. In the background, after three days of labor, Mina Purefoy is giving birth to a son; in the foreground, the reveling of the medical students who host Bloom and Stephen is presented in a pastiche of English prose styles, starting with the semblance of modern English translation of medieval Latin texts, through the alliterative Anglo-Saxon discourse ("Before born babe bliss had" 502), through Renaissance, Eighteenth-century, Victorian and Edwardian prose, the whole divided into movements that enact the nine months of gestation. Thus the dominant theme of development and new horizons is done "in style" (see Iser 1974: 179–95) as well as through symbolism. Paradoxically, this self-reflexive ("ipsorelative," 831) staging of the forward thrust recoups and co-opts an immense wealth of debris, both by way of literary allusions and by way of recycling the motifs of the previous chapters. And, as can well be expected, in the end of the episode the idea of progress is carnivalized when the drunken students' spilling out into the street is rendered in jargon, Cockney, and Pidgin English.

In "Circe" the relationship of the forward thrust of the vital impetus and lateral reabsorption of experience is reversed. The dominant technique of the chapter is that of nightmare reabsorption, a reassembling of all the cast of characters and motifs (a bow to Freud), and motifs-turned-into-characters. For example, among the throwaways we recover in this chapter, there is an "Irish Evicted Tenant," who demands that Bloom be sjamboked (616)—a personified reprise of the criticism against the Citizen leveled by the anonymous narrator of "Cyclops," who has recently entered the action of "Circe" as "The Nameless One," still resentful of Bloom's alleged winning on the Ascot race not being celebrated by a round of drinks (595). That avatar of Homer's No-man is a dun, a collector of bad or doubtful debts, one who recoups what is nearly lost back into private economy. An upholder of credit in the literal sense, he is also one whose memory keeps records of anything that is not to people's credit: he knows, for instance, that the Citizen, the Polyphemus of the "Cyclops" episode, is "not as green as he's cabbagelooking" (405; see Hayman 1974: 246–47): his loud-mouthed Irish nationalism goes hand in hand with his "grabbing the holding of an evicted tenant" (426)—and so now it is not safe for him to return to his own county. This information, incidentally, is not presented as available to either Stephen or Bloom—the deed is, anyway, registered in the Akasic records. It is culturally quite significant, however, that in the nightmare episode 15 the wrath of the dispossessed peasant is turned not against the Irish nationalist who has hypocritically benefited by the eviction but against the novel's avatar of the proverbial scapegoat, the Jew Bloom.

Yet though the handling of the recurrent motifs of the chapter can be thematized as lateral reabsorption, another prominent structural feature actually effects a totally new artistic development, one little dreamt of from within the noble tradition carnivalized in "Oxen of the Sun": the technique of seamless transitions between outer action and inner experience (which characterizes Dujardin's inner monologues and Joyce's own narrative in a number of previous chapters) is here translated into the language of drama, with the narrative intrusions confined to stage directions. Thus, in the chapter that celebrates the long-awaited achievement of Bloom's and Stephen's encounter, the reabsorption, reassembly, recycling of throwaways, is part of the forward motion of the vital impulse.

As can be expected in view of the fate suffered by other ideas infused into and tested in *Ulysses,* the philosophical theme of the lateral reabsorption of the discarded back into the life of the spirit is also carnivalized. A piece of garbage, a throwaway flyer, is followed on its itinerary through the city on June 16, 1904. The horse that wins the Ascot race on that day is an outsider named "Throwaway"—oxymoronically, an *objet trouvé*—if this had not been true, it could not have been more aptly invented. The thematic significance and the artistic games played with the issues of the human body—urination, defecation, flatulence, menstruation—likewise participate in this carnivalization of a serious thought, Bergson's or Joyce's own. And so do hilarious references to revivalism, to mystical events, the prālāyā; or the return of the ghost of a father to his son—not to demand revenge, as in *Hamlet,* but to advise that a missing boot is in the "return room," and that when it is found the pair must be resoled (390).

Bergson's figurative language likewise comes in for its share of carnivalization—in the jocoserious treatment of the extended metaphor of fireworks. At least twice in *Creative Evolution* is the movement of consciousness presented through the image of a fireworks rocket; both are associated with the statement that the creation of matter takes place when the creative current of consciousness is "momentarily interrupted" (262). At privileged moments of insight into organization between the reverse fluxes, "we catch a glimpse of a simple process, an action which is making itself across and action of the same kind which is unmaking itself, like the fiery path torn by the last rocket of a fireworks display through the black cinders of the spent rockets that are falling dead" (274). And later: "Consciousness, or supra-consciousness, is the name for the rocket whose extinguished fragments fall back as matter; consciousness, again, is the name for that which subsists of the rocket itself, passing through the fragments and lighting them up into organisms" (284–85)—the latter an impressive alternative metaphor for lateral reabsorption. The fate of this image in *Ulysses* is memorable: Bloom masturbates on the same strand where Stephen wasted a discharge of creative energies on composing a derivative quatrain, and it is there that Gerty McDowel seems to have an exhibitionist orgasm to the accompaniment of fireworks:

> She would fain have cried to him chokingly, held out her snowy slender arms to him to come, to feel his lips laid on her white brow the cry of a young girl's love, a little strangled cry, wrung from her, that cry that has rung through the ages. And then a rocket sprang and bang shot blind and O! then the Roman candle burst and it was like a sign of O! and everyone cried O! O! in raptures and it gushed out of it in a stream of rain gold hard threads and they shed and ah! They were all greeny dewey stars falling with golden, O so lively, O so soft, sweet, soft.
> Then all melted away dewily in the grey air: all was silent. (477)

A few pages later, Bloom's ironic comment deprecates his own transports and, indirectly, Bergson's tropes: "My fireworks. Up like a rocket, down like a stick" (483). So much for the creation of matter when the movement of the spirit is brought to a temporary halt.

One of the reasons why the economy of lateral reabsorption is carnivalized in the novel is its association with prudence, the Aristotelian middle way cherished by the English mainstream culture: the paradox is that whereas Odyssean prudence is the golden mean between excesses, between supererogation and sordidness, between promiscuity and stinginess, between recklessness and cowardice (see chapter 4), there may also be an excess of prudence itself—this, in fact, is demonstrated by the all too circumspect and at times insufferably flabby language of episode 16, "Eumaeus," in which prudent conduct is also a dominant theme. The chapter is presented in an enervated style replete with comically para-academic wary reservations ("not to put too fine a point on it," 706; "a sentrybox, or something like one" 708; "this had happened, or had been mentioned as having happened," 708; "so to speak," 754; "not particularly redolent sea," 727; "choppy, not to say stormy, weather," 728; "or something like that," 761), or needless repetitions seeking, as it were, foolproof clarity. And though Bloom has rescued Stephen from the madam's wrath and from the British soldiers in "Circe"— rescued, too, the remnants of Stephen's salary—and practically succeeded in restoring the young man to consciousness after his drunken bout, his fight with Mulligan offstage, and his fall, the paterfamilias's prudent advice that Stephen should drop the false friend Mulligan is notoriously commented on by the horse who deposits three turds. Bloom, "the prudent member" (384, 392) disliked in Dublin for his very prudence, is, on June 16, 1904, a man who will not give of himself to Zion, to wife, or to garden (Glasheen 1974: 59–60), though he will spare some funds in charity for Dignam's orphaned family and in recompense for his pen pal Martha ("I paid my way," as his antipode Deasy might say). Yet though in Joyce's Aristotelian ethics prudence indicates a deterioration of a person's character as a result of experience, Bloom's negative view of promiscuous friendships with drinking boons gains support in the last chapter of the novel, in Molly's comment on the excesses of Irish conviviality: "and they call that friendship killing and then burying one another" (920).

And yet Molly herself is infatuated with Blazes Boylan, a master of conviviality codes. This may suggest another reason why prudence is carnivalized in the novel, with or without respect to the treatment accorded to Bloom. There may be a sociological reason why the custom of young gentlemen wastefully "sowing their wild oats" (cf. the recycling of this topos in "After the Race" in *Dubliners*) seems to have survived and to have been placidly tolerated in Ireland much longer than in England, where it began to be frowned upon by the end of the Regency period. The wild youthful profligacy helps to defuse political rebelliousness. In Ireland this effect was, for obvious reasons, in demand for a much longer time than in England. Joyce's own ironic acceptance of his native country as the "isle of dreadful thirst" (50) may have been associated with his lack of sympathy for armed resistance to English rule. The latter, in its turn, is well in tune with his determined antimilitarism, and with the pacifist notes that, in *Ulysses*, employ the vocabulary of destructive evolution, of vicious waste that is the photonegative of that other moral problem, the survival of the fittest. In the prudent language of the "Eumaeus" episode, Bloom is presented as "only too conscious of the casualties invariably resulting from propaganda and displays of mutual animosity and the misery and suffering it entailed as a foregone conclusion on fine young fellows, chiefly, destruction of the fittest, in a word" (764–65). Molly, thinking of her dead lover, puts the same idea in her own words: "they could have made their peace in the beginning or old oom Paul and the rest of the old Krugers go and fight it out between them instead of dragging on for years killing any finelooking men there were with their fever" (886). The grim determinacies of war (politics conducted by "other means"), violence, terror, are the opposite of creative evolution of any kind. Often as Stephen Dedalus will find himself quoting Swinburne, he will not allow us to forget "old Algy's" poem in defense of an officer in command of concentration camps in South Africa (240); nor will he applaud the ending of Shakespeare's *Hamlet:* "nine lives for his father's one." Yet even this serious antimilitarist thought does not escape mild carnivalization: there are only eight throwaway deaths among the personages of *Hamlet;* the ninth is actually Joyce's feline throw-in, to bring tragic grandeur back to an everyman's Eccles Street basement kitchen, where a resilient modern Odysseus is shown feeding his cat.[15]

The creative-evolutionary "agenda" of the protagonists of *Ulysses* is but one example of the possibility of following the novel's themes from their nucleus to the fringes at which they peter out. Further nuclei of conceptual development may be expected to germinate out of loose ends. Bergson, indeed, discusses evolution as "an indistinct fringe" that forms around the "bright nucleus" of an intellectual concept and that "fades off into darkness." The nucleus, the "pure intellect," is a "contraction, by condensation, of a more extensive power" (53), a contraction in which creative evolution is forced into readymade conceptual slots. It is the fringe of intuition that impels creative reality, a reality "productive of effects in which it expands and transcends its own being" (59). Joyce's friendly, artistic, semiparodic concurrence in Bergson's views on the limited and matter-ridden place of the intellect in human experience constitutes, among other things, an invitation to the reader—to overinterpret, misread, go off on tangents, carnivalize in search of the intuitive move that would keep the text and the world of

---

15. This image is a link in an intertextual intersubjective strand of similar unforgettable felicities, wedged between the bird in a cage that Henchard brings to his daughter's wedding in *The Mayor of Casterbridge* (and then forgets and allows to die neglected) and the dog whom Nabokov's Pnin feeds on getting the news of his imminent dismissal from Waindel ("there was no reason a human's misfortune should interfere with a canine's pleasure," 1957: 171). Among the historical episodes that Nabokov would have liked to have on film is Melville "feeding a sardine to his cat," 1981: 61.

Ulysses (and, eventually, the reader's own world) from falling behind, being left, with other culture-determined baggage, by the side of the forward flux.

———

While working on *Finnegans Wake* Joyce toyed with the idea that someone else, appropriately programmed, could complete the book for him, letting its wheels roll in the set grooves—somebody (James Stevens?) could, as it were, continue Joyce's play with the text, or else become a part of this play. Among the Nabokov scholars who disapproved of the interpretive procedures in Alfred Appel's annotations to *Lolita* a joke circulated once: was Appel not invented by Nabokov, just like John Ray, Jr., to whom the Foreword to Humbert's narrative is ascribed? The joke eventually extended to Appel's critics, and Nabokov scholars in general: perhaps they too are Nabokov's inventions, or at least, his galley slaves, who have been "foreseen"—just like a twentieth-century decipherer of a nineteenth-century assassination plot feels "foreseen" at the end of Borges's story about Ireland, "The Theme of the Traitor and the Hero" (1964: 75). The reader of *Ulysses* likewise often feels "foreseen" and perhaps made fun of—teased, flattered and humbled, trapped and released, provoked to invent further intricacies and ascribe them to the text, led to credit the novel with excess depth.

I believe that this feeling, a form of "the suspicion of fraudulence" that, according to Stanley Cavell (1976: 188–89), is an intrinsic feature of aesthetic response to modernist art, actually lays bare not just a specific device but the very nature of the aesthetic play of the text. Just as the images of the novel can only temporarily be ascribed to the consciousness of its separate character, so the main play of the text reverses the relationship of instrumentality between the reader and the book: literary works tend to dethrone us from the position of the subject who uses the text as an object or a path towards aesthetic experience; rather, they turn us into parts of their own aesthetic play, their own "self-presentation" (Gadamer 1989: 105).[16] The ethics of narrative form in Joyce's mature work involves making us aware, conceptually or intuitively, of this loss of the subject's position; the resentment resulting from this loss helps us to break free from the text-play itself just as this text-play helps us out of conventional deadwood attitudes and mental habits. Joyce's carnival not only creates liberating cultural remissions; it also fragments the counterculture of its own magic. Nor does this double

16. "The structure of play absorbs the player into itself, and thus frees him from the burden of taking the initiative, which constitutes the actual strain of existence" (Gadamer 1989: 105).

effect of casting and releasing the spell escape "ipsorelative" carnivalization: at the end of episode 4, in the jakes, Bloom's "yielding but resisting" (84) describes both the process of defecation and the process of reading—and what Bloom is reading on this occasion is a story that echoes a discarded piece of Joyce's own juvenilia.

Caesura

IT HAPPENED.

Neither humanistic literature, nor enlightened philosophy, nor progressive political thought has prepared us for (let alone preempted) what happened in 1914, 1915, 1918, 1921, 1933, 1937, 1939, 1941, 1942 (etc.). Not only the start of World War I (1914), the Armenian genocide (1915), or the official start of World War II (1939) but also the 1918 creation of the CheKa (the nucleus of the Soviet and post-Soviet political police) and the dissolution of the Constituent Assembly in Petersburg, the ban on factionalism proclaimed at the Tenth Congress of the Communist Party (1921), and the Wannsee Conference (1942) were events of cosmic magnitude, though known to only a few and recognized by still fewer. It is probably with the benefit of hindsight that similar later events will be recognized as radically changing our world—unless there is no hindsight because, as, Einstein predicted, World War IV will be fought with clubs.

The history of the twentieth century, with what Philippe Lacoue-Labarthe has called the "caesura" (71–72) in the middle, has shown that actuality can surpass both the grimmest and the most ingenious artistic imagination. This, in addition to the ethical agenda of testimony, apologia, consciousness-raising, and homage to the dead, has contributed to the unprecedented popularity of life-writing since the mid-twentieth century.

Among the most prominent issues raised by literary critical studies of the different kinds of memoirs, biographies, autobiographies, nonfiction novels (Truman Capote, Norman Mailer), or identity-seeking travelogues (e.g., Michael Arlene's *Passage to Ararat*[1]), are questions about the relationship between the fictional and the factual, ranging from extreme hermeneutic nihilism to the admission that even nonreferential fictional narratives may accurately testify to the structures of historical reality.[2]

Those of us who study both life-writing and classical literature, especially English,[3] waver between seeing ourselves as oscillating from one of these two different worlds to the other or seeing these two worlds as not separable. At the moment, though ready to confess that it is classical English literature that helps me to keep sane, I lean to the latter view—provided the connections are drawn not only as lines of influence but also as negations of negations.[4] The frame of the current research does not accommodate unfolding this argument, but the one point I have to make here is that, despite addressing a different target audience, the best of the documentary prose of the second half of the twentieth century is akin to the literary modernism of the first half. In fictional prose narrative modernism may be seen as culminating in the works of Kafka, Joyce, and, in Russia, Andrey Bely. Varlam Shalamov (1907–82), the most distinguished artist among Gulag authors, considered himself the scion of the modernist writers of the Russian Silver Age.

One of the central features shared by these bodies of literature is the hesitation that resembles the "suspicion of fraudulence" (Cavell 1976: 188–89), so important in the aesthetic response to modernism (see p. 172). In reading documentary prose such a suspicion translates into the concern with

1. For a useful discussion of this work in the context of relational autobiography, see Eakin 2009.

2. Cf. the dialogue between the positions of Hayden White and Martin Jay in Friedlander 1992.

3. I single out the literature of the European country that has not been radically ravaged by a socialist revolution or a Nazi onslaught (though it did not remain untouched by and unimplicated in such events), whether because of its democratic-reform tradition or, as I have been taught in a course on historical materialism, because of the ruling classes' calculated redistribution of the profits derived from the exploitation of the colonies.

4. Postcolonial studies have made it amply clear that the world conjured up in the classical English novels is the same world in which colonial oppression took place. The exact links between nineteenth-century (including Victorian-era) science and culture, the birth of the concentration camp (Cuba, South Africa—see Kotek and Rigoulot 2000: 47–94), the birth of eugenics, its practice in the colonies such as German Namibia and British Tasmania, the Armenian Genocide, the Jewish Holocausts, as well as mass slaughters in Cambodia, Rwanda, and Darfur are still awaiting a sustained scholarly investigation. At the moment, I believe that oppositional writers such as Jane Austen were critical of the same mind-sets that could be seen as implicated in the latency of the developments that twentieth-century readers know with the benefit of hindsight.

the truth-value of each individual testimony—in particular, into wonder-ing about its *modality*—is it factographic or fictional? This goes beyond our possible wondering whether one or another detail is accurate or even whether an author's whole representation of the events is not opportunisti-cally mendacious. The need to know the modal status of a work of testimony is especially urgent when a narrative that we have been reading mainly "for the facts" suddenly offers us an unexpected aesthetic experience, too mixed to be called pleasure. What forces are responsible for such a bonus effect? We have counted as little on it as we may have counted on a semiotic cogni-tive enrichment from an exposure to abstractionist plastic arts. According to conventional expectations, in memoir literature, and especially in survivor narratives, the *arête,* the sense of difficulty overcome, pertains not to the composition of the work but to the experience with which it deals, because the composition is believed to follow not the creative imagination but the pregiven causal logic or temporal contingencies of the materials; hence *novels* about the times of atrocity are more readily but often less deservedly granted the status of art than factographic accounts, such as Primo Levi's *If This Is a Man* or Solzhenitsyn's *The Gulag Archipelago.* Or at least, this used to be the case: in recent decades the expectations of the audience seem to have been changing. A Duchamp-like framing of bowls or an autobiographer's straight-forward account of her experience are less and less frequently perceived as *too easy,* hence too trivial: what Keats called the "pinnacle and steep of godlike hardship" is more widely understood to have been attained not so much in the process of crafting the fair copy as in the cultural and biographical prehistory of the works, and in the intensity of the fermentation that their crudities and contexts have undergone in the creative consciousness.

The amount and quality of the scholarship devoted to life-writing in recent decades suggests that writers such as Levi or Shalamov have been allowed to teach large parts of the reading public not only to trust them but also *to treat their narratives as factual while asking of them the kind of questions we would ask of fiction:* questions about motifs and themes (internal reference) in addition to topics and issues (external reference), questions about symbols in addition to signs, about aesthetic and ethical congruence in addition to ideological emplotment. In terms of the semiological triad (see pp. 18–19), we have been taught to ask questions about syntactics in addition to those of semantics.

This new reading convention may reflect back on narratives packaged as fictional works—such as, for instance, Kafka's "A Hunger Artist"—of them, conversely, we may ask questions not only on the workings of narrative art but also of the accuracy of the historical representation, or rather, the consistency of their internal reference with the extratextual information on the episodes of cultural history in which their stories are set. This approach is not to be confused with the so-called use of a work of art as a historical document, which is a legitimate if ultimately unsatisfying procedure with documentary prose. Rather, it is a variation on "backward mimesis" (I. Armstrong 2000: 6), the external field of reference enriching our understanding of the meanings of intratextual narrative details—meanings in the Wittgensteinian terms of what "hangs together" with what.

The permeability of the borderlines between fictionalized and factographic narratives further suggests that the narratological features that distinguish fictional works from factography, such as, for instance, the inside views of characters who are not the first-person authorial "I"[5] or the absence of public verification landmarks, are sometimes a matter of pragmatically oriented choices: an author can say about a fictionalized third-person avatar what he cannot say about him- or herself in the first person; a narrative whose protagonist bears a name different from the author's (e.g., Krist in a number of Shalamov's stories) but undergoes the experience that was actually the author's, may use the conventional authority of narrative omniscience to forestall troubling moral questions of the target audience.[6] Such choices, combining the artistic and the pragmatic considerations, are likewise part and parcel of the ethics of narrative form.

To complete a paradigm of cultural remissions by adding the morphology of Lent to that of the carnival, I now propose to compare Kafka's "A Hunger Artist" and Shalamov's story "The Artist of the Spade." Since the latter is not part of the selection of Shalamov's stories widely accessible in John Glad's translation, it is reproduced here in the translation of Nedda Strazhas, with the kind permission of Berghahn Books, in whose volume *Cold Fusion: Aspects of the German Cultural Presence in Russia,* edited by Gennady Barabtarlo, it was published first, along with an earlier version of chapter 10 of the present book.

---

5. For a systematic discussion of the signals that a narrative is fictionalized, see Cohn 1999: 109–31.

6. I discuss this possibility in detail in "Testimony and Doubt" (2007), which compares two of Shalamov's stories, one factographic and one fictionalized but both written in the same year, 1964, and dealing with the same year, 1938. It must be added that pragmatic considerations have, more notoriously, led to some authors' passing of fictional narratives for factual ones, strictly imitating all the conventions of eyewitness narratives.

VARLAM SHALAMOV

The Artist of the Spade

Translated by N. Strazhas

ON SUNDAY, AFTER WORK, Krist was told that he was being transferred to the brigade[1] of Kostochkin to reinforce the rapidly melting gold-
mining brigade. The news was important. Whether good or bad—for Krist
there was no point in thinking about it, for it was irrevocable. But about
the man Kostochkin Krist had heard a lot on this rumourless mine, in the
deafened, mute barracks. Like any other convict, Krist did not know from
where the new people came into his life—some for a short time, others for
longer. They always vanished from his life without having said anything
about themselves; they went away as if dying, they died as if going away.
Chiefs, foremen, cooks, storage-men, neighbours on the plank-beds, brothers at the wheelbarrow, comrades at the hack...

This kaleidoscope, this movement of endless faces, was not tiresome for
Krist. He simply gave it no thought. Life left no time for such reflections.
"Don't worry, don't think about the new bosses, Krist. You are one, but your
bosses shall be many,"—so a certain joker and philosopher would say; who
he was Krist had forgotten. Krist could not recall either the name or the
face or the voice that had spoken these important jocular phrases. Important

---

1. The action of the story takes place in a Kolyma labor camp; a "brigade" is a convicts' work
team.

precisely because jocular. He was someone who dared to joke, to smile, if only a deeply concealed innermost smile, but nevertheless a smile, doubtless a smile. Such people did exist, but Krist himself was not one of them.

What foremen had Krist had? Either those of one's own kind, the fifty eighth,[2] who had taken upon themselves too serious a task and were soon demoted, degraded before they had the time to turn into murderers. Or, again, one's own kind, the fifty-eighth, "fraiers,"[3] but experienced—slick customers who could not only give orders at work but also organize the work, and, in addition, get along with the rate-setters, the office, and different bosses, who could bribe, persuade. But these too, one's fellow fifty-eighth, would not admit the thought that ordering people around at this forced labor was the worst camp sin, that where the reckoning is in blood, where man has no rights, to take upon oneself the responsibility to command somebody else's will to live or die was too big a sin, a deadly sin, not to be forgiven. There had been foremen who died together with the brigade. There had also been those whom this dreadful power over the life of others promptly corrupted, and then the hack, the handle of the spade in their hands began to help them speak to their comrades. And when they recollected this, they would quote, repeating it like a prayer, a grim camp maxim: "You die today, and I tomorrow." Yet it was not the rule that Krist's foremen should be convicts under the fifty eighth article. Much more often, and during the most terrible years—always, his foremen were common criminals, sentenced for murder, for dereliction of duties. These were ordinary people, and only the guilt of power and the heavy pressure from above—the stream of deadly instructions—drove them to acts they would not, perhaps, have dared to commit in their former life. The borderline between felonies and "nonpunishable acts" in the regulations of official duties, as well as in most criminal law articles, is very thin, at times indefinable. Frequently sentences were passed today for something they were not passed for yesterday, to say nothing about the means of suppression—all this judicial gamut of shades from misdemeanor to felony.

Common-criminal foremen were brutes by order. Foremen from among professional criminals were also brutes but not just by order. The worst thing that could happen to a brigade was to get a thug for a foreman. But Kostochkin was neither a professional sharper nor a common criminal. Kostoch-

2. Convicts sentenced in accordance with the "political" article fifty-eight of the Soviet criminal code.

3. A contemptuous thieves-jargon term for political prisoners, especially intellectuals, which eventually acquired wider currency and was applied to the easily victimized "slickers" inside and outside the camps.

kin was the only son of a big party or administrative boss on the KVZhD, prosecuted and killed in connection with the "KVZhD case."[4] Kostochkin's only son, who studied in Kharbin, and had seen nothing except Kharbin, was at the age of 25 sentenced to...fifteen years, as a *ChS*,[5] a member of the family. Brought up in the foreign Kharbinian life-style, where the innocently convicted were only known from novels—translated novels mainly, deep down the young Kostochkin was not convinced that his father had been innocent of the charges. His father had inculcated in him a belief in the infallibility of the NKVD;[6] young Kostochkin was totally unprepared for a different judgment. And when his father was arrested, when Kostochkin himself was sentenced and dispatched from the Very Far East to the Very Far North, Kostochkin grew first and foremost resentful against his father who had spoiled his life by his mysterious crime. What does he, Kostochkin, know about the life of adults? He, who had mastered four languages, two European and two Oriental, the best dancer in Kharbin who had learned all kinds of blues and rumbas from visiting experts, the best boxer in Kharbin, middle-weight to heavy-weight, who had been trained in uppercuts and jabs by a former European champion—what did he know about all this big politics? If the father was shot—there must have been something. Maybe the NKVD had been hasty, maybe he should have been given ten, fifteen years. And he, the young Kostochkin, should have been given five instead of fifteen—if anything at all.

Kostochkin kept repeating the same words, arranging them in a different order, and every time it came out bad, alarming: "Then something must have been there. Then there must have been something."

Having aroused Kostochkin's hatred for his executed father and a passionate wish to rid himself of the stigma, of this paternal curse, the investigating body had achieved an important success. But the interrogator did not know that. The interrogator in charge of Kostochkin's case had, in his turn, been shot in connection with one of the "NKVD cases."

It was not only fox-trots and rumbas that the young Kostochkin had studied in Kharbin. He graduated from the Kharbin politechnical institute, with a degree in mechanical engineering.

When Kostochkin was brought to the mine, his assigned place, he managed to get an appointment with the chief of the mine and asked to be given

4. KVZhD, the Chinese Eastern Railway, was sold to China in 1935, whereupon most of its employees moved to the Soviet Union, only to be persecuted on suspicions of espionage.

5. Acronym of *chlen sem'i* ("a member of the family"). Wives and children of the victims of Stalin's terror were liable to administrative incarceration.

6. Acronym for People's Commissariat for Internal Affairs and euphemism for the Soviet secret police.

a job in his specialty, promising to work honestly, condemning his father, pleading with the local authorities. "He'll write labels on tins," said the chief of the mine dryly, but the local police operative, who was present at the meeting, caught faintly familiar notes in the tone of the young Kharbinian engineer. The chiefs talked it over among themselves, then the police agent spoke with Kostochkin, and suddenly the news spread among the pit-face brigades: a newcomer, one of their own, the fifty-eighth, was appointed foreman of one of the brigades. The optimists saw this appointment as a sign of coming change for the better; the pessimists muttered something about a new broom. But all were surprised, except, of course, those who were long past surprise—Krist was not surprised.

Each brigade lives its own life, in its own section, in a barrack with a separate entrance; it meets the other inmates of the barrack only in the dining-hall. Krist often met Kostochkin who was so conspicuous—red mug, broad shoulders, powerful build. The cuffs of his bell-shaped gloves were of fur. The poorer foremen's cuffs are made of rags sewn together from wadded trousers. And Kostochkin's cap was that of a free man, fur with ear-flaps, and his felt-boots were the real stuff, not rag boots or string-tied bast shoes. All this singled out Kostochkin. He had been working as foreman for the winter month—which meant that he had fulfilled the plan, the percentage; how much that was could be found out on the blackboard by the guard-house. But such a question did not interest an old convict like Krist.

Krist had composed the biography of his future foreman mentally, on the plank-bed. But he was sure he was not wrong, could not be wrong. The Kharbinian could not have had any other ways of getting a foreman's job.

Kostochkin's brigade was melting away, as was the case with all the brigades working in the gold pit-face. From time to time—this should read from week to week rather than from month to month, a reinforcement was sent to Kostochkin's brigade. Today this reinforcement was—Krist. "Most likely Kostochkin even knows who Einstein is," thought Krist falling asleep in the new place.

As a newcomer, Krist was given a place further away from the stove. Whoever came to the brigade earlier—occupied a better place. This was the general rule, and Krist was well aware of it.

The foreman was sitting at the table in the corner, close to the lamp, reading a book. Even though the foreman, as master over the lives and deaths of his sloggers, could for the sake of his convenience put the only lamp on his own little table, depriving all the other inmates of the barrack of light—not that they would read or talk...One can talk in the dark just as well, but then there were neither subjects nor time for conversation.

But foreman Kostochkin settled down at the common lamp and went on reading; at times he drew his chubby childish heart-shaped lips into a smile and screwed up his big beautiful grey eyes. Krist was so appreciative of this peaceful picture of the foreman and the brigade at rest, something he had not seen for so long, that he decided to stay in this brigade by all means, to give all his strength to his new foreman.

There was also a deputy foreman in the brigade, the shortish fatigue-man Os'ka, old enough to be Kostochkin's father. His duties were to sweep the barrack, bring the brigade's food, help the foreman—same as everywhere. And on the point of falling asleep, Krist thought for some reason, that, most probably, his new foreman knew who Einstein was. And, made happy by the thought, warmed by the mug of boiling water he had just drunk for the night, Krist fell asleep.

Nor was there any noise in the new brigade when it was taken to work. Krist was shown the toolshed—everyone received his tool, and Krist adjusted his spade, as he had adjusted it a thousand times before: knocked off the short handle with the lug fixed to the American scoop-spade, with the butt of the axe unbent this scoop a little wider on a stone, picked out a very long new haft from the many standing in the corner of the shed, passed it into the ring of the spade, fixed it, placed the spade with its bent blade at his feet, took the measure and made a "notch" on the haft against his own chin, then cut it at this mark. With his sharp ax Krist scraped off the rough edge of the new handle, thoroughly smoothing it out. He got up and turned around. In front of him Kostochkin was standing, carefully watching the movements of the newcomer. Not that Krist had not expected this. Kostochkin did not say a word, and Krist understood, that the foreman was deferring judgment till the beginning of work, till the pit-face.

The pit-face was not far away and the work started. The haft broke into motion, a dull pain crept into his back, the palms of both hands fell into their usual position, the fingers clutched the haft. It was a tiny bit too thick, but Krist would repair it in the evening. He would also sharpen the spade with a file. His hands swung the spade time after time, and a quickened rhythm entered into the melodious grating of metal against stone. The spade screeched, rustled; the stone would slide off the spade at each sweep and drop onto the bottom of the wheel-barrow, and the bottom would respond with a wooden thump, and then stone would respond to stone—all this music of the pit-face was well known to Krist. In every place stood the same wheel-barrows, the same spades screeched, the stone, helpfully hewn with the hack, rustled and slid down the landslip, and the spades screeched again.

Krist put down the spade to replace his mate at the "machine OSO[7]—two handles, one wheel" as the convicts in Kolyma called the wheel-barrow (not in thieves' jargon, but something like it). Krist set the wheel-barrow bottom on the trap board, handles turned in the opposite direction of the pit-face, and quickly filled the wheel-barrow. Then he grasped the handles, arched his back straining the stomach and, catching his balance, wheeled his barrow to the pan, the gold washing appliance. On the way back Krist wheeled the barrow according to all the rules of the wheel-barrowers, inherited from centuries of penal servitude—handles upward, wheel forward; his hands resting on the handles. Then he put down the wheel-barrow and again took up the spade. The spade started screeching.

The Kharbinian engineer, the foreman Kostochkin, stood listening to the pit-face symphony and watching Krist's movements.

"Well, well, I can see that you are an artist of the spade," said Kostochkin and burst out laughing. His laughter was childish, irrepressible. With his sleeve the foreman wiped his lips. "What category did you get where you have come from?"

What he meant was the categories of nourishment, "the stomach scale," driving on the convict. These categories, Krist knew, were discovered on the White-Sea canal,[8] during the "reforging."[9] The slobbery romanticism of the reforging had a realistic foundation, cruel and sinister, in the shape of this "stomach scale."

"The third," answered Krist, emphasizing with his voice, as clearly as possible, his contempt for his previous foreman who had not appreciated the talent of the artist of the spade. Realizing the benefit, Krist, as usual, lied a little.

"I shall give you the second. Right as of today."

"Thanks," said Krist.

In the new brigade it seemed to be a little quieter than in the other brigades where Krist had to live and work; the barrack was a little cleaner; there was a little less swearing. Out of a long-time habit Krist wanted to fry

7. Acronym of *Osoboe Soveshchanie* (Special Council) that passed conveyor-line administrative sentences to victims of large waves of arrests. In the original saying "OSO" rhymes with *koleso*, "wheel."

8. The first major Stalinist construction project accomplished through convict labor, from September 1931 to April 1933. The estimates of convict mortality during the digging of the canal range between 50,000 and 200,000.

9. "Reforging" (*perekovka*) was a much-publicized early-1930s campaign of, as it were, re-educating prisoners through labor. It gave birth to the Gulag version of "incentive," which consisted in not giving the prisoners an assured flat subsistence but tying their rations to their production output.

a little piece of bread that had remained from his supper on the stove, but his neighbour—Krist didn't yet know and would never learn his surname—gave him a nudge and said that the foreman didn't like them to fry bread on the stove.

Krist went up to the lively burning iron stove, spread his fingers wide above the flow of heat, and put his face into the current of hot air. From the nearest plank-bed Os'ka, the deputy foreman, got up and with a strong arm led the newcomer away from the stove: "Go to your place. Don't block the stove. Let everybody be warm." This was, generally speaking, fair, but it is very difficult to restrain one's own body, its longing for the fire. The convicts of Kostochkin's brigade had mastered restraint. And Krist would have to master it too. Krist returned to his place, took off his pea-jacket. He thrust his feet into the sleeves of the pea-jacket, adjusted his cap, curled up, and fell asleep.

On the point of falling asleep, Krist still saw somebody come into the barrack and give an order. Kostochkin swore, without moving away from the lamp or stopping to read his book. Os'ka ran up to the newcomer, and seizing him by the elbows with quick deft movements, pushed him out of the barrack. In his former life Os'ka had been a history teacher in some institute.

For many following days Krist's spade went on screeching; the sand went on rustling. Kostochkin soon understood that behind the refined technique of Krist's movements there had for long been no strength and, no matter how hard Krist tried, his barrows were always filled a little bit less than prescribed. This did not depend on one's own will: measure is dictated by some inner feeling which controls the muscles—all kinds—healthy and powerless, young and worn out, exhausted. Every time the output was measured, it turned out that not as much had been achieved at the pit-face where Krist worked as the foreman had expected from the highly professional movements of the artist of the spade. But Kostochkin did not take it out on Krist, did not scold him more than he did the others, did not abuse him, did not preach to him. Perhaps he understood that Krist was putting all his strength into his work, saving only what could not be spent to please any foreman in any camp of the world. Or perhaps he felt it rather than understood—our feelings are much richer than thoughts; the bloodless tongue of the convict does not reveal all there is in his heart. Feelings also pale, grow weaker, but much later than thoughts, much later than human speech, language. And Krist was indeed working harder than he had worked in a long time, and, although his output was not sufficient for the second category, he was receiving this second category, for his assiduity, for his efforts...

The second category, indeed, was the most that Krist could possibly get. The first was given to the record-setters who fulfilled 120 percent of the quota, and more. There were no record-setters in Kostochkin's brigade. There were those in the brigade who received the third category, that is, who fulfilled the quota, and those who received the fourth category, who did not fulfill the quota but only 70 or 80 percent of it. Still these were not the obvious idlers who deserved penal rations, the fifth category; there were none of those in Kostochkin's brigade.

Day followed day, and Krist grew weaker and weaker, and the submissive silence in the barrack of Kostochkin's brigade pleased him less and less. But then one evening, Os'ka, the history teacher, took Krist aside and said to him in a low voice: "The cashier is coming today. The brigadier ordered money for you, have it in mind..." Krist's heart was pounding. So, Kostochkin did appreciate Krist's diligence, his skill. This Kharbinian engineer, who knows about Einstein, is, after all, no stranger to conscience.

In the brigades where Krist had worked before, he had never received any money. Each brigade inevitably appeared to contain more deserving people: either really physically stronger and better workers or just friends of the foreman—Krist never indulged in such futile reflection, accepting every dinner check (the categories were changed every ten days, the percentage being determined for the output of the recent period) as the finger of fate, as good or bad fortune, success or failure, that would pass, change, and would not be eternal.

The news about the money he would be paid that night filled Krist's soul and body with a great, irrepressible joy. It appears that for joy there are enough feeling and strength. How much money could he be paid?...Even five or six rubles would mean five or six kilograms of bread. Krist was ready to worship Kostochkin and couldn't wait for work to end.

The cashier arrived. He was a very ordinary man but wore a good tanned sheepskin coat; he was a civilian. He was accompanied by a guard who was concealing his revolver or pistol or had left his weapon in the guard-house. The cashier sat down at the table, opened his briefcase packed with much used many-coloured banknotes that looked like laundered rags. The cashier took out a list, densely lined, covered with all kinds of signatures—made by people either happy or disappointed with the sums they had got. The cashier called Krist and pointed to a ticked-off spot.

Krist, all attention, felt something special in this premium. Nobody, except Krist, went up to the cashier. There was no queue. Maybe the members of the brigade had been so trained by their solicitous foreman. Well, what is there to think about! The money has been ordered, the cashier pays out. That's Krist's luck.

The foreman himself was not in the barrack; he had not yet returned from the office, and the identification of the recipient was taken care of by the foreman's deputy, Os'ka, the history teacher. With his forefinger Os'ka showed Krist the place for his signature.

"And...and...how much?" Krist wheezed, choking.

"Fifty rubles. Satisfied?"

Krist's heart began to sing, to pound. Here's luck. Hurriedly, tearing the paper with the sharp pen and almost overturning the non-drip inkstand, Krist signed the payroll.

"Atta boy," said Os'ka approvingly.

The cashier clapped the briefcase shut.

"Nobody else in your brigade?"

"No."

Krist still could not understand what was going on.

"And the money? the money?"

"I gave the money to Kostochkin," said the cashier. "Already in the morning." And the small Os'ka tore Krist away from the table with an iron arm, with a force no hewer in this brigade had ever had, and hurled him into the darkness.

The brigade was silent. Not a single person stood up for Krist or asked a question. No one even cursed Krist for a fool...This for Krist was more terrible than the brute Os'ka and his clawing iron hand. More terrible than the childish chubby lips of foreman Kostochkin.

The door of the barrack was flung open, and with quick and light steps foreman Kostochkin walked to the lighted table. The floor of the barrack, made of beams and planks, hardly shook under his light, springy gait.

"Here's the foreman himself—speak to him," said Os'ka, stepping back. Pointing at Krist, he explained to Kostochkin: "He wants money!"

But the foreman had already understood everything while crossing the threshold. Kostochkin immediately felt as he had in the ring in Kharbin. He stretched out his hand towards Krist with the habitual handsome boxing movement "from the shoulder," and Krist fell onto the floor, stunned.

"Knockout, knockout," wheezed Os'ka, hopping around the half dead Krist and acting the referee in the ring, "eight...nine...Knockout."

Krist did not rise from the floor.

"Money? Money he wants?" Kostochkin, was saying, unhurriedly seating himself at the table and taking a spoon out of Os'ka's hands to get down to a bowl of peas.

"These trotskyites," said Kostochkin slowly and instructively, "they are the undoing of me and you, Osia." Kostochkin raised his voice. "They've ruined the country. And are ruining us. He needs money, the artist of the spade, money. Hey, you!" shouted Kostochkin to the brigade. "You fascists! Do you hear! You won't knife *me* down. Dance, Os'ka!"

Krist was still lying on the floor. The huge figures of the foreman and the orderly stood between him and the light. Suddenly Krist saw that Kostochkin was drunk, very drunk. Those same fifty rubles, which had been assigned to Krist...How much spirit could they buy, alcohol rationed out to the whole brigade...

Os'ka, the foreman's deputy, obediently started to dance, repeating all the while:

I have bought two washing-troughs,
And my wife Rosita...

"That's ours, from Odessa, foreman. It is called 'From the bridge to the slaughter-house.'" And Os'ka, history teacher in some capital city institute, father of four children, again went into a dance.

"Stop, fill up."

Fumbling, Os'ka found a bottle under the plank-beds and poured something into a tin. Kostochkin drank it and ate the remains of the peas in the bowl, picking them up with his fingers.

"Where is that artist of the spade?"

Os'ka raised Krist up and pushed him into the light.

"Why, no strength? Aren't you getting your rations? Who is getting the second category? That's not enough for you, you trotskyite swine?"

Krist kept silent. The brigade kept silent.

"I'll smash all of you! Damned fascists," raged Kostochkin.

"Go, go to your place, artist of the spade, or else the foreman may hit you again," advised Os'ka peaceably, holding the drunken Kostochkin and pushing him into the corner, turning him over onto the foreman's splendid single trestle-bed—the only trestle-bed in the barrack where all the plank-beds were double and two-tiered, "the railway type." Os'ka himself, the foreman's deputy and orderly, who slept on the last cot, was taking up his important third and quite official duties, those of the bodyguard, the night watchman of the foreman's sleep, rest, and life. Krist, groping, reached his bed.

But neither Kostochkin nor Krist had a chance to fall asleep. The door of the barrack opened, letting in a current of white steam, and a man came in wearing a fur cap with ear-flaps and a dark winter overcoat with an astrakhan fur collar. The overcoat was very crumpled, the astrakhan worn out; nevertheless it was a real overcoat and real astrakhan.

The man crossed the whole barrack to the table, to the light, to Kostochkin's trestle-bed. Os'ka greeted him respectfully and started shaking the foreman out of his stupor.

"Minia the Greek is calling you." This name was familiar to Krist. He was the foreman of the thugs. "Minia the Greek is calling you." But Kostochkin had already come to and sat up on the trestle-bed with his face to the light.

"Still carousing, Tamer?"

"Well, you see...they've driven me to this, the skunks..."

Minia the Greek uttered a sympathetic grunt.

"One day, Tamer, you'll be blown up into the air. Eh? They'll lay ammonium under your cot, set fire to the cord, and there you go..." The Greek pointed his finger upwards. "Or they'll saw off your head with a saw. Here, your neck is thick, it will take a long time to saw."

Kostochkin, slowly regaining his wits, was waiting to hear what the Greek had to tell him.

"How about a little one? Say, we'll find something in two seconds."

"No. We've got plenty of this liquor in our brigade, you know that. My business is more serious."

"Pleased to be of service."

"'Pleased to be of service,'" laughed Minia the Greek. "This is how they taught you to speak to people in Kharbin."

"Well, I didn't mean anything," Kostochkin hurried on. "I just don't know what you want."

"Here's what." The Greek started speaking rapidly, and Kostochkin nodded in agreement; the Greek drew something on the table, and Kostochkin started nodding understandingly. Os'ka was following the talk with interest. "I went to see the rate-setter," said Minia the Greek. His manner was neither sullen nor lively; he spoke in a most usual voice. "The rate-setter said it is Kostochkin's turn."

"But they took off from me last month as well..."

"What can I do..." And the Greek's voice became merrier. "Our guys, where can they get...the cubes?[10] I told the rate-setter. The rate-setter says— it's Kostochkin's turn."

"But..."

"Look. You yourself know our situation..."

"Well, all right," said Kostochkin. "You'll count it in the office, and then tell them to take it off from us."

---

10. Cubic meters. Professional criminal élite would not do any work in the camps, but their rations were still supposed to be calculated according to the output.

"No fear, fraeir," said Minia the Greek and patted Kostochkin on the shoulder. "Today you helped me out—tomorrow I'll do the same for you. I pay my debts. You do for me today, I do for you tomorrow."

"Tomorrow we shall kiss together,"[11] said Os'ka starting to dance, overjoyed at the decision finally taken and afraid that the foreman's hesitation could only spoil the matter.

"Well, good-bye, Tamer," said Minia the Greek, rising from the bench. "The rate-setter says: go boldly to Kostochkin, to the Tamer. There is a drop of the rogue's blood in him. Don't be afraid, don't be shy. Your fellows will manage. You have such artists of the spade..."

11. Allusion to a popular gypsy romance.

CHAPTER TEN

Discourse of Lent

Kafka's "A Hunger Artist" and
Shalamov's "The Artist of the Spade"

THE DISCUSSION OF THE ETHICS OF FORM in carnivalesque narrative would be incomplete without taking into account the literary refractions of fasting, the carnival's uneasy counterpart.

In her 1989 essay "Karneval und Fasten: Excess und Mangel in der Sprache des Körpers," Ruth Ginsburg argues that Lent, with its body language of deficiency rather than excess, is not the opposite of carnival but, like carnival, the opposite of the quotidian realities of social life. Her main literary example is Kafka's "A Hunger Artist," in which the person who used to stage widely advertised feats of forty-day fasting loses his hold on the interest of the public and eventually starves himself to death in an unmonitored and unlimited fast. Canonical works of fiction contain few similar examples of rendering the body language of Lent;[1] and this raises the question whether it is possible to draw meaningful extrapolations from Kafka's extraordinary story.

The discourse of Lent may, however, take derivative shapes—for instance, in novels that present the protagonists' voluntary acceptance of a period of privation and hard work on the way to future rewards—*per aspera ad astra.*

---

1. One might think, however, of Knut Hamsun's *Hunger,* or, *mutatis mutandis,* Orwell's *Down and Out in Paris and London.* For a study of the actual hunger disease see Winick 1979; for an account of an historical experiment in hunger see Tucker 2006.

Elsewhere (Toker 2007) I have made a case for Dickens's *Nicholas Nickleby* being such a novel, complete with the forceful evocation of the children's hunger in Squeers's school; to some extent, Charlotte Brontë's *Jane Eyre* might be another example. But while Nicholas's and his sister Kate's readiness to brave honorable hardships, like Jane Eyre's consent to physical hardship in preference to moral compromise, lay the foundation for a Lenten narrative, the episodes of *unhedged* chronic starvation in Dotheboys Hall and Lowood represent a *corruption* of Lent.

But the discourse of corrupted Lent is displayed, with overwhelming intensity, in another body of literature—the large corpus of documentary narratives that deal with concentration camp experience, among them the narratives of the veterans of the Gulag, including such stories by Varlam Shalamov as "At Night," "The Individual Assignment," "Sententia," "Rain," and, among numerous others, "The Artist of the Spade."

Since I first started thinking about the discourse of Lent, I have changed my mind about its being, as Ruth Ginsburg has put it, the carnival's "second self." Rather, this discourse bears what Wittgenstein called "a family resemblance" to both the carnivalesque and the oppositional narratives: it shares some features with the one and other features with the other. I shall attempt to demonstrate how this works by a comparative analysis of Kafka's "A Hunger Artist" and Shalamov's "The Artist of the Spade."

Shalamov may have been familiar with "A Hunger Artist" in 1964, when he wrote "The Artist of the Spade." The January 1964 issue of the Soviet journal *Inostrannaya literatura* (*Foreign Literature*) published Russian translations of two works by Kafka, "Metamorphosis" and "In the Penal Colony"; other Kafka stories in Russian translation circulated in the Samizdat at the time. "A Hunger Artist" was among the latter[2]—its story of a secular fast turning into lethal starvation must have been deemed inappropriate for the Soviet press: indeed, it could trail in the memories of what had not yet been publicly disclosed during Khrushchev's half-measure de-Stalinization—the near-genocidal artificial famine in the Ukraine in the early thirties, the postwar famine in former Rumanian territories, and the multimillion-person death toll caused by starvation in Stalin's camps; in the sixties, moreover, chronic hunger was again resorted to in the camps, mainly as a punitive measure.[3]

2. I thank Omri Ronen for making this suggestion, which I then found confirmed by references to "A Hunger Artist" (Russ. "Golodar'") in the memoirs of the dissident Anatoly Murzhenko (1985: 118).

3. This is a pervasive theme of Marchenko's *My Testimony* (1969).

What matters, however, is not the actual possibility of Kafka's influence on Shalamov but the overlap in the morphology of the two stories, in the form and the Lenten repertoire of their content. The action of "The Artist of the Spade" takes place in a Kolyma gold mine during one of the worst periods in Gulag history, when the supply of convict labor to the camps was, seemingly, inexhaustible and individual human life of no value. The work team lead by young Kostochkin, an intellectual from Kharbin, periodically melts away—its members, hunger artists despite themselves, die of exhaustion and hunger-related diseases. The protagonist, Krist, is sent to this work team as a reinforcement. Physically weak at the start of the story, he keeps further losing his strength, even though, in recognition of his virtuoso handling of the spade, Kostochkin assigns him somewhat higher rations. One day, Kostochkin selects Krist as the recipient of a monetary reward. However, it turns out that all the money is going to Kostochkin himself. Drunk on the alcohol purchased with Krist's prize, Kostochkin displays his boxing skills, sending Krist into a knockout.

The same night Kostochkin is himself humbled by the visit of Minia the Greek, head of the team of professional criminals whose code does not allow them to do any work in the camps. In order to get provisions, the thieves' team has to show production results, and, there not being any, Minia imposes contributions on the other teams. This time, like a month ago, it is Kostochkin's turn. Kostochkin submits to the racket, even though the falsification of his own team's production reports will lead to a further reduction in his own hungry workers' diet.

The period of Lent, variously defined at different times in different places, involves a fast for the sake of physical and spiritual purification. This is a time set apart for asceticism, when the Will, to use Schopenhauer's concepts, is silenced and subdued. Schopenhauer, indeed, is a philosophical authority on the subject of Lent, just as Nietzsche is the philosophical presence behind Bakhtin's carnivalesque. Elsewhere (1997a) I have argued that Schopenhauer and Shalamov provide useful indirect comments on each other's work:[4] the descriptive part of Schopenhauer's exploration of asceticism is partly confirmed by Shalamov's works, but not the prescriptiveness of his praise of asceticism. A Schopenhauerian saint starves himself to death not because, like Kafka's hunger artist, he has never found any food to his liking, but because he (often, she) wishes to subdue the Will and disperse the illusion of discrete individuality, removing "the veil of Maya" (Schopenhauer I: 352, 380). What Kafka's *Hungerkünstler* seeks through his feats of fasting

---

4. Satz and Ozsvath (1978) make a similar point about Kafka's relationship to Schopenhauer.

is not to dissolve but to affirm his identity: rejecting physical nourishment, he seeks public admiration.[5]

Concentration camp inmates do not starve voluntarily: they are *denied* sufficient food for unlegislated periods—in concentration camps "prescribed hunger" (Levi 1990: 42) is one of the main instruments of discipline and torture. Yet if the imposition of the fast is corrupt, the victim's response to it may display genuine Lenten attitudes—indeed, a great number of concentration camp narratives, and Gulag narratives in particular, display the morphology of Lent, both in terms of body language and in ethical terms. What such works tend to suggest is that, up to a point, *the answer to hunger is fasting.* The point where this rule can no longer hold is that of the physiological changes, such as niacin deficiency, after which the onset of dementia can no longer be staved off by moral self-discipline.

Fasting, indeed, was one of the ways of maintaining personal dignity in the camps. Literal fasting took the shape of hunger strikes (held in the earliest and the latest periods in the history of the Gulag) or of Jewish observances of the Day of Atonement. A related but more pragmatic self-discipline could be observed in the attempts of veteran prisoners to avoid talking or thinking about food (the less experienced kept fantasizing about food and thus, actually, stimulated the secretion that damaged the walls of the stomach). Mainly, however, it was in a figurative sense that the Lenten abstention from carnivorousness was practiced by individual prisoners—those who refused to become cannibals, that is, refused to prolong their own lives at the expense of the lives of others,[6] to adopt the "you die today and I tomorrow" maxim of the criminal world, to hold jobs that involved bending the will of others, to fawn, to sell out. Such principles of behavior were also oppositional: while forcing themselves to obey official camp regulations, the angrily independent prisoners, in contrast to the toadies, informers, and "trusties," withheld consent and cooperation with the forces that were destroying them.

In Shalamov's stories, camp Lent is a communal experience but not a comprehensive one: alongside the majority of the starved there is an aggressive minority (professional criminals such as Minia the Greek, brutal team-leaders such as Kostochkin, and their loyal servants such as Os'ka) who seek power, safety, and food at all costs. The relationship between the two groups

5. This may be a Nietzschean moment in Kafka (see Bridgewater 1974: 134–35).

6. Interesting in this respect is Joseph Conrad's extraordinary 1901 short novella "Falk," based on the same period of the author's experience as "The Secret Sharer."

is a version of the carnivalesque hierarchy reversals: intellectuals and other formerly influential people are here reduced to the most downtrodden of victims, and the criminal underworld has joined the masters of their fate. Krist is surprised at getting an intellectual for an omnipotent team-leader— he would like to interpret this as a deviation from the pattern, perhaps even a sign of change; soon enough, however, Krist discovers the radical moral degradation of this once promising young man. In Kafka's story the vertical reversals first take the shape of the body's depletion to the state of almost irreversible dystrophy and then its gradual rising to the normal state. Towards the end of the story the reversal is the transformation of the admired to the abject, the star of the show turning into neglected refuse.

Lent, which usually follows the carnival in a religious calendar, is in these stories acted out in the spatial proximity of the carnival's corrupt look-alike. In the second part of Kafka's story, the cage, the oxymoronically public *oubliette* in which the Hunger Artist is eventually left to die, belongs to a sideshow of a circus, that fake carnival island amidst everyday burgher life. Instead of being placed center stage, on the arena, his cage serves as a peripheral extra attraction—or obstacle—on the way to the menagerie that the spectators visit during intermissions. Every day raw meat is taken to the animals past the Hunger Artist's cage. When the Hunger Artist dies, the same cage is assigned to a panther, the predatory untamed cat. In Shalamov's stories, it is carnival rather than fast that is insular, in the lifestyle of professional criminals and of the camp "prominents."[7] Corrupting the conventional temporary hierarchy reversal, the middle-aged Os'ka, a paterfamilias history professor, serves as young Kostochkin's bodyguard and court jester; Kostochkin himself is known as "the Tamer," and meat, metaphorically speaking, is taken past the barracks of political prisoners into the menagerie of the professional predators, the so-called honest thieves.

The difference between the carnivalesque narratives and the discourse of Lent is associated with the treatment of the boundary transgression. The carnival presents spectacles in which the borderlines between the actors and the spectators are erased, whereas in the experience of Kafka's and Shalamov's "artists" the spatial positions are not blended but reversed. The artist of the spade is first a spectator, then a participant: he first hears of Kostochkin's team and then is sent to join it—the common lot of the doomed others becomes his own lot. In the camp toolshed Krist is an actor, an artist in the handling of the spade; the audience is Kostochkin, who observes him and

---

7. This is also the case in Tadeusz Borowski's Auschwitz stories, which partly accounts for their complex, at times almost carnivalesque, effect.

rewards him with better rations. Later, Krist is again a spectator: from the dark "orchestra" of the sleeping-planks he observes Kostochkin, observer-turned-actor, in the only illuminated part of the barrack. And later Krist has to join Kostochkin in that footlighted arena, in the role of a martyr: he is beaten for an attempt to assert his rights, and this spectacle is silently observed by noninterfering teammates. After Kostochkin himself joins the tacit chorus of the sleepers at the walls of the barrack, it is Minia, symbolically nicknamed *the Greek*,[8] who appears on the stage in what looks like an ironic perversion of Nietzsche's account of Greek tragedy—as a king-subduing demigod, evoked, as it were, by Dionysian intoxication[9] (Kostochkin having consumed the alcohol that should have been distributed among the whole tacit chorus). Hinting at a vertical reversal, Minia, a would-be magician, intimates that the Tamer may one day be blown to pieces or have his head sawed off (cf. Bakhtin 1968: 303–67 on carnivalesque dismemberment), in the best tradition of the criminals' code of justice: predator would thus become prey.

Kafka's Hunger Artist is observed by the public while he, in his turn, observes and studies the spectators' behavior: on the two sides of the bars of his cage, both freedom and its lack are *relative* (Krist defines Kostochkin's education as "knowing who Einstein was"—a vague reminiscence of the theory of relativity). The bars of the cages give two-way views: the actors are also the spectators, but there is a boundary between the two groups. This boundary, however, is transparent and psychologically permeable; indeed, the primary responsibility for the hunger show lies with the public: it is the public who stages an experiment in survival, using the artist as a projection of its hopes and fears. At the expiration of the forty days, the period chosen for expediency (270) but also alluding to Christ's forty-day fast in the wilderness, the public watches as its representatives retrieve the hunger artist from his cage—his head lolling, his body hollowed out, his legs clinging to each

---

8. There can, of course, be several explanations of Minia's nickname. The topographical deployment of the story is reminiscent of the chorus and the stage in Greek tragedy but the name Minia the Greek also has a plain reality-effect: most of the "honest thieves" were known by their first names and nicknames that reflected either their origin, or the details of their specialization in the criminal world, or a feature of their character. For all we know, Shalamov may be describing an actual person of Greek origin, one who may, like Os'ka, have come from Odessa, which had substantial Jewish and Greek populations. On the other hand, his name may allude to Maksim the Greek, who translated the Psalms from Greek into Slavonic in 1552 and was known for his "'correction of the books' which later contributed to the schism of Old Belief" (Friedberg 1997: 22).

9. In "The Birth of Tragedy" Nietzsche notes that the "choral parts with which tragedy is interlaced are, as it were, the womb that gave birth to the whole of the so-called dialogue, that is, the entire world of the stage, the real drama. . . . the scene, complete with the action, was basically and originally thought of merely as a vision; the chorus is the only 'reality' and generates the vision, speaking of it with the entire symbolism of dance, tone, and words" (1966: 65).

other at the knees and barely scraping the ground. The smiling ladies who, in a parody on Pieta (cf. Ginsburg 1989: 36), are delegated to lead him to the table, grow pale with disgust or else with fear of his insidious touch; the one closest to him bursts into tears, "to the great delight of the spectators" (272).

The ritual of carnivalesque laughter partly distances the spectacle from the crowd that has financed—and thereby produced—the depletion and the revival of the Hunger Artist's body. Significantly, the Hunger Artist, the crowd's scout to the frontiers of the *Liebestod* (Neumarkt 1970: 110), is discarded at about the time the mass "destruction of the fittest" (Joyce, *Ulysses* 765), looming down from the proud towers of World War I, cancels the public interest in—or its need for—protracted shows of individual brinkmanship.[10] What attracts the observers at the end of the story, defining their new desires, is not the Hunger Artist's endurance but the robust vitality of the panther.

In carnivalesque narratives identities blend into a crowd when customary partitions, decorum, and self-restraint are voluntarily removed; in narratives of concentration camp experience, the discreteness of personality is likewise lost—but through lack instead of excess. From other stories by Shalamov (as well as from Solzhenitsyn 1978, Panin 1976, Kopelev 1977, Margolin 1952, Ginzburg 1981, Herling 1987, Razgon 1997, and others) we learn of the inroads that the environment makes on the convict's famished body, through untreated bruises, scurvy sores, frostbites, osteomyelytis, and on his peace of mind—through, among other things, absence of privacy. Body and mind, moreover, are causally related: the chronic starvation that depletes the limbs also contracts the brain, leading—at best—to a stunting of long-term memory. And yet the emotional experience of Shalamov's characters is more akin to the "secret sharing" than to the carnivalesque communion: each prisoner suffers his own hunger, his own bitterness, his own shame, his own fear of or indifference to death.[11]

In Gulag literature, indeed, the commonness of experience takes the shape not of the manifest pooling of affects but of seriality: this is forcefully evoked in the story of Volodin's arrest in Solzhenitzyn's *The First Circle:* the reader is given to understand that the processing Volodin undergoes in the

10. It seems, indeed, to be a historical fact that show fasts were largely discontinued at the outbreak of World War I; see Mitchell 1987: 250–51.

11. Newcomers to the camps can sometimes still produce choric scandal scenes—some are described in the memoirs of Julius Margolin. Even newcomers would soon learn, however, that group protest of any kind was a harshly punishable offense. It is only in the accounts of the camp rebellions of the fifties, described, for instance, in the third volume of Solzhenitsyn's *The Gulag Archipelago,* that the pooling of affects is prominently represented.

Lubianka prison upon his induction routinely replicates the experience of thousands of victims brought there before and after. What happens to Shalamov's characters is, with variations, what happens to thousands in Kolyma. Shalamov's ethically oriented exploration of their responses to their experience likewise enhances the sense of seriality: his characters seek to maintain some sense of their moral identity, on the basis of moral qualities that are culturally generalizable. It therefore often does not matter whether his separate stories are directly autobiographical or representative, fictionalized: what happens to one morally staunch and physically depleted former intellectual also happens, with minor variations, to another, whether the protagonist is "Shalamov," or "Andreev," the anonymous "I," or "Krist."

In Kafka's "A Hunger Artist" the sense of seriality is produced by iterative episodes:[12] at the beginning of the story the descriptions of the fasting ritual seem to be representative of the art of show-fasting as it was generally practiced; the definite article in "the hunger artist" is perceived as generic. Then the narrative passes from an account of the general practice to the repeated experience of one particular hunger artist whose name is withheld (some time after one loses track of his fasting days, the placards bearing his name get dirty and are torn down). Yet the story contains one singulative scene—that of the Hunger Artist's last words and death—as in Kafka's "Before the Law" (3–4), the gate that is then closed is the one that has been kept open for him alone. Here a touch of mystical respect for the individual breaks through the absurdity of the human condition. Yet in "A Hunger Artist," the circus overseer's command "Well, clear this out now," uttered in lieu of a funeral oration, is one that could well be used in Shalamov's Gulag world, in which even the passage through the ultimate gate would be imagined as serial. Shalamov's characters are generally driven to unheroic slow death, at the threshold of which they are denied outward dignity. The second story of the cycle to which "The Artist of the Spade"[13] belongs is "The Funeral Oration"—an attempt to restore to the dead the respectful attention that the regime had denied them to the very end.

According to Schopenhauer (I: 324), each man's life in its particulars is a comedy, but viewed as a whole, in retrospect, it is tragic. The cumulative tragedy of Shalamov's characters lies in the very absence of tragic grandeur in their individual suffering and death: individual claims to attention are erased by communal unconcern, by statistics, and by the emotional depletion of

12. An "iterative" scene (Genette 1980: 116) presents events that are supposed to have happened many times; episodes that present (once) what happened once are "singulative."
13. *Kolyma Tales*, Shalamov's main work, consists of three story cycles; later he composed several other story and sketch cycles.

the fellow sufferers who would have been best qualified to respond to such claims. Whereas Kafka's narrator has not lost the sense of the tragedy of the Hunger Artist's existential predicament, Shalamov's narratives emphasize the routinely serial character of in-camp deaths.[14] Only occasionally is a touch of the sublime added to his protagonists' near-death condition: like the biblical Job, Shalamov's goners are sometimes shown to be vaguely comforted by being "at peace with the beasts of the field" and "in league with the stones,"[15] that is, by versions of a mystical insight into the life of things. "The Artist of the Spade," however, belongs to those stories in which, instead of a mystical insight, the *morituri* get insights into the social semiotics of the system that is grinding them down.

In the corrupt Lent of Kafka's and Shalamov's stories, the unlimited fast that does not lead to moral or physical purification is also associated with corrupt forms of *ilinx,* the game of vertigo that is forced on the protagonist. Vertigo is a by-product of carnivalesque intoxication, but it can also result from the weakening of the chronically starved body. The predator and the victim in "The Artist of the Spade" experience vertigo—no playing matter—for these two diametrically opposite reasons.

As noted in the Introduction (pp. 15–17), game shares the structural features of carnival as another licensed subversion of the everyday order of things; it reinvigorates this order by forcing it to lose itself in order to find itself again (cf. Huizinga 1955: 10). Like carnival and Lent, this culture-bound cultural remission is circumscribed in time; unlike them, it is usually also circumscribed in space. Game is corrupted when it is not contained by spatio-temporal boundaries, and when it is not entered into voluntarily: in such cases loss does not lead to finding. Indeed, so long as the impresario is in charge of the Hunger Artist's forty-day fast and does not allow it to continue indefinitely, the game framework is maintained; this framework is abandoned when the artist and the impresario part and no one updates the notice board stating which day of the fast has been achieved. Death ceases to be symbolic or to lead to symbolic resurrection: it becomes real and stark;

14. As Nietzsche has noted in the essay "On the Genealogy of Morals," "Man, the bravest of animals and the one most accustomed to suffering, does not repudiate suffering as such; he desires it, he even seeks it out, provided he is shown a meaning for it, a purpose of suffering" (1966: 598).

15. Cf. Nietzsche's "The Birth of Tragedy" on the Dionysian reconciliation of man and nature: "Freely, earth proffers her gifts, and peacefully the beasts of prey of the rocks and deserts approach" (1966: 37).

the fast, once a form of *imitatio Christi,* no longer ends in even a parody of Pieta.

The drunken Kostochkin, who has been taught uppercuts and jabs by a former European champion, displays his own boxing virtuosity not in a fair competition but on the frail and unresisting body of Krist. In Shalamov's story, *ilinx* is catastrophically linked to *arête* that is divorced from *agôn.* Krist's economically precise movements in adjusting the spade, handling it, and handling the wheelbarrow earn him the title of "the artist of the spade," but, in the absence of physical strength, this technical perfection does not lead to good production results, and Krist knows that the deceptiveness of his visible skills, his self-protective *mimicry,* will soon become apparent. The Hunger Artist considers himself a fraud for a different reason. The public suspects that he might be cheating, secretly eating food smuggled into his cage; hence the spectators' round-the-clock vigils by his cage in the first part of the story—a difficulty incurred by a public that wants to make sure that there is a difficulty overcome by an artist. Actually, however, the fraud lies in the Artist's enjoyment of the attention that these vigils signify (a debased version of that prolonged attention which in "Art as Technique" Shklovsky demands for reality-defamiliarizing works of art). Insofar as both the stories contain elements of autodescriptive allegory (cf. also Rolleston 1995) they *thematize* the "suspicion of fraudulence" inherent in the experience of modernist art. Kafka's Hunger Artist does, indeed, cheat—in that he does not suffer the way the public expects him to suffer: for him the suffering comes not during the fast but when he has to break it, not in the period of Lent, the remission, but in the return to the quotidian. Shalamov's protagonist is a fraud not in that he gets better rations on false pretenses but in that most of the time he manages to conceal his inner resistance underneath external obedience. Insofar as Krist is also the avatar of the author, he also conceals—even from himself—a different kind of artist under the exterior of the depleted artists of the spade.

Shalamov's stories, unlike Kafka's, are not philosophical tales ("We were not philosophers. We were workers," he writes in "Sententia," 1978: 886; 1998, I: 358–59), but bifunctional documentary narratives whose aesthetic and communicative aspects become marked at different periods of reception.[16] As works of testimony, they have their own urgencies. Nor can they have the self-sufficiency of Kafka's narrative: the metaphysical vision that is implicit in

16. On the multifunctionality of any work of art see Mukařovský 1970 and 1978: 3–88.

Shalamov's work can only emerge from the interrelations between a number of his stories in combination with their broader contextual links.

Without the activation of the historical and philosophical *hors-text* Kafka's story can be underread but not misread; its intertextual reading creates surplus significances. In the case of Shalamov, intertextuality is mandatory rather than optional. Here the *hors-text* provides, as it were, the annotations without which the text may remain plainly misunderstood. Intertextual seepage is, in general, characteristic of the literature of testimony, if only because no internal evidence can vouch for a documentary text's historical veracity. Shalamov's work, however, occupies a special place in the literature of Gulag testimony: the intertext that it claims is not limited to corroborating testimony from similar geographical and social settings. The reading of his stories leaves one with a sense of unfinished business, of gnomonic gaps that open up his texts to precursor battlegrounds of images and ideas, to literary and philosophical backgrounds, the way the frostbitten, scurvy-scarred, lice-infested osteomyelytic bodies of the goners who populate his text are forced to open up to what is not themselves. At the same time, Shalamov's matter-of-fact insistence on the referentiality of the setting and on the testimonial function of his works holds the intertextual seepage in check, calling for a limit on the interpretive license of the reader. If in reading modernist literature one becomes conscious of not knowing how far interpretation can go, which of the far-fetched intra- or intertextual links are, as Samuel Johnson once put it, "worth the carriage" (1955, I: 15), and how much the reader becomes a part of the game of the text, hesitations of this kind are more urgent in the reading of documentary prose: here at issue is not the expense of the carriage but the reader's responsibility for not leaving the weight of the literal testimony too far behind.

CONCLUDING REMARKS

One day someone should write the history of "purity."

—Gadamer, *Truth and Method*, 92n177

AS NOTED THROUGHOUT THIS STUDY, the common denominator of aesthetic experience, of the carnivalesque, and of play is cultural remission, itself culturally or counterculturally constituted: the concerted marches of the social and intellectual causalities are interrupted, the rat race temporarily stopped, disciplined purities of principle are suspended, and new rules and options can be tried out. Even if such pauses help to perpetuate the order of things oppositionally, by perforating it, what they allow us to catch a glimpse of through the loopholes can no longer remain unseen.

With this common denominator in mind, I have examined the carnivalesque in narrative and the phenomena that bear a family resemblance to it (the discourse of non-carnivalesque oppositionality and the discourse of Lent). My immediate aim was to see whether the proposed method of analysis could yield new insights into well-loved texts, into their art of oppositional morphology and the specific ethical significance of their formal features. A remoter goal—to the remoteness of which these concluding remarks are devoted—was to begin to systematize the bearings that this analysis has on the ethics of narrative form.

The ethics of narrative form may be sought in the balance between, on the one hand, striving for maximal perfection according to a specific set of poetic principles and, on the other hand, the pragmatics of addressing specific target and hurdle audiences as well as the general reader. Finding such a balance between the opposite terms of the Author-Text-Reader communicative model often means negotiating a conflict between the aesthetic goal and the pragmatic objective.

Most of the findings of this book pertain to the construction of the Author-Text relationship, that "purposiveness without purpose" which Kant saw as an integral part of aesthetic excellence. Analysis of the narrative representations and reenactments of cultural remissions points to the ethical significance of the congruence (and, potentially, lack of it) between the form of content, the form of expression, and the substance of the content. Well aware of the impossibility of uncoupling form from content even under laboratory conditions, I have made use of these three coordinates of the Hjelmslev net[1] to extend the notion of "form" from narrative technique to the deployment of the themes, motifs, and the shape of the *fabula* in a narrative, their place in the semiological triad of semantics, syntactics, and pragmatics.

Two criteria, borrowed from anthropology, were used to determine the position of the work in the scale of the carnivalesque mode: the reversal of hierarchies and the blurring of boundaries between the self and its human, social, and natural environment. The analysis of the relationship between these features of the form of content has demonstrated the following narratological regularities also involving (1) the form of expression and (2) the substance of content.

(1) Carnivalesque narratives (here, specific works by Fielding, Sterne, Hawthorne, Dickens, Hardy, and Joyce) focus on crisis situations and involve corresponding limitations on the time frame of the main action; the beginning of the narrative tends to be at a point of a near-critical intensification of a tendency—rather than associated with the event of arrival or departure, death or birth, or similar troupe redeployment characteristic of non-carnivalesque ("biographical") narratives; the events of the story culminate in the temporary dissolution of identity; the story (the *fabula*) usually ends not with the return to the previous stabilities but with a shift, a change, a new beginning.

(2) The substance of the carnivalesque narratives' content usually includes a high view of human possibility, a longing for a deontological ethics, and an

---

1. The fourth coordinate, the substance of expression, the written narrative medium, is here a given. Lessing's *Laokoön,* which focuses on the effects of the medium of time and space arts, can actually be redescribed as the study of the relationship between the form of content and the substance of expression.

exploration of its versions and limits; by contrast, the ethical system inferable from non-carnivalesque narratives tends to be of the middle-way kind, with rule-utilitarian or contractarian skepticism about both the possibility of a totally selfless virtue and, conversely, the existence of ultimate evil.

As examples of the non-carnivalesque oppositional, I have discussed narratives by Austen and Conrad that likewise constitute cultural remissions. These narratives stage the turning of the alienating system's force vectors against the system itself in order to create loopholes for individual survival or self-realization. In the contractarian ethics constructed in these narratives (and in Conrad partly yielding to a protoexistentialism), even moments of supererogation represent a quest for individual splendor instead of, or at least in addition to, a self-sacrificial commitment to a goal outside the self.

Whereas the oppositional element in Jane Austen's fiction consists in her pointing to a system of values alternative to the ruling principles of her social setting yet mainly in such a way as to suggest that this alternative ethos is, in fact, the original contract on which society tends to renege, Conrad's more radical oppositionality privileges individual commitment over institutionalized ethics and social regulation. In both cases, however, a reconciliation with the hurdle audiences is largely effected when the subversion of some ethical conventions is balanced by a reaffirmation of other conventions or shared beliefs.

Whereas an artistic narrative usually serves as a testing ground for ideas, in some of the works discussed here, in particular in *Daniel Deronda* (an intermediate formation between the poles of the carnivalesque and the non-carnivalesque), the ethical *Weltanschauung* seems to be prior to its narrative refraction; in other cases (e.g., *Tristram Shandy*) the narrative clearly participates in the elaboration of the ethical system. The "Doctrine" inferable from the narrative of *Tom Jones* has developed unexpected ramifications in response to the pragmatic challenge of mystification; in Austen's novels, by contrast, the pragmatics of addressing the target and the hurdle audience leads to downplaying the oppositional force through poetic-justice endings that are, however, deftly integrated into the syntactic deployment of the novels' motifs.

Most of Conrad's fiction ("The Secret Sharer" being an apt example) stages test situations. Non-carnivalesque narratives of test tend to start not when a specific tendency in the protagonist comes to a head but when he is faced with an unexpected contingency—which, however, is the result of the swelling of a tendency elsewhere. As the protagonist is faced with the challenges for which he is not ripe, he recognizes in another the inclinations that he himself shares and that might, eventually, lead him to a crisis that has already overtaken the other. This "secret sharing," a recognition of a psychological kinship, does not lead to the carnivalesque pooling of affects; nevertheless, it has the power to reinforce oppositional attitudes.

Oppositionality is a broader phenomenon than the carnivalesque—the latter is, almost by definition, also oppositional. Joyce's *Ulysses* takes the liberating effect of a cultural remission almost to its logical completion when it carnivalizes its own sufficiently subversive brand of high seriousness—its own intellectual repertoire, one that aligns Joyce with some of the most innovative thinkers of his time but that, in its turn, is restrained by an aesthetic misrule that leaves the audience its intellectual freedom.

Modernist literature, of which *Ulysses* is one of the most admirable monuments, practically celebrates a liberation from its own artistic heritage—a liberation that, in retrospect, has proved to be a prolonged cultural remission with permanent effects rather than a radical aesthetic revolution. I believe that the end of this remission coincided with the historical "caesura," whose deepest abyss opened towards the middle decades of the twentieth century. The massive body of literature that testified to and processed that caesura— prominently including narratives of concentration camp experience—has formed, as a by-product, the critical mass necessary for a retrospective recognition of a new kind of discourse, the discourse of Lent—or rather the discourse of the corruption of Lent, in which some of the morphological features of the carnival, such as the blurring of borderlines between the individual and the environment, are produced, in a stifled form, not by excess but by lack, not through festiveness but through extreme deprivation, not through temporally circumscribed pleasure but through continuous, chronic, inexorably depleting pain. Lent stands in the relationship of family resemblance to carnival and non-carnivalesque oppositionality in that its dominant interpersonal relationship is not the carnivalesque pooling of affects but a serial enactment of the same fate, at times punctuated by moments of "secret sharing," tacit mutual understanding of people who do not even need to project themselves into each other in imagination because they know, or have known, the same experience in reality.

As the notion of family resemblance may also suggest, the discourse of Lent, which cannot be identified with the carnival even as its photonegative, cannot be fully identified with oppositional discourse either—if only because it does not seek to merely lighten the oppressive system responsible for the experience that such narratives recount: it may describe but does not seek to effect loopholes that can make this regime more livable when slightly subverted. What such multifunctional narratives seek to accelerate is, rather, the cancellation of the regime, or, if it has already fallen, a reversal of its consequences (for instance, salvaging its defaced victims from the common grave of oblivion) and a preemption of its recidivistic resurgence. The history of Russia, China, North Korea, Cambodia, Bosnia, Rwanda, and Darfur, to give but the best known examples, shows that the latter goal has not been achieved.

This issue is far beyond the question of the ethics of form in narrative, but it may be seen as its horizon. Representation of the carnival, the non-carnivalesque oppositional, play, "discharge" in the crowd, and aesthetic experience (with mystical transcendence remaining beyond, but only just, the threshold of these concerns) as cultural remissions entails viewing the logic of cultural determinacies as a disease, one likely to be lethal. I do not wish to retract this suggestion: it is, indeed, not an intrusion from outer space or an outbreak of madness but a concatenation of cultural causalities, with reactions to reactions and negations of negations, that, in the century which, some believe, started in 1914—or more likely in 1904 (the Herero genocide), or in 1896 (the first concentration camps, in Cuba)—has led states and communities over the brink of "caesurae" and may still lead to new precipices in the century that started with September 11, 2001. England may be seen as one of the few countries that have so far skirted the precipice, some of its literary works (e.g., the World War I poetry of Wilfred Owen and Siegfried Sassoon) coming sufficiently close to it. Though its charity would begin, and sometimes end, at home, its mainstream literary and philosophical tradition may well be credited with disseminating a culture that is complete with wholesomely endemic remissions. As noted above, the wilder offshoots of that march of mind and their further windings await a separate investigation.

I do not wish to end on that note any more than to make idealistically exaggerated claims either for literature or for aesthetics in general. In his book on "athletic beauty," Hans Ulrich Gumbrecht, one of the intellectuals who are painfully trying to conceptualize the movements towards and the aftermath of twentieth-century cataclysms, notes that he has never claimed that "enjoying sports—or enjoying beauty in general—has much of anything to do with moral improvement" (2006: 200). Not much, indeed. Moral improvement is predominantly a matter of individual moral commitment, whether instinctive, instilled by education, or endorsed by conscious choice—never an automatic effect of aesthetic experience, literary or other. Yet this does not deny the faith underneath my narratological analyses—that aesthetic experience can help fine-tune the ethical commitment by educating sensitivity, or perhaps even create the kind of *individual* cultural remission that is propitious for forming commitments. There is an indubitable ethical component in the history of the response that a text elicits from the beginning of the first reading to the end of the second, especially when it involves changes or reassessments of our attitudes—this is the ethics of the second half of the Author-Text-Reader communicative scheme. One should not, however, develop complacency on the basis of having lived through such literary experience: the ethical functioning that deserves credit is elsewhere, not in front of a book.

The regularities of the carnivalesque morphology, like other instruments of analysis, may be helpful in estimating and accounting for the aesthetic congruence that is perceived as striving for *arête*—which is also an ethical obligation of narrative form, whatever other ethical goals it may end up promoting or impeding. However, the possibility of different standards of perfection also means that, in view of a specific substance of content, the ethics of form may account for noncongruence, for self-contradictions, or for gaps.

One of the criteria for evaluating the measure of aesthetic congruence is the relationship between the modal status of the text and the predominant type of response that it elicits. The carnivalesque narrative mode need not entail carnivalesque experience on the part of the reader. Of the four games distinguished by Caillois, it is *mimicry*—in the sense of sympathetic identification and vicarious experience—that is the closest to a carnivalesque communion on the reader's part. Though cultural conditions largely determine our readiness to forget ourselves when absorbed in the joys and troubles of fictional characters or real-life narrators (as the case may be), narrative techniques, which can be only partly effective in creating such experience, can be fully effective in terminating or preempting it. The question whether the latter effect is an achievement or a failure is another juncture of aesthetic excellence and the ethics of form.

The substance of the narrative content includes ideas that belong to specific historically rooted ethical theories and to specific corrections to the schemata of those theories; narrative form produces effects that may or may not be congruent with the shape an ethical theory takes in the narrative's repertoire of ideas. These effects may be local or cumulative. The local effects produce a connected sequence of reader reactions, involving various combinations of surmises, expectations, readjustments, suspense, surprise, alternations of vicarious and analytic responses. They also produce the local felicities, minor aesthetic achievements which, as Housman and Nabokov have put it, we appreciate with the spine (literal or metaphoric) rather than with the head; thereby they also influence (but cannot control) the unstructurable oscillation between moments of aesthetic heightening and stretches of agonistic or aleatic engagement with the text. But it is mainly the cumulative effect of a work of art that gives us the sense of *arête,* a major difficulty overcome, an accomplishment in which an individual reader somehow becomes a participant, or a party, or a part.

Both types of effects are ethical and aesthetic in the broad (rather than laudatory) sense of these terms—in the sense that they are appropriate fields of study for the two branches of philosophy—ethical theory and aesthetics. They are also appropriate objects of criticism on ethical as well as aesthetic grounds.

Aesthetic experience is nothing to be particularly proud of. It is true that on seeing a rainbow Mr. Wordsworth might have a sense of his heart leaping up whereas his neighbor might just say that this is a nice day, but that same neighbor might not even know that his disinterested fascination with the elegant pacing of a thoroughbred horse or with the slow motion of a ship leaving the harbor is a form of ennobling aesthetic experience—a Mr. Wordsworth (or rather a Mr. Thoreau) might see in those only humdrum links in the chain of economic transactions.

Like happiness, aesthetic experience seldom comes when expected and often takes one unawares: one may fail to be awed in front of Mona Lisa in the Louvre but be arrested by a still life on the way to the cafeteria. Nor is this experience more pure than it is reliable. As I walked to an end of a block in a Paris street, map tucked away, the grim bulks of the Conciergerie swam into my field of vision from across the river. In the rush that transfixed me there were emotions, memories, thoughts of connotations, visual presence, the illusion of the prison's motion produced by a change of my own location in space. I recall that spot of time more vividly than more important events, and I recall that the indubitable aesthetic heightening of the moment was embittered by an unease about its source.

I sometimes suspect that in academic circles the hostility to the notion of aesthetic experience stems not only from the ideological critique of its being pressed into the service of bourgeois and imperial interests, and not only from a revolt against the highbrow scorn for "bad taste," but also from our lack of control over aesthetic experience in our own exposure to the beautiful and from the lack of cognitive mastery over the production of aesthetic effect.

The fascination that at times takes over in the reading of narrative, even when the reading has been initially undertaken for academic credit or in quest of "facts," is likewise unpredictable—and impure. At times it is practically indistinguishable from absorption in the "human interest" content of the narrative; it may actually be profoundly intermixed with it and extend towards imaginative identification, the game of *mimicry*. At other times it is produced not during the reading but on reflection about the semantic and syntactic patterns of the text—this is the case with the "effects of meaning" rather than the effects of imagined presence. The aesthetic enjoyment of the effects of meaning is not impaired even by the possibility that what we enjoy is not the intrinsic feature of a text but a construct of our own making, in response to the conditions created by the text.

More amenable to analysis, however, are points at which this experience of communion with something in the world of the text is interrupted by the consciousness of the vicissitudes of processing the flow of textual data—stumbling blocks that force us to backtrack and change our attitudes, conflicting instructions, surprises, veiled reference that points to the inadequacies of our training or attention (my *Eloquent Reticence* was devoted to some of these techniques of activating the reader's nonvicarious and not-disinterested analytic response to narrative). The experience of reading a narrative is that of a to-and-fro movement, with various and varying rhythms, an oscillation between self-forgetfulness and self-awareness, disinterestedness and vested interest, communion and self-assertion.

The ethics of narrative form is, among other things, a matter of the conditions that set the rhythms of this movement in individual works.

WORKS CITED

Abel, Elizabeth, Marianne Hirsch, and Elizabeth Langland. 1983. "Introduction," in *The Voyage In: Fictions of Female Development,* ed. Elizabeth Abel, Marianne Hirsch, and Elizabeth Langland. Hanover, N.H.: University Press of New England. 3–19.

Abraham, Nicolas, and Maria Torok. 1994. *The Shell and the Kernel: Renewals of Psychoanalysis.* Trans. Nicholas Rand. Chicago: University of Chicago Press.

Adamson, Jane. 1991. "Who and What Is Henchard? Hardy, Character and Moral Inquiry." *Critical Review* 31: 47–74.

Alter, Robert. 1968. *Fielding and the Nature of the Novel.* Cambridge, Mass.: Harvard University Press.

———. 1984. *Motives for Fiction.* Cambridge, Mass.: Harvard University Press.

Amis, Martin. 2002. *Koba the Dread: Laughter and the Twenty Million.* New York: Hyperion.

Aristotle. 1945. *The Nicomachean Ethics.* Trans. H. Rackham. London: Heinemann.

———. 1954. *Rhetoric and Poetics.* Trans. (respectively) by W. Rhys Roberts and Ingram Bywater. New York: Random House.

Armstrong, Isobel. 1988. *Jane Austen: Mansfield Park.* Harmondsworth, U.K.: Penguin Critical Studies.

———. 2000. *The Radical Aesthetic.* Oxford: Blackwell.

Armstrong, Nancy. 1987. *Desire and Domestic Fiction: A Political History of the Novel.* New York: Oxford University Press.

Austen, Jane. 1952. *Jane Austen's Letters to Her Sister Cassandra and Others.* Ed. R. W. Chapman. London: Oxford University Press.

———. 1954. *Minor Works* (*The Works of Jane Austen,* vol. VI). Ed. R. W. Chapman. London: Oxford University Press.

―――. 1978 [26 November 1771]. "The History of England." In *Love and Freindship and Other Early Works.* London: Women's Press. 67–79.

―――. 1994 [1811]. *Sense and Sensibility.* Harmondsworth, U.K.: Penguin Popular Classics.

―――. 1998 [1814]. *Mansfield Park.* Ed. Claudia L. Johnson. New York: Norton Critical Editions.

―――. 2000 [1816]. *Emma.* Ed. Stephen M. Parrish. 3rd ed. New York: Norton Critical Editions.

Auerbach, Nina. 1998. "Jane Austen's Dangerous Charm: Feeling as One Ought about Fanny Price." In Norton Critical Edition of *Mansfield Park,* 445–57. Reprinted from Todd 1983.

Averintsev, Sergei S. 1992. "Bakhtin and the Russian Attitude to Laughter." In *Bakhtin, Carnival, and Other Subjects: Selected Papers from the Fifth International Bakhtin Conference, University of Manchester, July 1991,* ed. David Shepherd. *Critical Studies* 3–4: 13–19.

Babb, Howard S. 1962. *Jane Austen's Novels: The Fabric of Dialogue.* Columbus: The Ohio State University Press.

Baker, Sheridan. 1967. "Bridget Allworthy: The Creative Pressures of Fielding's Plot." *Papers of the Michigan Academy of Science, Arts, and Letters* 52: 345–56. Reprinted in Henry Fielding, *Tom Jones,* ed. Sheridan Baker. New York: Norton Critical Editions, 1973.

Bakhtin, Mikhail. 1968. *Rabelais and His World.* Trans. Helene Iswolsky. Cambridge, Mass.: MIT Press. Reprinted by Indiana University Press, 1984.

―――. 1979. "Avtor i geroi v esteticheskoi deiatel'nosti." *Estetika slovesnogo tvorchestva.* Moscow: Iskusstvo.

―――. 1981. *The Dialogic Imagination. Four Essays.* Ed. Michael Holquist; trans Caryl Emerson and Michael Holquist. Austin: University of Texas Press.

―――. 1984 [1929]. *Problems of Dostoevsky's Poetics.* Ed. and trans. Caryl Emerson. Minneapolis: University of Minnesota Press.

Baldridge, Cates. 1998 [1990]. "Alternatives to Bourgeois Individualism in *A Tale of Two Cities.*" In *Critical Essays on Charles Dickens's "A Tale of Two Cities,"* ed. Michael Cotsell. New York: Hall. 168–86. Previously published in *Studies in English Literature* 30 (1990): 633–54.

Barnard, Teresa. 2009. "Anna Seward's 'Terrestrial Year': Women, Poetry, and Science in Eighteenth-Century England." *Partial Answers* 7, no. 1: 3–17.

Baron, Marcia. 1987. "Kantian Ethics and Supererogation." *Journal of Philosophy* 84:237–62.

Barthes, Roland. 1974 [1970]. *S/Z: An Essay.* Trans. Richard Miller. New York: Hill and Wang.

Battestin, Martin C. 1974. *The Providence of Wit: Aspects of Form in Augustan Literature and the Arts.* Oxford: Clarendon.

―――. 2000. *A Henry Fielding Companion.* Westport, Conn.: Greenwood Press.

Baudelaire, Charles. 1965. *Art in Paris 1845–1862: Salons and Other Exhibitions.* Trans. and ed. Jonathan Mayne. London: Phaidon Press.

Baumgarten, Murray. 1983. "Writing the Revolution." *Dickens Studies Annual* 12: 161–76.

Belcher, Margaret E. 1982. "Bulwer's Mr Bluff: A Suggestion for *Hard Times.*" *The Dickensian* 78: 105–9.

Bell, Robert H. 1991. *Jocoserious Joyce: The Fate of Folly in Ulysses.* Ithaca, N.Y.: Cornell University Press.

Bergson, Henri. 1944. *Creative Evolution.* Trans. Arthur Mitchell. New York: Random House.

———. 1956. "Laughter." In *Comedy.* Garden City, N.Y.: Doubleday Anchor Books. 61–190.

Berlin, Isaiah. 1990. *The Crooked Timber of Humanity: Chapters in the History of Ideas.* London: John Murray.

Bernheimer, Richard. 1952. *Wild Men in the Middle Ages: A Study in Art, Sentiment, and Demonology.* Cambridge, Mass.: Harvard University Press.

Bernstein, Michael André. 1992. *Bitter Carnival: Ressentiment and the Abject Hero.* Princeton, N.J.: Princeton University Press.

Berrong, Richard M. 1986. *Rabelais and Bakhtin: Popular Culture in* Gargantua *and* Pantagruel. Lincoln: University of Nebraska Press.

Berthoud, Jacques. 1984. "Shandeism and Sexuality." In Myer 1984, 24–38.

Birk, John F. 1991. "New Roots for *Merry Mount:* Barking Up the Wrong Tree?" *Studies in Short Fiction* 28: 345–53.

Blackwell, Bonnie. 2001. "*Tristram Shandy* and the Theater of the Mechanical Mother." *ELH* 68, no. 1: 81–133.

Bloom, Edward A. and Lillian D. Bloom. "'This Fragment of Life': From Process to Mortality." In Myer 1984, 57–72.

Bloom, Harold, ed. 1987. *Charles Dickens's A Tale of Two Cities.* New York: Chelsea House.

Booth, Wayne. 1961. *The Rhetoric of Fiction.* Chicago: University of Chicago Press.

———. 1988. *The Company We Keep: An Ethics of Fiction.* Berkeley: University of California Press.

Borg, Ruben. 2003. "A Fadograph of Whome: Topographies of Mourning in *Finnegans Wake.*" *Partial Answers* 1, no. 2: 87–110.

———. 2007. *The Measureless Past of Joyce, Deleuze and Derrida.* New York: Continuum Press.

Borges, Jorge Luis. 1964. *Labyrinths: Selected Stories and Other Writings.* Ed. Donald A. Yates and James E. Irby. New York: New Directions.

———. 1972 [1932]. "Narrative Art and Magic." *Triquarterly* 25: 209–15. Originally published as "El arte narrativo y la magia," in *Discusion* (Buenos Aires: Manuel Gleizer, 1932, 111–24).

Bradford, William. 1967 [1620–47]. *Of Plymouth Plantation.* Ed. Samuel Eliot Morison. New York: Modern Library.

Brewer, Michael. 1995. "Authorial, Lyric, and Narrative Voices: A Close Reading of Shalamov's *Sentenciia.*" Paper presented at the 1995 AATSEEL conference in Chicago.

Bridgwater, Patrick. 1974. *Kafka and Nietzsche.* Bonn: Bouvier.

Bristol, Michael D. 1985. *Carnival and Theater: Plebeian Culture and the Structure of Authority in Renaissance England.* New York: Methuen.

Broes, Arthur T. 1964. "Journey into Moral Darkness: *My Kinsman, Major Molineux* as Allegory." *Nineteenth-Century Fiction* 19: 171–84.

Brown, Julia Prewitt. 1979. *Jane Austen's Novels: Social Change and Literary Form.* Cambridge, Mass.: Harvard University Press.

Brownstein, Rachel M. 1997. "*Northanger Abbey, Sense and Sensibility, Pride and Preju-

214 / Works Cited

dice." In *The Cambridge Companion to Jane Austen,* ed. Edward Copeland and Juliet McMaster. Cambridge: Cambridge University Press. 32–57.

Budick, Emily Miller. 1986. "The World as Specter: Hawthorne's Historical Art." *PMLA* 101: 218–32.

———. 1989. *Fiction and Historical Consciousness: The American Romance Tradition.* New Haven, Conn.: Yale University Press.

Burkhardt, Sigurd. 1961. "*Tristram Shandy*'s Law of Gravity." *ELH* 28: 70–88.

Butler, Lance St John. 1994. "'Bosh' or: Believing Neither More nor Less—Hardy, George Eliot and God." In *New Perspectives on Thomas Hardy,* ed. Charles P. C. Petit. New York: St. Martin's Press. 108–15.

Butler, Marilyn. 1990 [1975]. *Jane Austen and the War of Ideas.* 2nd ed. Oxford: Clarendon.

Caillois, Roger. 1961 [1958]. *Man, Play, and Games.* Trans. Meyer Barash. New York: Cowell-Collier. Originally published as *Les Jeux et les Hommes* (Paris: Gallimard, 1958).

Canetti, Elias. 1978 [1962]. *Crowds and Power.* Trans. Carol Stewart. New York: Seabury Press.

Carey, John. 1993. *The Intellectual and the Masses: Pride and Prejudice among the Literary Intelligentsia, 1880–1939.* New York: St. Martin's Press.

Carlyle, Thomas. 1888 [1837]. *The French Revolution: A History.* London: Chapman and Hall.

Casarino, Cesare. 2002. *Modernity at Sea: Melville, Marx, Conrad in Crisis.* Minneapolis: University of Minnesota Press.

Cash, Arthur H. 1968. "The Birth of Tristram Shandy: Sterne and Dr Burton." In *Studies in the Eighteenth Century: Papers Presented at the David Nichol Smith Memorial Seminar,* Canberra, 1966, ed. R. F. Brissenden. Toronto: University of Toronto Press.

Castle, Terry. 1984. "The Carnivalization of Eighteenth-Century English Narrative." *PMLA* 99, no. 5: 903–16.

Cavell, Stanley. 1976. *Must We Mean What We Say? A Book of Essays.* Cambridge: Cambridge University Press.

———. 1987. *Disowning Knowledge in Six Plays of Shakespeare.* Cambridge: Cambridge University Press.

———. 1988. *In Quest of the Ordinary: Lines of Skepticism and Romanticism.* Chicago: University of Chicago Press.

Certeau, Michel de. 1984. *The Practice of Everyday Life.* Trans. Steven Rendall. Berkeley: University of California Press.

Chase, Cynthia. 1978. "The Decomposition of the Elephants: Double-Reading *Daniel Deronda.*" *PMLA* 93: 215–27.

Chambers, Ross. 1991. *Room for Maneuver: Reading (the) Oppositional (in) Narrative.* Chicago: University of Chicago Press.

Chazal, Roger. 1991. "*Mansfield Park* et l'embleme de l'oiseleur." *Études Anglaises* 44, no. 2: 185–201.

Christophersen, Bill. 1986. "*Young Goodman Brown* as Historical Allegory: A Lexical Link." *Studies in Short Fiction* 23: 202–4.

Clabough, Casey. 2003. "Cwmrhydyceirw and the Art of Resistant Otherness: The Everyday Spaces and Consumer Practices in Kingsley Amis's *Lucky Jim.*" *Partial Answers* 1, no. 2: 111–23.

Clowes, Edith. 1988. *The Revolution of Moral Consciousness: Nietzsche in Russian Literature 1890–1914*. DeKalb: Northern Illinois University Press.

———. 1994. "Kafka and Russian Experimental Fiction in the Thaw, 1956–1965." *Modern Language Review* 89: 149–65.

Cohn, Dorrit. 1999. *The Distinction of Fiction*. Baltimore: Johns Hopkins University Press.

Colacurcio, Michael. 1984. *The Province of Piety: Moral History in Hawthorne's Early Tales*. Cambridge: Cambridge University Press.

Collins, Irene. 1994. *Jane Austen and the Clergy*. London: Hambledon Press.

Conrad, Joseph. 1998 [1910]. "The Secret Sharer." In *Typhoon and Other Tales*, ed. Cedric Watts. Oxford: Oxford University Press. 177–217.

Copeland, Edward. 2006. "Introduction." In Jane Austen, *Sense and Sensibility*. Cambridge: Cambridge University Press. xxiii–lxv.

Coronato, Rocco. 2003. *Jonson versus Bakhtin: Carnival and the Grotesque*. Amsterdam: Rodopi.

Cott, Nancy F. 1978. "Passionlessness: An Interpretation of Victorian Sexual Ideology, 1790–1850." *Signs: Journal of Women in Culture and Society* 4, no. 1: 219–36.

Crews, Frederick C. 1966. *The Sins of the Fathers: Hawthorne's Psychological Themes*. New York: Oxford University Press.

Curtis, James M. 1986. "Michael Bakhtin, Nietzsche, and Russian Pre-Revolutionary Thought." In Rosenthal 1986, 331–54.

Curtius, Ernst Robert. 1953. *European Literature and the Latin Middle Ages*. Trans. Willard R. Trask. New York: Pantheon Books, Bollingen Series 36. Originally published as *Europäissche Literatur und leteinisches Mittelalter* (Bern: A. Crancke, 1948).

Daleski, H. M. 1970. *Dickens and the Art of Analogy*. London: Faber and Faber.

———. 1977. *Joseph Conrad: The Way of Dispossession*. London: Faber and Faber.

———. 1985. *Unities: Studies in the English Novel*. Athens: University of Georgia Press.

———. 1987. "Joyce's 'Circe': A Tale of Dragons." In *Essays on English and American Literature and a Sheaf of Poems Presented to David Wilkinson*. Amsterdam: Rodopi. 151–63.

———. 1997. *Thomas Hardy and Paradoxes of Love*. Columbia: University of Missouri Press.

Day, Robert Adams. 1980. "How Stephen Wrote His Vampire Poem." *James Joyce Quarterly* 17, no. 2: 183–97.

Dazey, Mary Ann. 1986. "Shared Secret or Secret Sharing in Joseph Conrad's 'The Secret Sharer.'" *Conradiana* 18: 201–3.

Deleuze, Gilles. 1991 [1966]. *Bergsonism*. Trans. Hugh Tomlinson and Barbaraa Habberjam. New York: Zone Books.

Deleuze, Gilles, and Félix Guattari. 1992. "1933: Micro Politics and Segmentarity." *A Thousand Plateaus: Capitalism & Schizophrenia II*. London: Athlone Press.

Derrida, Jacques. 1981 [1968]. "Plato's Pharmacy." Trans. Barbara Johnson. In *Dissemination*. Chicago: University of Chicago Press. 61–156. Originally published as "La Pharmacie de Platon" in *Tel Quel* 32 (1968): 3–48; 33: 118–59.

Devlin, David Douglas. 1975. *Jane Austen and Education*. London: Macmillan.

Dever, Carolyn. 2006. "Psychoanalysing Dickens." In *Palgrave Advances in Charles Dickens Studies*, ed. John Bowen and Robert L. Patten. Basingstoke: Palgrave Macmillan. 216–33.

Dickens, Charles. 1969 [1854]. *Hard Times.* Ed. David Craig. London: Penguin.
———. 1977 [1853]. *Bleak House.* Ed. George Ford and Sylvère Monod. New York: Norton Critical Editions.
———. 1993 [1965]. *The Letters of Charles Dickens.* Ed. Madeline House and Graham Storey; assoc. ed. Kathleen Tillotson. Oxford: Clarendon.
———. *A Tale of Two Cities.* 2000 [1859]. Ed. Richard Maxwell. London: Penguin Classics.
Diamond, Cora. 1991 [1983]. "Having a Rough Story about What Moral Philosophy Is." In *The Realistic Spirit: Wittgenstein, Philosophy, and the Mind.* Cambridge, Mass.: MIT Press. 367–81. First published in *New Literary History* 15 (1983): 155–69.
———. 1997. "Moral Differences and Distances: Some Questions." In *Commonality and Particularity in Ethics,* ed. Lilli Alanen, Sara Heinamaa, and Thomas Wallgren. New York: St. Martin's Press. 197–234.
Docherty, Thomas. 2003. "Aesthetic Education and the Demise of Experience." In Joughin and Malpas 2003, 23–35.
Dollimore, Jonathan. 2003. "Art in Time of War: Towards a Contemporary Aesthetics." In Joughin and Malpas 2003, 36–50.
Duckworth, Alistair M. 1971. *The Improvement of the Estate: A Study of Jane Austen's Novels.* Baltimore: Johns Hopkins University Press.
During, Lisabeth. 1998. "The Concept of Dread: Sympathy and Ethics in *Daniel Deronda.*" In *Renegotiating Ethics in Literature, Philosophy, and Theory,* ed. Jane Adamson, Richard Freadman, and David Parker. Cambridge: Cambridge University Press. 65–83.
Eakin, Paul John. 2009. "Eye and I: Negotiating Distance in Eyewitness Narrative." *Partial Answers* 7, no. 2: 201–12.
Eagleton, Terry. 1990. *The Ideology of the Aesthetic.* Malden, Mass.: Blackwell.
Easterly, Joan Elizabeth. 1991. "Lachrymal Imagery in Hawthorne's *Young Goodman Brown.*" *Studies in Short Fiction* 28: 339–43.
Eco, Umberto. 1990 [1988]. *Foucault's Pendulum.* Trans. William Weaver. New York: Ballantine.
Eigner, Edwin M. 1987. "Charles Darnay and Revolutionary Identity." In Bloom 1987, 37–56. Reprinted from *PMLA* 93, no. 3 (1978).
———. 1989. *The Dickens Pantomine.* Berkeley: University of California Press.
Ek, Grete. 1979. "Glory, Jest, and Riddle: The Masque of Tom Jones in London." *English Studies* 60: 148–58.
Elias, Norbert. 1982. *The Civilizing Process, Volume 2: State Formation and Civilization.* Trans. Edmund Jephcott. Oxford: Basil Blackwell.
Eliot, George. 1901. [1879]. *Impressions of Theophrastus Such: Essays and Leaves from a Note-Book.* Edinburgh: William Blackwood. X: 356–96.
———. 1977. *Middlemarch.* Ed. Bert G. Hornback. New York: Norton Critical Editions.
———. 1990. *Daniel Deronda.* Ed. Terence Cave. Harmondsworth, U.K.: Penguin.
Ellmann, Richard. 1983. *James Joyce.* Oxford: Oxford University Press.
Facknitz, Mark R. A. 1987. "Cryptic Allusions and the Moral of the Story: The Case of Joseph Conrad's *The Secret Sharer.*" *The Journal of Narrative Technique* 17: 115–30.
Faulkner, William. 1960 [1940]. "The Pantaloon in Black." In *Go Down, Moses.* Harmondsworth: Penguin. 107–25.

Ferguson, Frances. 2005. "On Terrorism and Morals: Dickens's *A Tale of Two Cities*." *Partial Answers* 3, no. 2: 49–74.

Fielding, Henry. 1972 [1743]. "Of Good Nature." In *Miscellanies,* ed. Henry Knight Miller. Oxford: Oxford University Press, vol. I: 30–35.

———. 1987 [1742]. *Joseph Andrews, with Shamela and Related Writings.* Ed. Homer Goldberg. New York: Norton.

———. 1995 [1750]. *Tom Jones: The Authoritative Text, Contemporary Reactions, Criticism.* Ed. Sheridan Baker. 2nd ed. New York: Norton.

Fisher, Joe. 2000 [1992]. "*The Mayor of Casterbridge:* Made of Money." In Wolfreys 2000, 132–52. Reprinted from Joe Fisher, *The Hidden Hardy* (Basingstoke, U.K.: Macmillan, 1992, 115–35).

Fitzpatrick, Tony. 2005. "The Trisected Society: Social Welfare in Early Victorian Fiction." *Partial Answers* 3, no. 2: 23–47.

Fleishman, Avrom. 1967. *A Reading of Mansfield Park: An Essay in Critical Synthesis.* Minneapolis: University of Minnesota Press.

Fontanier, Pierre. 1977 [1827–30]. *Les Figures du discours.* Paris: Flammarion.

Fox, Kate. 2004. *Watching the English: The Hidden Rules of English Behaviour.* London: Hodder and Stoughton.

Fraiman, Susan. 1993. *Unbecoming Women: British Women Writers and the Novel of Development.* New York: Columbia University Press.

Frank, Lawrence. 1984. *Charles Dickens and the Romantic Self.* Lincoln: University of Nebraska Press.

Frankl, Victor. 1962. *Man's Search for Meaning: An Introduction to Logotherapy.* Trans. Ilse Lasch. Boston: Beacon. Originally published as *Ein Psycholog erlebt das Konzentrationslager* in 1946.

Freud, Sigmund. 1955 [1919]. "The Uncanny." In *The Standard Edition of the Complete Psychological Works of Sigmund Freud,* ed. James Strachey. London: Hogarth. XVII: 217–56.

———. 1961 [1929]. *Civilization and Its Discontents.* Trans. and ed. James Strachey. New York: Norton.

Friedberg, Maurice. 1997. *Literary Translation in Russia: A Cultural History.* University Park: Pennsylvania State University Press.

Friedlander, Saul, ed. 1992. *Probing the Limits of Representation: Nazism and the "Final Solution."* Cambridge, Mass.: Harvard University Press.

Frye, Northrop. 1957. *The Anatomy of Criticism: Four Essays.* Princeton, N.J.: Princeton University Press.

Gadamer, Hans-Georg. 1989 [1960]. *Truth and Method.* 2nd rev. ed. Trans. and rev. by Joel Weinsheimer and Donald G. Marshall. London: Sheed and Ward.

Gallagher, Catherine. 1987 [1983]. "The Duplicity of Doubling in *A Tale of Two Cities*." In Bloom 1987, 73–94. Reprinted from *Dickens Studies Annual* 12 (1983): 125–45.

Garber, Marjorie, with Barbara Johnson. 1987. "Secret Sharing: Reading Conrad Psychoanalytically." *College English* 49: 628–40.

Garson, Marjorie. 2000 [1991]. "*The Mayor of Casterbridge:* The Bounds of Propiety." In Wolfreys 2000, 80–115. Reprinted from Marjorie Garson, *Hardy's Fables of Integrity: Woman, Body, Text* (Oxford: Clarendon, 1991, 94–130).

Gatrell, Simon. 2000 [1993]. "*The Mayor of Casterbridge:* The Fate of Michael

Henchard's Character." In Wolfreys 2000, 48–79. Reprinted from Simon Gatrell, *Thomas Hardy and the Proper Study of Mankind* (Basingstoke, U.K.: Macmillan, 1993, 68–96).

Genette, Gérard. 1980. *Narrative Discourse: An Essay in Method.* Trans. Jane E. Lewin. Ithaca, N.Y.: Cornell University Press.

Gennep, Arnold van. 1960 [1908]. *The Rites of Passage.* Trans. Mokina V. Vizendom and Gabrielle L. Caffee. London: Loutledge and Kegan Paul.

Gibbon, Frank. 1982. "The Antiguan Connection: Some New Light on *Mansfield Park.*" *Cambridge Quarterly* 12: 298–305.

Gifford, Don, with Robert J. Seidman. 1988. *Ulysses Annotated: Notes for James Joyce's Ulysses.* Rev. and exp. ed. Berkeley: University of California Press.

Gilbert, Sandra M., and Susan Gubar. 1979. *The Madwoman in the Attic: The Woman Writer and the Nineteenth-Century Literary Imagination.* New Haven, Conn.: Yale University Press.

Gilbert, Stuart. 1952 [1930]. *James Joyce's Ulysses: A Study.* London: Faber and Faber.

———. 1957. "Introduction." In *Letters of James Joyce,* ed. Stuart Gilbert. London: Faber and Faber. 21–41.

Gillespie, Michael Patrick. 1983. *Inverted Volumes Improperly Arranged: James Joyce and His Trieste Library.* Ann Arbor, Mich.: UMI Research Press.

Ginsburg, Ruth. 1989. "*Karneval und Fasten: Exzess und Mangel in der Sprache des Körpers.*" *Poetica* 21: 26–42.

Ginzburg, E. 1967. *Journey into the Whirlwind.* Trans. Paul Stevenson and Max Hayward. San Diego: Harcourt Brace Jovanovich.

———. 1981. *Within the Whirlwind.* Trans. Ian Boland. San Diego: Harcourt Brace Jovanovich.

Girard, René. 1977 *Violence and the Sacred.* Trans. Patrick Gregory. Baltimore: Johns Hopkins University Press. Originally published as *La Violence et le sacré* (Paris: Bernard Grasset, 1972).

Glasheen, Adaline. 1974. "Calypso." In Hart and Hayman 1974, 51–70.

Goldberg, Michael. 1972. *Carlyle and Dickens.* Athens: University of Georgia Press.

Grabes, Herbert. 2007. "Culture or Literature." *Partial Answers* 5, no. 2: 153–64.

Graef, Ortwin de. 2004. "Encrypted Sympathy: Wordsworth's Infant Ideology." *Partial Answers* 2, no. 1: 21–51.

———. 2010 (forthcoming). "'A Common Humanity Is Not Yet Enough': Shadows of the Coming Race in George Eliot's Final Fiction."

Greene, Donald J. 1953. "Jane Austen and the Peerage." *PMLA* 68: 1017–31.

Greimas, Algirdas Julien. 1974 [1966]. *Sémantique structurale: Recherche de méthode.* Paris: Librairie Larousse.

Groys, Boris. 1994. "Nietzsche's Influence on the Non-Official Culture of the 1930s," in Rosenthal 1994, 367–89.

Guerard, Albert. "Introduction," in Joseph Conrad, *The Secret Sharer and Heart of the Darkness.* New York: Signet, 1950. 7–15.

Gumbrecht, Hans Ulrich. 2004. *Production of Presence: What Meaning Cannot Convey.* Stanford, Calif.: Stanford University Press.

———. 2006. *In Praise of Athletic Beauty.* Cambridge, Mass.: Belknap Press of Harvard University Press.

Hammond, Brean S. 1993. "The Political Unconscious in *Mansfield Park.*" In Wood 1993, 56–90.

Harding, D. W. 1962. "The Psychological Processes in the Reading of Fiction." *British Journal of Aesthetics* 2: 133–47.

Hardy, Barbara. 1970. *The Moral Art of Dickens*. London: Athlone Press.

Hardy, Florence Emily. 1928. *The Early Life of Thomas Hardy: 1840–1891*. New York: Macmillan.

Hardy, Thomas. 1977 [1886]. *The Mayor of Casterbridge*. Ed. James K. Robinson. New York. Norton Critical Editions.

———. 1981 [1895]. *Jude the Obscure*. Ed. C. H. Sisson. Harmondsworth, U.K.: Penguin.

———. 1991 [1891]. *Tess of the D'Urbervilles*. Ed. Scott Elledge. 3rd ed. New York. Norton Critical Editions.

Harrison, Bernard. 1975. *Henry Fielding's Tom Jones: The Novelist as Moral Philosopher*. London: Sussex University Press.

———. 1989. "Morality and Interest." *Philosophy* 64: 303–22.

———. 1991. *Inconvenient Fictions: Literature and the Limits of Irony*. New Haven, Conn.: Yale University Press.

———. 1993/1994. "Gaps and Stumbling-Blocks in Fielding: A Response to Cerny, Hammond and Hudson." *Connotations: A Journal for Critical Debate* 3, no. 2: 147–72.

———. 1994. "Sterne and Sentimentalism." In *Commitment in Reflection: Essays in Literature and Moral Philosophy*, ed. Leona Toker. New York: Garland. 63–100.

———. 2006. *The Resurgence of Anti-Semitism: Jews, Israel and Liberal Opinion*. Lanham, Md.: Rowman and Littlefield.

Harshaw (Hrushovski), Benjamin. "Fictionality and Fields of Reference: Remarks on the Theoretical Framework." *Poetics Today* 5 (1984): 227–51.

Hart, Clive, and David Hayman, eds. 1974. *James Joyce's "Ulysses": Critical Essays*. Berkeley: University of California Press.

Hawthorne, Nathaniel. 1937. *The Complete Novels and Selected Tales of Nathaniel Hawthorne*. Ed. Normal Holmes Pearson. New York: Modern Library.

Hayman, David. 1974. "Cyclops." In Hart and Hayman 1974, 234–75.

Henry, Nancy. 2002. *George Eliot and the British Empire*. Cambridge: Cambridge University Press.

Herling (Herling-Hrudzinski), Gustav. 1987 [1951]. *A World Apart*. Trans. Joseph Marek. Oxford: Oxford University Press.

Herman, David. 2007. "Narrative Theory and the Intentional Stance." *Partial Answers* 6, no. 2: 233–60.

Hinnant, Charles H. 2006. "Jane Austen's 'Wild Imagination': Romance and the Courtship Plot in the Six Canonical Novels." *Narrative* 14, no. 3: 294–310.

Hill, Bridget. 2001. *Women Alone: Spinsters in England 1660–1850*. New Haven, Conn.: Yale University Press.

Hjelmslev, Lewis. 1969. *Prolegomena to a Theory of Language*. Madison: University of Wisconsin Press.

Hoffman, Daniel. 1961. *Form and Fable in American Fiction*. New York: Oxford University Press.

Hopkins, Robert. 1978. "General Tilney and Affairs of State: The Political Gothic of *Northanger Abbey*." *Philological Quarterly* 57: 213–24.

Howe, Irving. 1980. "Beyond Bitterness." *The New York Review of Books* 27 (August 14): 36–37.

Huizinga, Johan. 1955 [1950]. *Homo Ludens: A Study of the Play Element in Culture.* Boston: Beacon.

Humphrey, Mary Jane. 1991. "Mrs. Palmer and Her Laughter." *Persuasions* 13: 13–15.

Hunt, Lynn. 1992. *The Family Romance of the French Revolution.* Berkeley: University of California Press.

Hutter, Albert D. 1987. "Nation and Generation in *A Tale of Two Cities.*" In Bloom 1987, 37–56. Reprinted from *PMLA* 93, no. 3 (1978): 448–62.

Ingersoll, Earl. 1990. "Writing and Memory in *The Mayor of Casterbridge.*" *ELT* 33, no. 3: 299–309.

Iser, Wolfgang. 1974 [1972]. *The Implied Reader: Patterns of Communication in Prose Fiction from Bunyan to Beckett.* Baltimore: Johns Hopkins University Press.

———. 1978 [1976]. *The Act of Reading: A Theory of Aesthetic Response.* Baltimore: Johns Hopkins University Press.

———. 1988. *Laurence Sterne. Tristram Shandy.* Trans. David Henry Wilson. Cambridge: Cambridge University Press.

———. 1989. *Prospecting: From Reader Response to Literary Anthropology.* Baltimore: Johns Hopkins University Press.

———. 1993 [1991]. *The Fictive and the Imaginary: Charting Literary Anthropology.* Baltimore: Johns Hopkins University Press.

Ivanov, V. V. 1976. "The Significance of Bakhtin's Ideas on Sign, Utterance and Dialogue for Modern Semiotics." *Papers on Poetics and Semiotics,* no. 4. Tel Aviv: Institute for Poetics and Semiotics, Tel Aviv University.

James, Henry. 1987. *The Critical Muse: Selected Literary Criticism.* Ed. Roger Gard Harmondsworth, U.K.: Penguin.

Jarvis, William. 1996. *Jane Austen and Religion.* Witney, Oxon, U.K.: Stonesfield Press.

Johnson, Barbara, and Marjorie Garber. 1987. "Secret Sharing: Reading Conrad Psychoanalytically." *College English* 49: 628–40.

Johnson, Bruce. 1983. *True Correspondence: A Phenomenology of Thomas Hardy's Novels.* Tallahassee: University Press of Florida.

Johnson, Claudia L. 1988. *Jane Austen: Women, Politics, and the Novel.* Chicago: University of Chicago Press.

———. 1993. "Gender, Theory and Jane Austen Culture." In Wood 1993, 91–120.

Johnson, Samuel. 1955 [1781]. *Lives of the English Poets.* London: Oxford University Press, 2 vols.

Johnston, Kenneth. 1983. "The Politics of 'Tintern Abbey.'" *The Wordsworth Circle* 14: 6–14.

Johnstone, Peggy Fitzhugh. 1994. "The Pattern of the Myth of Narcissus in *Daniel Deronda.*" In *The Transformation of Rage: Mourning and Creativity in George Eliot's Fiction.* New York: New York University Press. 159–80.

Joughin, John J., and Simon Malpas, eds. 2003. *The New Aestheticism.* Manchester, U.K.: Manchester University Press.

Joyce, James. 1960 [1916]. *A Portrait of the Artist as a Young Man.* Harmondsworth, U.K.: Penguin.

———. 1999 [1939]. *Finnegans Wake.* London: Penguin.

———. 2000 [1922]. *Ulysses.* London: Penguin Classics.

Kafka, Franz. 1976. *Complete Stories.* Ed. Nahum N. Glatzer. New York: Schoken.

Kant, Immanuel. 1946 [1785]. *Fundamental Principles of the Metaphysics of Ethics.* Trans. Thomas Kingsmill Abbott. London: Longmans, Green.

————. 1951 [1790]. *Critique of Judgment.* Trans. J. H. Bernard. New York: Hafner.

Kelly, Gary. 1982. "Reading Aloud in *Mansfield Park.*" *Nineteenth-Century Literature* 37: 29–49.

Klarer, Mario. 1999. "Cannibalism and Carnivalesque: Incorporation as Utopia in the Early Image of America." *New Literary History* 30, no. 2: 389–410.

Klawitter, Robert. "Henri Bergson and James Joyce's Fictional World." *Comparative Literature Studies* 3 (1966): 429–37.

Klein, Scott W. 1994. *The Fictions of James Joyce and Wyndham Lewis: Monsters of Nature and Design.* Cambridge: Cambridge University Press.

Knowles, Ronald. 1998. *Shakespeare and Carnival: After Bakhtin.* Basingstoke, U.K.: Macmillan.

Knox-Shaw, Peter. 2004. *Jane Austen and the Enlightenment.* Cambridge: Cambridge University Press.

Krzychylkiewicz, Agata. 2006. *The Grotesque in the Work of Bruno Jasieński.* Bern: Peter Lang.

Koestler, Arthur. 1941. *Darkness at Noon.* Trans. Daphne Hardy. New York: Macmillan.

————. 1945. *The Yogi and the Commissar and Other Essays.* London: Hutchinson.

Kopelev, Lev. 1977 [1975]. *To Be Preserved Forever.* Trans. Anthony Austin. Philadelphia: J. B. Lippincott. Also published as *No Jail for Thought* (London: Secker and Warburg).

Kotek, Joël, and Pierre Rigoulot. 2000. *Le Siècle des camps: Détention, concentration, extermination. Cent ans de mal radical.* Paris: JCLattès.

Krook, Dorothea. 1959. *Three Traditions of Moral Thought.* Cambridge: Cambridge University Press.

Kuhns, Richard. 1983. "The Strangeness of Justice: Reading *Michael Kohlhaas.*" *NLH* 15, no. 1: 73–91.

Kumar, Krishan. 1987. *Utopia and Anti-Utopia in Modern Times.* Oxford: Blackwell.

Lacoue-Labarthe, Philippe. 1987. *La Fiction du Politique: Heidegger, l'art et la politique.* Paris: Christian Bourgois.

Lakoff, George, and Mark Johnson. 1980. *Metapohors We Live By.* Chicago: University of Chicago Press.

Lamb, Jonathan. 1989. *Sterne's Fiction and the Double Principle.* Cambridge: Cambridge University Press.

Lejeune, Philippe. 1989. *On Autobiography.* Ed. Paul John Eakin; trans. Katherine Leary. Minneapolis: Minnesota University Press.

Le Roy Ladurie, Emmanuel. 1979. *Carnival in Romans.* Trans. Mary Feeney. New York: George Braziller. Originally published as *Le Carnaval du Romans* (Paris: Gallimard, 1979).

Levi, Primo. 1988. *The Drowned and the Saved.* Trans. Raymond Rosenthal. Harmondsworth, U.K.: Sphere Books.

————. 1990. *If This is a Man / The Truce.* Trans. Stuart Woolf. London: Abacus.

Levine, David. 1962. "Shadows of Doubt: Specter Evidence in *Young Goodman Brown.*" *American Literature* 34: 335–43.

Levine, George. 1994. "Introduction: Reclaiming the Aesthetic." In *Aesthetics and Ideology,* ed. George Levine. New Brunswick, N.J.: Rutgers University Press. 1–30.

————. 2001. "Saving Disinterest: Aesthetics, Contingency, and Mixed Conditions." *New Literary History* 32: 907–32.

Levinson, Jerrold. 2003. "Philosophical Aesthetics: An Overview." In *The Oxford Handbook of Aesthetics,* ed. Jerrold Levinson. Oxford: Oxford University Press. 3–24.

Lewis, Wyndham. 1957 [1927]. *Time and the Western Man.* Boston: Beacon.

Lodge, David. 1982. "Double Discourses: Joyce and Bakhtin." *James Joyce Broadsheet* 11.

Longstaffe, Stephen. 1998. "'A Short Report and not Otherwise': Jack Cade in *2 Henry VI.*" In Knowles 1998, 13–35.

Lotman, Yu M., and Ba A. Uspenskij. 1984. *The Semiotics of Russian Culture.* Ed. Ann Shukman. Ann Arbor: University of Michigan (Michigan Slavic Contributions).

Loveridge, Mark. 1992. "Stories of COCKS and BULLS: The Ending of *Tristram Shandy.*" *Eighteenth-Century Fiction* 5, no. 1: 35–54.

Mackey, Peter Francis. 1999. *Chaos Theory and James Joyce's Everyman.* Gainesville: University Press of Florida.

Magnet, Myron. 1985. *Dickens and the Social Order.* Philadelphia: University of Pennsylvania Press.

Mannheim, Karl. 1955. *Ideology and Utopia: An Introduction to the Sociology of Knowledge.* Trans. Louis Wirth and Edward Shils. New York: Harcourt, Brace.

Marchenko, Anatolii. 1969. *Moi pokazaniia.* Frankfurt: Possev. Eng. trans. Michael Scammell: *My Testimony* (London: Pall Mall Press).

Marcus, Amit. 2005. Kazuo Ishiguro's *The Remains of the Day:* The Discourse of Self-Deception." *Partial Answers* 4, no. 1: 129–50.

Margolin, Julius. 1952 [1949]. *Puteshestvie v stranu zelka [Journey into the Country of Z/K].* New York: Chekhov Publishing House. First published in the French translation by Nina Berberova and Mina Journot as *La condition inhumaine: Cinq ans dans les camps de concentration soviétiques* (Paris: Calmann-Lévy, 1949).

Marshall, David. 1986. *The Figure of Theater: Shaftesbury, Defoe, Adam Smith, and George Eliot.* New York: Columbia University Press.

McCarthy, Justin, ed. 2007. *Irish Literature* X. http://books.google.co.il/books?id= eJMMR8Hjr-QC&dq=justin+Mccarthy+%22Irish+literature (October 27, 2009).

McCobb, E. A. 1985. "*Daniel Deronda* as Will and Representation: George Eliot and Schopenhauer." *Modern Language Review* 80: 533–49.

McKenzie, Alan T. 1985. "The Derivation and Distribution of 'Consequence' in *Mansfield Park.*" *Nineteenth-Century Literature* 40, no. 3: 281–96.

Mendelson-Maoz, Adia. 2007. "Ethics and Literature: Introduction." *Philosophia* 35: 111–16.

Meyer, Susan. 1993. "'Safely to Their Own Borders': Proto-Zionism, Feminism, and Nationalism in *Daniel Deronda.*" *ELH* 60, no. 3: 733–58.

Meyersohn, Marylea. 1983. "What Fanny Knew: A Quiet Auditor of the Whole." In Todd 1983, 224–30.

Miller, Andrew. 2008. *The Burdens of Perfection: On Ethics and Reading in Nineteenth-Century British Literature.* Ithaca, N.Y.: Cornell University Press.

Miller, David A. 1981. *The Narrative and Its Discontents: Problems of Closure in the Traditional Novel.* Princeton, N.J.: Princeton University Press.

———. 1988. *The Novel and the Police.* Berkeley: University of California Press.

Miller, J. Hillis. 1970. *Thomas Hardy: Distance and Desire.* Cambridge, Mass.: Harvard University Press.

Miller, John N. 1989a. "*The Maypole of Merry Mount:* Hawthorne's Festive Irony." *Studies in Short Fiction* 26: 111–23.

———. 1989b "The Pageantry of Revolt in *My Kinsman, Major Molineux.*" *Studies in American Fiction* 17: 51–64.

Minma, Shinobu. 1996. "General Tilney and Tyranny: *Northanger Abbey.*" *Eighteenth Century Fiction* 8, no. 4: 503–518.

Mintz, Alan. 1976. "*Daniel Deronda* and the Messianic Vocation." In *Daniel Deronda: A Centenary Symposium,* ed. Alice Shalvi. Jerusalem: Jerusalem Academic Press. 137–56.

———. 1978. *George Eliot and the Novel of Vocation.* Cambridge, Mass.: Harvard University Press.

Mitchell, Breon. 1987. "Kafka and the *Hunger Artists.*" In *Kafka and the Contemporary Critical Performance: Centenary Readings, ed.* Alan Udoff. Bloomington: Indiana University Press. 236–55.

Monaghan, David. 1978. "*Mansfield Park* and Evangelicalism: A Reassessment." *Nineteenth-Century Fiction* 33: 215–30.

Monod, Sylvère. 1970. "Some Stylistic Devices in *A Tale of Two Cities.*" In *Dickens the Craftsman: Strategies of Presentation,* ed. Robert B. Partlow, Jr. Carbondale: Southern Illinois University Press. 165–86.

Montaigne, Michel de. 1958. *Essays.* Trans. J. M. Cohen. Harmondsworth, U.K.: Penguin.

Morris, Charles. 1946. *Signs, Language, and Behavior.* New York: Prentice-Hall.

Moses, Michael Valdez. 2000 [1988]. "Agon in the Marketplace: *The Mayor of Casterbridge* as Bourgeois Tragedy." In Wolfreys 2000, 170–201. Reprinted from *South Atlantic Quarterly* 87, no. 2 (1988): 219–49.

Moynahan, Julian. 1956. *The Mayor of Casterbridge* and the Old Testament's First Book of Samuel: A Study of Some Literary Relationships." *PMLA* 71: 118–30.

Mudrick, Marvin. 1952. *Jane Austen: Irony as Defense and Discovery.* Princeton, N.J.: Princeton University Press.

Muka ovský, Jan. 1970. *Aesthetic Function, Norm and Value as Social Facts.* Trans. Mark E. Suino. Ann Arbor: University of Michigan (Michigan Slavic Contributions).

———. 1978. *Structure, Sign, and Function: Selected Essays by Jan Muka ovský.* Trans. and ed. John Burbank and Peter Steiner. New Haven, Conn.: Yale University Press.

Mullan, John. 1988. *Sentiment and Sociability: The Language of Feeling in the Eighteenth Century.* Oxford: Clarendon.

Murdoch, Iris. 1956. "Vision and Choice in Morality." *Proceedings of the Aristotelian Society,* Supplementary Volume 30: 32–58.

Murphy, Michael. 1986. "*The Secret Sharer:* Conrad's Turn of the Winch." *Conradiana* 18: 193–200.

Murry, John Middleton. 1956. "In Defense of Fielding." In *Unprofessional Essays.* London: Jonathan Cape. 9–52.

Murzhenko, Anatoly. 1985. *Obraz schastlivogo cheloveka, ili pis'ma iz lagerya osobogo rezhima [An Image of a Happy Man, or Letters from a Special-Regime Camp].* Ed. Michail Kheifetz. London: Overseas Publications Interchange.

Myer, Valerie Grosvenor, ed. 1984. *Laurence Sterne: Riddles and Mysteries.* London: Vision.

Myers, William. 1971. "George Eliot: Politics and Personality." In *Literature and Politics in the Nineteenth Century: Essays,* ed. John Lucas. London: Methuen. 105–29.

Nabokov, Vladimir. 1957. *Pnin.* London: Heinemann.

————. 1970. *The Annotated Lolita*. Ed. Alfred Appel. New York: McGraw-Hill.

————. 1972. *Transparent Things*. New York: McGraw-Hill.

————. 1980. *Lectures on Literature*. New York: Harcourt Brace Jovanovich.

————. 1981. *Strong Opinions*. New York: McGraw-Hill.

Neumarkt, Paul. 1970. "Kafka's *A Hunger Artist:* The Ego in Isolation." *American-Imago: A Psychoanalytic Journal for Culture, Science, and the Arts* 27: 109–21.

New, Melvyn. 1994. *Tristram Shandy: A Book for Free Spirits*. New York: Twayne.

Newman, Karen. 1983. "Can This Marriage Be Saved: Jane Austen Makes Sense of an Ending." *ELH* 50, no. 4: 693–710.

Nietzsche, Friedrich. 1966. *Basic Writings of Nietzsche*. Trans. and ed. Walter Kaufman. New York: Modern Library.

————. 1968. *The Will to Power*. Trans. Walter Kaufmann and R. J. Hollingdale. New York: Modern Library.

————. 1983. "Schopenhauer as Educator." In *Untimely Meditations*. Trans. R. J. Hollingdale. Cambridge: Cambridge University Press. 127–94.

Noon, William T. 1957. *Joyce and Aquinas*. New Haven, Conn.: Yale University Press.

Nussbaum, Martha C. 1983. "Flawed Crystals: James's *The Golden Bowl* and Literature as Moral Philosophy." *NLH* 15, no. 1: 25–50. Reprinted in *Love's Knowledge: Essays on Philosophy and Literature* (New York: Oxford University Press, 1990, 125–47).

————. 1986. *The Fragility of Goodness: Luck and Ethics in Greek Tragedy and Philosophy*. Cambridge: Cambridge University Press.

————. 1995. *Poetic Justice: The Literary Imagination and Public Life*. Boston: Beacon.

Panin, D. 1976 [1973]. *The Notebooks of Sologdin*. Trans. John Moore. New York: Harcourt Brace Jovanovich.

Paris, Bernard J. 1997. *Imagined Human Beings: A Psychological Approach to Character and Conflict in Literature*. New York: New York University Press.

Parrinder, Patrick. 1984. *James Joyce*. Cambridge: Cambridge University Press.

Paulits, Walter J. 1970. "Ambivalence in *Young Goodman Brown*." *American Literature* 41: 577–84.

Pearce, Harvey. 1954. "Hawthorne and the Sense of the Past." *ELH* 21:327–49.

Phelan, James. 1987. "Character, Progression, and the Mimetic-Didactic Distinction." *Modern Philology* 84: 282–99.

————. 2003. "The Beginning and Early Middle of *Persuasion;* Or, Form and Ideology in Austen's Experiment with Narrative Comedy." *Partial Answers* 1, no. 1: 65–87.

————. 2005. *Living to Tell about It: A Rhetoric and Ethics of Character Narration*. Ithaca, N.Y.: Cornell University Press.

————. 2006. "Judgment, Progression, and Ethics in Portrait Narratives: The Case of Alice Munro's 'Prue.'" *Partial Answers* 4, no. 2: 115–29.

Polhemus, Robert M. 1982. *Comic Faith: The Great Tradition from Austen to Joyce*. Chicago: University of Chicago Press.

Poovey, Mary. 1984. *The Proper Lady and the Woman Writer: Ideology as Style in the Works of Mary Wollstonecraft, Mary Shelley, and Jane Austen*. Chicago: University of Chicago Press.

————. 1988. *Uneven Developments: The Ideological Work of Gender in Mid-Victorian England*. Chicago: University of Chicago Press.

Rabinowitz, Peter J. 1977. "Truth in Fiction: A Reexamination of Audiences." *Critical Inquiry* 4, no. 1: 121–41.

———. 1987. *Before Reading: Narrative Conventions and the Politics of Interpretation*. Ithaca, N.Y.: Cornell University Press.

Raine, Craig. 1994. "Conscious Artistry in *The Mayor of Casterbridge*." In *New Perpectives on Thomas Hardy*, ed. Charles P. C. Pettit. New York: St. Martin's Press. 156–71. First published as the Everyman's Library Edition of *The Mayor of Casterbridge*.

Razgon, Lev. 1997 [1989]. *True Stories*. London: Souvenir.

Reed, Walter R. 1981. *An Exemplary History of the Novel: The Quixotic versus the Picaresque*. Chicago: University of Chicago Press.

Ressler, Steve. 1984. "Conrad's *The Secret Sharer:* Affirmation of Action." *Conradiana* 16: 195–214.

Rickard, John S. 1998. *Joyce's Book of Memory: The Mnemotechnic of Ulysses*. Durham, N.C.: Duke University Press.

Rimmon-Kenan, Shlomith. 1983. *Narrative Fiction: Contemporary Poetics*. London: Methuen.

———. 1985. "Qu'est-ce qu'un thème?" *Poètique* 64: 397–406.

———. 1996. *A Glance Beyond Doubt: Narration, Representation, Subjectivity*. Columbus: The Ohio State University Press.

Rivinus, Timothy M. 1992. "Tragedy of the Commonplace: The Impact of Addiction on Families in the Fiction of Thomas Hardy." *Literature and Medicine* 11, no. 2: 237–65.

Roberts, W. Rhys, ed. 1989. *Longinus on the Sublime*. Cambridge: Cambridge University Press.

Rolleston, James. 1995. "Purification unto Death: *A Hunger Artist* as Allegory of Modernism." In *Approaches to Teaching Kafka's Short Fiction*, ed. Richard T. Gray. New York: MLA. 135–42.

Rorty, Richard. 1989. *Consistency, Irony, and Solidarity*. Cambridge: Cambridge University Press.

Rosenwein, Babara H. 2002. "Worying about Emotions in History." *The American Historical Review* 107: 821–45.

———. 2006. *Emotional Communities in the Early Middle Ages*. Ithaca, N.Y.: Cornell University Press.

Rosenthal, Bernice Glatzer, ed. 1986. *Nietzsche in Russia*. Princeton, N.J.: Princeton University Press.

Rosenthal, Bernice Glatzer, ed. 1994. *Nietzsche and Soviet Culture: Ally and Adversary*. Cambridge: Cambridge University Press.

Rotenstreich, Nathan. 2007. *Zionism: Past and Present*. Albany, N.Y.: State University of New York Press.

Rougemont, Denis de. 1956. *Love in the Western World*. Trans. Montgomery Belgion. Rev. and aug. edition. New York: Pantheon.

Sacks, Sheldon. 1966. *Fiction and the Shape of Belief: A Study of Henry Fielding with Glances at Swift, Johnson, and Richardson*. Berkeley: University of California Press.

Said, Edward. 1993. *Culture and Imperialism*. New York: Knopf.

———. 1980. *The Question of Palestine*. London: Routledge and Kegan Paul.

Sartre, Jean Paul. 1962. *Literary and Philosophical Essays*. Trans. Annette Michelson. New York: Collier Books.

Satz, Martha, and Zsuzsanna Ozsvath. 1978. "*A Hunger Artist* and *In the Penal Colony* in the Light of Schopenhauerian Metaphysics." *German Studies Review* 1: 200–10.

Scarry, Elaine. 1985. *The Body in Pain: The Making and Unmaking of the World.* Oxford: Oxford University Press.

Schiller, Friedrich. 1965 [1954, 1795]. *On the Aesthetic Education of Man, in a Series of Letters.* Trans. Reginal Snell. New York: Frederick Ungar.

Schopenhauer, Arthur. 1969. *The World as Will and Representation.* Trans. E. F. J. Payne. New York: Dover.

Schor, Hilary Margot. 1999. *Dickens and the Daughter of the House.* Cambridge: Cambridge University Press.

Senderovich, Savelii, and Shvarts, Elena. 2000. "Balagan smerti: zametki o romane V. Nabokova *Bend Sinister*" ["The Carnival-Booth of Death: Notes on V. Nabokov's Novel *Bend Sinister*"]. In *Kultura russkoi diaspory: Vladimir Nabokov—100.* Tallinn, Estonia: TP Kirjastus. 356–70.

Shalamov, Varlam. 1978. *Kolymskiye rasskazy* [*Kolyma Tales*]. Ed. M. Heller. London: Overseas Publications Interchange.

———. 1991. *Kolymskiye rasskazy.* Ed. I. Sirotinskaya. Moscow: Sovremennik.

———. 1992. "Correspondence with Nadezhda Mandelstam." *Znamia,* no.2: 158–77.

———. 1994. *Kolyma Tales.* Trans. John Glad. Harmondsworth, U.K.: Penguin.

———. 1994. "Zhuk" ["The Insect"]. In *Shalamovskii sbornik I,* ed. V. V. Esipov. Vologda: Teachers Training Institute Press. 15–16.

———. 1998. *Sobranie sochinenii v chetyrekh tomakh* [*Collected Works in Four Volumes*]. Ed. I. P. Sirotinskaia. Moscow: Khudozhestvennaia literatura/Vagrius.

———. 2000. "The Artist of the Spade." Trans. N. Strazhas. In *Cold Fusion: Aspects of the German Cultural Presence in Russia,* ed. Gennady Barabtarlo. New York: Berghahn Books. 292–302.

Sherman, Nancy. 1988. "Common Sense and Uncommon Virtue." *Midwest Studies in Philosophy* 13: 97–114.

Shklar, Judith. 1984. *Ordinary Vices.* Cambridge, Mass.: Belknap Press.

Shklovsky, Victor. 1968 [1929, 1921]. "A Parodying Novel: Sterne's *Tristram Shandy.*" Trans. W. George Isaak. In Traugott 1968, 66–89. The text is based on the 1929 version of the paper included in Shklovsky's book *O teorii prozy.* The text published in *Russian Formalist Criticism* (see under Shklovsky 1965) is based on the 1921 version of the article.

———. 1965. "Art as Technique." In *Russian Formalist Criticism: Four Essays,* ed. Lee T. Lemon and Marion J. Reis. Lincoln: University of Nebraska Press. 3–14.

Showalter, Elaine. 1979. "The Unmanning of the Mayor of Casterbridge." In *Critical Approaches to the Fiction of Thomas Hardy,* ed. Dale Kramer. London: Macmillan, 1979. 99–115.

Sicher, Efraim. 2003. *Rereading the City, Rereading Dickens: Representation, the Novel, and Urban Realism.* New York: AMS Press.

Slater, Michael. 1983. *Dickens and Women.* Stanford, Calif.: Stanford University Press.

Smith, Adam. 1853. *The Theory of Moral Sentiment.* London: Henry G. Bohn.

Solzhenitsyn, Alexandr. 1978 [1973–1975]. *The Gulag Archipelago: An Experiment in Literary Investigation.* Trans. Thomas P. Whitney (Parts I–IV) and Harry Willetts (Parts V–VII). New York: Harper and Row.

Southam, Brian. 1995. "The Silence of the Bertrams: Slavery and the Chronology of *Mansfield Park.*" *Times Literary Supplement,* 17 February: 13–14. Partly reprinted in Austen 1998, 493–98.

Spencer, Herbert. 1959 [1852]. "Philosophy of Style." In *Philosophy of Style by Herbert Spencer and Philosophy of Composition by Edgar Allan Poe*. New York: Pageant Press. 9–64.

Stallybrass, Peter and Allon White. 1986. *The Politics and Poetics of Transgression*. Ithaca, N.Y.: Cornell University Press.

Starr, G. A. 1965. *Defoe and Spiritual Autobiography*. New York: Gordian Press.

———. 1971. *Defoe and Casuistry*. Princeton, N.J.: Princeton University Press.

Steedman, Carolyn. 2002. "Service and Servitude in the World of Labor: Servants in England, 1750–1820." In *The Age of Cultural Revolutions: Britain and France, 1750–1820*, ed. Colin Jones and Dror Wahrman. Berkeley: University of California Press. 124–36.

Steiner, George. 1998 [1958]. *Language and Silence: Essays on Language, Literature, and the Inhuman*. New Haven, Conn.: Yale University Press.

Sternberg, Meir. 1978. *Expositional Modes and Temporal Ordering in Fiction*. Baltimore: Johns Hopkins University Press.

Stewart, Garrett. 1987. "Death by Water in *A Tale of Two Cities*." In Bloom 1987, 107–20. Reprinted from *Death Sentences: Styles of Dying in British Fiction* (Cambridge, Mass.: Harvard University Press, 1984).

Stokes, Peter M. 2001. "Bentham, Dickens, and the Uses of the Workhouse." *Studies in English Literature 1500–1900* 43, no. 4: 711–27.

Tandon, Bharat. 2003. ". . . Among the Ruins": Narrative Archeology in *The Mayor of Casterbridge*." *Studies in the Novel* 35, no. 4: 471–89.

Tanner, Tony. 1977. "Licence and Licencing: To the Presse or to the Spunge." *Journal of the History of Ideas* 38:3–18.

———. 1979. *Adultery in the Novel*. Baltimore: Johns Hopkins University Press.

———. 1986. *Jane Austen*. London: Macmillan.

Tave, Stuart M. 1973. *Some Words of Jane Austen*. Chicago: University of Chicago Press.

Terry, Judith. 1995. "Sir Thomas Bertram's 'Business in Antigua.'" *Persuasions* 17: 97–105.

Thompson, J. B. 2001. "Hardy's *The Mayor of Casterbridge*." *The Explicator* 59, no. 2: 83–85.

Thoreau, Henry David. 1951. *Walden*. New York: Bramhall House.

Timofeev, Lev. 1991. "Poetika lagernoi prozy: Pervoye chteniye *Kolymskikh rasskazov* Varlama Shalamova" ["The Poetics of Camp Prose: A First Reading of *Kolyma Tales* by Varlam Shalamov"]. *Russkaya mysl'*, no. 3859–3863 (8 March–5 April).

Tritt, Michael. 1991. "*Young Goodman Brown* and the Psychology of Projection." *Studies in Short Fiction* 28: 113–17.

Todd, Janet, ed. 1983. *Jane Austen: New Perspectives*. New York: Holmes and Meier.

Todorov, Tzvetan. 1980 [1970]. *The Fantastic: A Structural Approach to a Literary Genre*. Trans. Richard Howard. New York: Cornell Paperbacks. Originally published as *Introduction à la littérature fantastique* (Paris: Seuil, 1970).

Toker, Leona. 1989. *Nabokov: The Mystery of Literary Structures*. Ithaca, N.Y.: Cornell University Press.

———. 1991. "Philosophers as Poets: Reading Nabokov with Schopenhauer and Bergson." *Russian Literature Triquarterly* 24: 185–96.

———. 1993a. *Eloquent Reticence: Withholding Information in Fictional Narrative*. Lexington: University Press of Kentucky.

———. 1993b. "Varlam Shalamov's Kolyma." In *Between Heaven and Hell: The Myth of Siberia in Russian Culture,* ed. Galya Diment and Yuri Slezkine. New York: St. Martin's Press. 151–69.

———. 1994/1995. "If Everything Else Fails, Read the Instructions: Further Echoes of the Reception-Theory Debate." *Connotations: A Journal for Critical Debate* 4: 151–64.

———. 1995. "Représentation de la crise dans l'oeuvre de Nathaniel Hawthorne: Le Mode carnavalesque." Trans. Christine Raguet-Bouvart. In *Éclats de voix: Crises en représentation dans la littérature Nord-Américaine,* edited by Christine Raguet-Bouvart. La Rochelle: Rumeur des Ages. 97–109.

———. 1996a. "The Adventures of Jenny Jones: Fielding's 'Fine Old Moralism' Reconsidered." In *Rereading Texts / Rethinking Critical Presuppositions: Essays in Honour of H. M. Daleski,* ed. Shlomith Rimmon-Kenan, Leona Toker, and Shuli Barzilai. Frankfurt: Peter Lang. 149–61.

———. 1996b. "*Hard Times* and a Critique of Utopia: A Typological Study," *Narrative* 4: 218–34.

———. 1997a. "*Contra* Schopenhauer: Varlam Shalamov and the *Principium Individuationis.*" *REAL* (Germany) 13: 257–69.

———. 1997b. "Towards a Poetics of Documentary Prose—From the Perspective of Gulag Testimonies." *Poetics Today* 18: 187–222.

———. 1998. "Veblen, Dickens, and Martin Chuzzlewit's America," *Dickens Quarterly* 15, no. 3: 147–57.

———. 1999. "'The Dead Are Good Mixers': Nabokov's Version of Individualism." In *Nabokov and His Fiction: New Perspectives,* ed. Julian Connolly. Cambridge: Cambridge University Press. 92–108.

———. 2000. *Return from the Archipelago: Narratives of Gulag Survivors.* Bloomington: Indiana University Press.

———. 2005. "Target Audience, Hurdle Audience, and the General Reader: Varlam Shalamov's Art of Testimony." *Poetics Today* 26: 281–303.

———. 2006. "Narrative Enthymeme: The Examples of Sterne and Joyce." *Partial Answers* 4, no. 2: 163–74.

———. 2007. "*Nicholas Nickleby* and the Discourse of Lent." *Dickens Studies Annual* 38: 19–33.

———. 2008a. "Being Read by *Lolita.*" In *Approaches to Teaching Nabokov's Lolita, ed.* Zoran Kuzmanovich and Galya Diment. New York: Modern Language Association.

———. 2008b. "The Semiological Model in the Teaching of Literature: Discussing the Title of Austen's *Mansfield Park.*" *Literatūra* (Vilnius University) 50, no. 5: 91–97.

———. 2010 (forthcoming). "Syntactics—Semantics—Pragmatics (Still Having One's Cake?)." In *Theory and Teaching,* ed. Richard Bradford. Basingstoke, U.K.: Palgrave.

Traugott, John, ed. 1968. *Laurence Sterne: A Collection of Critical Essays.* Englewood Cliffs, N.J.: Prentice Hall.

Trevelyan, George Macaulay. 1942. *History of England.* 2nd ed. London: Longmans.

Trilling, Lionel. 1955. *The Opposing Self: Nine Essays in Criticism.* New York: Viking.

Tucker, Todd. 2006. *The Great Starvation Experiment: The Heroic Men Who Starved So That Millions Could Live.* New York: Free Press.

Turner, Paul. 1998. *The Life of Thomas Hardy.* Oxford: Blackwell.

Turner, Victor. 1982. *From Ritual to Theatre: The Human Seriousness of Play.* New York: Performing Arts Journal Publications.

Twain, Mark. 1994 [1885]. *The Adventures of Huckleberry Finn.* London: Penguin.

Valentino, Russell Scott. 2005. "The Oxymoron of Empathic Criticism: Readerly Empathy, Critical Explication, and the Translator's Creative Understanding." *Poroi* 4, no. 1 (http://www.uiowa.edu/~russian/texts/Empathy.pdf, April 6, 2009).

Vanden Bossche, Chris R. 1983. "Prophetic Closure and Disclosing Narrative: *The French Revolution* and *A Tale of Two Cities.*" *Dickens Studies Annual* 12: 209–21.

Veblen, Thorstein. 1899. *The Theory of the Leisure Class: An Economic Study of Institutions.* New York: Macmillan.

Waldron, Mary. 1999. *Jane Austen and the Fiction of Her Time.* Cambridge: Cambridge University Press.

Walzer, Michael. 1987. *Interpretation and Social Criticism.* Cambridge, Mass.: Harvard University Press.

Weisser, Susan Ostrov. 1990. "Gwendolen's Hidden Wound: Sexual Possibilities and Impossibilities in *Daniel Deronda.*" *Modern Language Studies* 20, no. 3: 3–13.

Wexler, Joyce. 1991. "Conrad's Dream of a Common Language: Lacan and *The Secret Sharer.*" *Psychoanalytic Review* 78: 599–606.

Wiltshire, John. 1997. "*Mansfield Park, Emma, Persuasion.*" In *The Cambridge Companion to Jane Austen,* ed. Edward Copeland and Juliet McMaster. Cambridge: Cambridge University Press. 58–83.

———. 2005. "Introduction." In Jane Austen, *Mansfield Park.* Cambridge: Cambridge University Press. xxv–lxxxvi.

Winick, Myron, ed. 1979 [1946]. *Hunger Disease: Studies by the Jewish Physicians in the Warsaw Ghetto.* Trans. Martha Osnos. New York: Wiley.

Wolf, Susan. 1982. "Moral Saints." *Journal of Philosophy* 79, no. 8: 419–39.

Wolfreys, Julian, ed. 2000. *The Mayor of Casterbridge: New Casebooks.* Basingstoke, U.K.: Macmillan.

Wolosky, Shira. 2004. "Poetry and Public Discourse, 1820–1910." In *The Cambridge History of American Literature,* vol. 4: *Nineteenth-Century Poetry 1800–1910,* ed. Sacvan Bercovitch. Cambridge: Cambridge University Press. 147–480.

Wood, Nigel, ed. 1993. *Mansfield Park.* Buckingham; Philadelphia: Open University Press.

Wordsworth, William. 1956 [1798]. "Preface to Lyrical Ballads." In *Wordsworth: Poetry and Prose.* Oxford: Clarendon. 150–76.

———. 1974. "Essays upon Epitaphs." In *The Prose Works of William Wordsworth,* ed. W. J. B. Owen and Jane Worthington Smyser. Oxford: Clarendon. II: 48–99.

Worsthorne, Peregrine. 2004. *In Defence of Aristocracy.* London: HarperCollins.

Wright, Andrew. 1965. *Henry Fielding: Mask and Feast.* London: Chatto & Windus.

Zamir, Tzachi. 2000. "Upon One Bank and Shoal of Time." *New Literary History* 31, no. 3: 529–51.

———. 2006. *Double Vision: Moral Philosophy and Shakespearean Drama.* Princeton, N.J.: Princeton University Press.

INDEX

Wolosky, Shira, 76n21

Woolf, Virginia, *Mrs. Dalloway,* 16, 54

Wordsthorne, Peregrine, 74n16, 84n37, 103n17

Wordsworth, William, 113n37; "Essays upon Epitaphs," 3; "Preface to Lyrical Ballads," 17, 113n37, 157, 208

Yeats, William Butler, 163n13

Zamir, Tzachi, 3n7, 128n20

Zionism, 122, 127, 130

THEORY AND INTERPRETATION OF NARRATIVE

James Phelan and Peter J. Rabinowitz, Series Editors

Because the series editors believe that the most significant work in narrative studies today contributes both to our knowledge of specific narratives and to our understanding of narrative in general, studies in the series typically offer interpretations of individual narratives and address significant theoretical issues underlying those interpretations. The series does not privilege one critical perspective but is open to work from any strong theoretical position.